The Guaranteed Goof-Proof Microwave Cookbook

The Guaranteed Goof-Proof MICROWAVE COOKBOOK

BY

Margie "The Microwhiz" Kreschollek

BANTAM BOOKS

TORONTO · NEW YORK · LONDON · SYDNEY · AUCKLAND

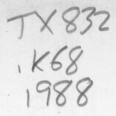

A very special thanks to Dorothy Jordan,
David Ferber, Donnkenny, Inc., and Rubbermaid, Inc.,
for helping to make my dream come true.

THE GUARANTEED GOOF-PROOF MICROWAVE COOKBOOK
A Bantam Book / January 1988

*Kitchen courtesy of Regba Diran, New York, NY
Fashions by Donnkenny, Inc.*

Library of Congress Cataloging-in-Publication Data

Kreschollek, Margie.
    The guaranteed goof-proof microwave cookbook.

    Includes index.
    1. Microwave cookery. I. Title.
    TX832.K68   1988   641.5'882   86-46801
    ISBN 0-553-34457-9

Published simultaneously in the United States and Canada

---

*Bantam Books are published by Bantam Books, Inc. Its trademark,
consisting of the words "Bantam Books" and the portrayal of a rooster, is
Registered in U.S. Patent and Trademark Office and in other countries. Marca
Registrada. Bantam Books, Inc., 666 Fifth Avenue, New York, New York 10103.*

PRINTED IN THE UNITED STATES OF AMERICA

MV   0 9 8 7 6 5 4 3 2 1

To my husband Willie,
sons Billie and Tommie

Without whose love, faith,
continual help,
and encouragement
this book
would never have been
a reality.

Contents

Introduction

I got my first microwave as a Christmas present some years ago. My husband worked all morning installing it over my stove. How could I possibly prepare Christmas dinner in my regular oven with this brand-new toy waiting to be played with?

I will never forget that poor ham as long as I live. I read the directions that came with the oven for cooking ham. It sounded real easy; place ham in shallow dish and cook. *Well,* thought I, *any dummy can microwave a ham, right?* Wrong!

The only edible part was the deep interior; the rest of the ham was bricklike. Unbelievable! Words cannot express the sight of my poor family trying to be polite eating this little portion of ham that remained soft enough to cut, while they were thinking, *This is what the microwave can do? Let's open a can.*

I called everyone I knew, trying to get some tips on how to make this expensive bun warmer do more than heat my leftovers, but not one of my friends with a microwave knew any more than I did. I refused to give up without a fight, so I began experimenting. I didn't know if it was possible, but I wanted to produce perfect-looking, perfect-tasting food in one-third the time it took with my gas stove. Let me tell you, I have made all the mistakes and blunders possible. My goal in writing this book is to teach you everything my years of practice have taught me.

When I first began cooking in my microwave, I gathered all the microwave cookbooks I could find. My biggest complaint was that not one of them had all the necessary techniques and problems one might encounter listed with each recipe. I would find a recipe that interested me and just begin following the directions. I must admit that as a new microwaver I didn't read the opening chapters, where most books list all the necessary procedures to make a microwave recipe work; I just began cooking.

My first whole meal completely from the microwave was a total disaster and the kids didn't even try to swallow it and smile. Critics are what I live with, and as my skills improved it became a game in my house to see if Dad and the boys could tell where Mom had cooked dinner. This was a real challenge: my husband is a professional chef, trained at the Culinary Institute of America. This game became the basis for my perfected recipes; if they couldn't tell where it had been cooked, then I had indeed accomplished making a conventional-oven–perfect recipe in the microwave. Years later, *I'm* the expert, with thousands of newspaper readers and radio listeners who call me The Microwhiz.

I have done all my experimenting and geared all my recipes to microwaves that range from 600 to 700 watts. This simply means that if the wattage in your oven is lower than 600 watts, you may have to increase the cooking times I list by 20% for each 100 watts under 600. Whenever you use a microwave recipe, always microwave for the shortest amount of time the recipe recommends; you can always add more time, but once you have overcooked, it becomes pooch material.

Look at it this way: you might spend $150 on tennis lessons just to learn how to hit a ball, so spend a few dollars on food and do some experimenting and get to know your oven. It won't take long for you to figure out if you need a turntable and where, if you have any, the hot spots in your oven are. If you find things always overcooking in one area of the oven, then you have a hot spot. A turntable made for the microwave will help distribute the microwaves evenly around your food.

You will also find that I have not included everyday kitchen items in my equipment list for each recipe. I want to make things as easy as possible for you, and I assume you have paper towels, plates, bowls, wax paper, plastic wrap, a whisk, glass measuring cups, and spoons.

In my opinion, anyone can write a recipe but not everyone can get it to come out of the microwave tasting and looking perfect, and that's what I want to teach you. I always think of Fred the waiter when

I try to explain this point. I was having breakfast with some dear friends one morning when one of them asked Fred if he would bring her an order of toast. Fred pulled out his little pad and with the most serious face I have ever seen said, "Would you like that toasted?" When we all stopped laughing and apologized to poor Fred, I thought, *This is my exact point.* Anyone can put a recipe together, but if you don't know the necessary techniques, the food may not look and taste the way it should.

So relax, and remember, you are the one who makes this new kitchen wizard work. I have done all the hard work for you; now you need only to follow my directions. Each recipe highlights all the necessary techniques and problems you might encounter and how to handle them. Read and follow the boxed tips that appear throughout the book; you will not only produce a perfect dish but will learn procedures you can apply when converting your own recipes to the microwave.

I have enjoyed putting my thoughts and recipes together for you and hope you will be as proud of your new skills as I am of mine. I have compiled favorites from both sides of our family and I hope your family will enjoy them as much as we do.

WHY GOOF-PROOF?

If you've ever turned out a disaster with your microwave, you know the terrible feelings that come over you. "I'll never make this recipe again," you swear; or, "I'm only going to heat things up from now on"; or, "This machine has got the best of me and it's time to admit it and give up." Those are the mild reactions; if you've just ruined a very expensive roast, rage may be the appropriate response.

It *does* take a while to get used to your oven and its peculiarities, and of course you'll make mistakes from time to time. But this book is the only one that tells you on the same page with the recipe *exactly* what to do, and *exactly* what might go wrong. The key techniques appear in bold type with each recipe. A few of them may seem so obvious that they don't need to be mentioned—like whisking, elevating, rotating—but they can make all the difference in the success of your dish. And that's why I highlight them for you everytime you need them. Follow them carefully, keep in mind the trouble areas, and you can't go wrong. If all else fails, write to me in care of my publisher and I'll guarantee you an answer to your microwave problem.

The Basics

HOW IT WORKS

Are you totally baffled about how your expensive new bun warmer really works? Let me try to explain as simply as I can. If you haven't already, you will learn to love and appreciate this great little machine for its speed, cleanliness, and cost efficiency.

Every microwave oven has a magnetron tube, which produces microwaves that come into your oven, bounce off the metal walls (and the metal in the glass door), and concentrate on whatever object is sitting in the oven.

Once the microwaves are released from the magnetron tube, they penetrate no more than 1 to 1½ inches into the food. At the point where they penetrate the food, they cause the molecules in the food—whether it is fat, sugar, or water—to vibrate. This vibration causes heat, and it is this heat—not the actual microwaves—that spreads through your food and cooks it.

The microwaves simply act as a starter mechanism to get the molecules vibrating and the heat going in the food. Once the molecules begin producing heat, it is spread from the outside to the center of the food by conduction, just as it is when you cook in a conventional oven. For this reason, when you turn the microwaves off, the molecules inside the food are still vibrating and the food is still cooking. Once the microwave energy is shut off—by pressing the Stop button or opening the door—the microwaves no longer exist.

Once the oven is stopped, the microwaves are gone—just like an ordinary light bulb turning off.

Now enter **standing time**. Because the food is still cooking when the oven cooking time finishes, you must always slightly *under*cook your food and allow it to finish cooking in the 5 to 10 minutes it must stand before serving, and this is logically called standing time. If you bake a potato until it is done to perfection it will shrivel up before you serve it because it continues to cook, and therefore overcooks, during the standing time.

To summarize microwave cooking:
1. The microwaves act as a catalyst to start the food cooking.
2. Once the microwaves are stopped from entering the food, it continues to cook during standing time.
3. There are no microwaves left over in the food after the oven is shut off.
4. Because the oven is encased in metal, the microwaves cannot get out, as long as the closures are kept clean and free of blockage.
5. It is a fast, energy-efficient, temperature-saving way to cook, and if you haven't tried it you should.

The microwaves cause no chemical change in your food, and they cook from the outside in to the center, contrary to common belief. Many people think microwaves start cooking in the center of the food and spread to the outside edges. You can better understand the cooking procedure when you microwave an eye round roast (see p. 47) because you can watch the meat go from raw around the edges to cooked, closer and closer to the center of the meat.

A lot of people are frightened by microwaves in the beginning, and in fact there are some important things to remember. They're all right here: The very serious ones are marked **DANGER** to help you remember.

Right here, let me stress the importance of *not* turning on the oven while it's empty.

If you are a new microwaver or if you have small children who you fear may turn on the oven accidentally, keep a glass measuring cup with 1 cup water in the oven when it is not in use. Instead of water, I always keep a box of baking soda in my oven, which helps absorb odors and leftover moisture. As long as you have something to absorb the microwaves, you won't risk damaging your oven should it be turned on accidentally.

There are a few things that you must *not* do in the microwave because they are dangerous and can harm your oven. First of all, your oven is for cooking; it is not a clothes dryer. Do not put underwear, stockings, or any other form of clothing in the microwave to dry. I recently received a letter from a couple in Texas who tried drying their underwear and burned all the wiring in their microwave as well as in the wall and blew the door off the oven. People are always telling me Julia Child dries off her wet newspaper in the microwave—maybe she does, but she shouldn't, and neither should you.

DANGER You cannot hardboil or reheat hardboiled eggs in the microwave. They have been known to explode and do a great deal of damage to the microwave, including blowing off the oven door. Popcorn is another very dangerous item if you use anything except a micro-safe popper or the disposable bags made for microwave popping. A regular brown paper bag may have metal particles or chemicals that can start a fire.

MICROWAVE DON'TS

1. Never operate your microwave if the door is cracked or if the glass has been broken.
2. Never microwave an egg in its shell, or an egg out of its shell without piercing the yolk with a toothpick. You must also pierce the casings on sausages, potatoes, hot dogs, squash, tomatoes, and peaches. If you do not allow the steam an avenue of escape, the casing will burst, sending the food all over the inside of your microwave.
3. Do not use any metal utensils, and do not use aluminum foil unless it is being used for shielding (see p. 10) and then use only a small, flat piece. Never put a twist-tie in the microwave, as it will arch (see p. 10) and ignite. Replace twist-ties with plastic closures that can be found in the supermarket produce section or on various bread bags.
4. Do not attempt to dry any type of clothing in your microwave; fabric gets very hot and can smoke and ignite.
5. Never attempt to use harsh oven-cleaning sprays, sharp objects, or steel wool to clean your microwave.

6. Never microwave anything so large that it touches the top or sides of the inside of the microwave.
7. Don't attempt to do any deep-frying in the microwave.

It's also a good idea to remember the following:
8. Avoid square-corner dishes in the microwave, as the microwaves tend to overcook anything they find in square corners.
9. Never allow flat-bottomed containers to sit flat on the floor of the microwave. Elevate them on an inverted saucer.
10. Drinks with a high portion of eggs, such as eggnog, can only be warmed or they will curdle.
11. Canning jars cannot be sterilized in the microwave. Don't melt parrafin in the microwave, either.
12. Don't bake cakes that use only the egg whites; they don't do as well as whole-egg cakes.
13. Don't bake two-crust pies in the microwave; the filling will not cook.
14. Don't microwave phyllo dough or puff pastry.
15. Any type of yeast bread dough is better cooked in a conventional oven. To my taste, I have not found a yeast bread dough that is satisfactory in the microwave.

THINGS ALWAYS TO DO

Try to get in the habit of doing these little tricks so that after a while you'll do them without thinking.

1. Microwave your frozen vegetables in the box or bag they come in, unless the box is wrapped in aluminum foil, in which case remove it. Make a vent slit or hole in the plastic bags but do not add water.
2. Cover your bread with paper towels before defrosting and reheating to absorb moisture; this will keep it from getting hard.
3. Place 2 layers of paper towels under any food sitting directly on the floor of the microwave.
4. Begin your red meat on HIGH for the first 5 minutes of cooking time, then reduce the power to 50 percent or MEDIUM to allow enough time for tenderizing.
5. When defrosting meat, cover it loosely with wax paper to keep it from drying out.

6. Be sure the inside of your microwave is clean before pre-heating your browning dish. The oven gets so hot during the preheat period that any spills or stains may bake on permanently.
7. Prebake the dough of a single-crust pie before adding filling to prevent it from getting soggy.
8. When defrosting, shield with small flat pieces of aluminum foil any areas that start to get warm. These areas will begin to cook if they are not protected.
9. Begin with uniformly sized and shaped meats and vegetables. Same-size pieces will cook in the same length of time.
10. Rotate dishes in the microwave either manually or with a turntable. You will achieve more even cooking if you rotate the dish every time you stir or check its progress.
11. Stir food in the microwave by bringing the center to the outside edges and the edges to the center.
12. Round containers cook food more evenly and should be used whenever possible.
13. Look inside the oven when you turn it on. If arching (see p. 10) occurs, be sure to fix the problem immediately.
14. Be sure that nothing blocks the vents on your microwave.
15. Be sure you completely clear the oven before programming time and temperature, as you may have previously pro-grammed a power level that will take over if not removed.

EQUIPMENT

If you're new to microwaving, you may not know which utensils are micro-safe and which are not, and I want you to understand and feel comfortable with the equipment you will be using.

Metal containers reflect microwave energy and do not allow it to penetrate to the food inside; therefore, metal cookware in the micro-wave is taboo. The only time metal can safely be used in the micro-wave is in very small, completely flat—not crimped, folded, or bended—pieces of aluminum foil to shield small areas of food you do not want to cook. This is covered completely in Arching and Shield-ing, p. 10.

Very shallow metal trays that TV dinners come in are allowed, but you would be better advised to take the food out and place it on a plate. When using these foil trays you will find that only the exposed surfaces sticking above the tray will heat, making even heating of the food very difficult.

There are many materials that allow microwave energy to pass through them and concentrate on the food inside. Among these are paper, plastic, glass, pottery, and china. Some plasticware can be used in the microwave for heating (no more than 50 percent power) but melts if used for cooking. Dishes that are safe for microwave use should get hot only where the food transfers heat. For plastic that is not micro-safe, this heat transference is enough to melt it. A dishwasher-safe plastic colander is fine for microwaving, and I often use it for cooking hamburger and sausage.

If you question the safety of any piece of cookware for use in your microwave, this simple test will help. First, check for any metal rims, handles, designs, or signatures. If the dish is free of metal, place a glass filled with 1 cup of water inside or right next to the test piece. Microwave on HIGH for 1 minute. Feel the test piece to see if it has remained cool. If it is hot, it will melt if you use it to cook in; however, if it remains cool, it will microwave with no problem.

Most of you have glassware that you could never use in your conventional stove but will be suitable for microwaving. All glassware suitable for conventional-oven use will also work well, including glass custard cups, casserole dishes, mixing bowls, measuring cups, and even glass pie and bread pans. Corning Ware will also do well; just be sure to check that it has no metal rims or handles. A piece of equipment I use constantly is the glass measure—I have 2-cup, 4-cup and 6-cup sizes.

Paper products are fine, but be careful with plastic storage containers and Styrofoam. They may be acceptable for quick reheating, but they may melt during actual cooking, so check their safety first (see above.) Both wax paper and paper towels are excellent food coverings, and paper towels are a must under any foods sitting directly on the floor of your microwave. You don't need to buy special microwave paper towels; just buy ordinary white ones, since the color sometimes transfers to the food.

A few wooden items are useful: toothpicks, wooden skewers, and chopsticks will all come in handy.

If you're in the process of outfitting a kitchen, you may want to purchase dishes made specifically for microwave use. Many companies manufacture microwave equipment in every size and shape imaginable. Some are even safe in conventional ovens up to 400 degrees. Many times you can incorporate both your microwave and conventional equipment when producing a recipe.

The one item of specialized microwave cookware you might want to buy is a meat rack—very useful for roasting, and other cooking jobs too. A browning dish is also a good idea if you're going to get really serious about microwaving. But see what you need as you go along—you can start microwaving right away with the equipment you already have.

A *word of caution:* take the time to test anything you question and thereby save ruining a dish that is not safe. Please remember, a simple saucer placed under all flat-bottomed cookware will help your microwave heat and cook more evenly and do a far better job.

COVERING AND VENTING

When your recipe calls for a cover of plastic wrap, it is usually with the assumption that you don't have a cover for the dish you are using. If you do have a cover that fits the dish tightly, by all means use it.

Venting is accomplished by completely covering the dish with plastic wrap, then turning back one corner just enough to let out the steam. If this is not done and too much steam builds up inside the dish, the plastic wrap may melt onto the food or you can easily burn yourself when you open it. This principle applies also to plastic bags full of vegetables. To microwave them you must make a slit or hole in the plastic bag to let the steam escape.

Plastic wrap or the casserole lid is used when you want something to steam and hold in all of the moisture while it cooks. Wax paper is used when you want the dish to steam but it isn't necessary to hold in all of the moisture. Paper is used as a covering only to hold in spatters, as it does not allow food to steam or hold in moisture.

Should your recipe call for a tight-fitting lid on your casserole dish, place a piece of wax paper between the dish and its lid to form a tight fit. Covering is very important in microwaving, since many items need to steam in order to cook properly, and without the proper coverings your recipe may not microwave as well as it should.

Your choice of coverings is determined by what you want the covering to do. When you want the food to steam and be soft, use plastic wrap; when you want to steam but don't need all the moisture to remain inside, wax paper works well; but if you want just a covering to keep food from spattering, paper towels will do. I suggest using white paper towels since the colored ones tend to release their color onto foods.

FREEZING AND DEFROSTING

One of the questions I am asked most often is, "How do you defrost in a microwave and what power do you use?" This is difficult to answer accurately because each oven manufacturer sets up its ovens differently. While some ovens come with a special defrost cycle, and others just have high, medium, and low power, today most ovens have power levels from 1 through 9 and then HIGH.

My rule for freezing meat that is to be defrosted in the microwave is first to remove the Styrofoam plate and freshness packet that is under most meat that comes from the supermarket. Microwaves are attracted to liquid before ice, so if you defrost meat on top of this packet it melts quickly and a great deal of the available power is drawn to it, taken away from the meat.

Second, if you tend to forget to remove the metal twist-tie from frozen foods before placing them in the microwave (you shouldn't have to learn that lesson more than once, though), substitute for the twist-tie a plastic closure that comes on some breads and can be found in the produce departments of most food stores.

When freezing hamburger, shape the meat into a big ball, flatten it, and make a depression in the center so that the microwave can defrost from the middle of the meat as well as around the sides. When freezing rolls, it's useful to separate them before freezing so it's easier to select just the number you need to defrost.

Remove the item you want to defrost from the freezer and if possible elevate it on an inverted saucer or a meat rack to help the microwaves get in from the bottom. If it is not in a container or plastic bag, place it on 2 paper towels. Bread must be completely wrapped in paper towels to absorb all the moisture that will be given off. However, again, if you're defrosting several rolls, place 2 paper towels under the rolls and one sheet on top. Place the rolls in a circle for more even defrosting.

My method for defrosting is to heat for short periods of time on 30 percent or LOW, unless your oven has a defrost cycle. By short periods of time I mean 4 to 5 minutes on defrost, LOW, or 30 percent, then 5 minutes of just standing in the oven. I repeat this procedure one to a few times more, depending on the size of the frozen food, until the food is defrosted. I find that when you defrost for long periods of time without letting the food stand, the food begins to cook.

If you are defrosting bread or rolls, 4 to 5 minutes is far too long; you might want to start with 1 minute. As with everything you will be cooking, defrosting will take some experimenting as to time for your particular oven. You can always repeat these short cycles if necessary, and by doing it this way you will save your food from cooking on the outside edges.

KEEPING YOUR OVEN CLEAN

Both new and experienced microwavers have the same problem of keeping the insides of their microwaves clean and odor-free. Unfortunately, there is no such thing as a self-cleaning microwave, but once you know the tricks you'll find your microwave is much easier to maintain than a conventional oven.

One of the biggest problems often overlooked by new microwavers is the buildup of lingering odors from strong-smelling foods. The problem goes beyond the awful smell you get every time you open the microwave door. If not removed, these odors will be absorbed by milder foods while cooking, causing them to acquire a strange taste.

To remove odors and stuck-on food, place a solution of 2 cups of water plus 2 tablespoons of lemon juice in a microwave-safe bowl or 4-cup glass measure. Should you happen to have lemon or lime rinds handy, add them to the solution. Bring the mixture to a boil on HIGH and let it boil rapidly inside the oven for 12 minutes. This boiling will cause steam to form and then condense on the walls and floor of your oven.

With a soft cloth or sponge, thoroughly wipe the interior dry, including the door seals. Whether you detect an odor or not, you should routinely wipe down the interior of your oven with a solution of baking soda and water (1 tablespoon soda per quart) to maintain freshness and remove spattered food particles.

In between cleanings, I keep a box of baking soda in my microwave when it is not in use. This also helps to absorb odors and moisture that linger inside the oven after cooking certain foods. *Be sure to remove the box of baking soda before you begin microwaving.*

Never use abrasive cleaners, commercial oven cleaners, steel-wool pads, kitchen knives, or other utensils to clean the interior or exterior. If your oven has a removable glass tray or shelf, wash it in warm sudsy water but do not use abrasive cleaners on it, as tiny scratches on the surface will allow food spatters to become lodged in them.

Always check and wipe down your door seals and the glass on your oven door to help maintain the oven's attractiveness and safety of operation. The exterior should be cleaned with soap and water or glass cleaner and a soft cloth. To prevent damage to the working parts, do not allow water to seep into ventilation openings.

OVEN CLEANING

To clean and deodorize your microwave, combine 2 cups of water with 2 tablespoons of lemon juice in a 4-cup glass or micro-safe measure. Microwave on HIGH for 12 minutes. Remove the container of water and immediately wipe out the inside of your oven with a soft cloth.

Do not use abrasives, oven cleaners, scouring pads or powders, or knives to remove stains and food. Be sure to clean the glass door of your microwave with window cleaner, and keep the door closures and seal clean. Always wipe all around the door to prevent any food buildup where the door meets the oven.

METAL IN THE MICROWAVE

One of the main things drummed into our heads is not to use metal in a microwave. That is generally true except for some very careful use of aluminum foil, and then only if your oven manufacturer allows it.

ARCHING AND SHIELDING

Before trying to use foil in your oven, check your manufacturer's instruction book—some ovens will not allow the use of any metal at all. Aluminum foil is used in the microwave only to *shield* something you do not want to cook. The cardinal rule for foil is that it must be *flat*—no crimps, no folds, and it cannot touch itself or it will arch and ignite.

DANGER The best example to picture is a twist-tie. If you should forget to remove one before putting a bag of rolls in the microwave to defrost, here is what will happen: the microwaves will cause the metal wire that is touching itself to arch. The resulting spark will cause the paper covering the metal to ignite, and from there it will ignite the plastic bag, and then the entire inside of your oven will be in flames. (Should this happen to you, shut off the oven immediately, remove the bag and place it in your sink, and turn on the water. This is not a grease fire, so water will extinguish it.)

I am not trying to scare you, only to make you aware of what will happen if you're not careful. Get used to looking inside your oven as soon as you turn it on. If anything is going to happen, it will do so immediately.

When you're using foil for shielding, lay it flat over the area you *do not* want to cook—for instance, an overcooking chicken wing. If your oven has a blower and the foil will not stay in place, try using a wooden toothpick to anchor it. It helps to reflect the microwaves if you place the shiny side of the foil on the outside, away from the area you wish to shield. Also be sure the foil never touches the top or sides of the interior of your oven, as it will burn the plastic wherever it touches.

As long as you are careful, aluminum foil works very well for shielding. But *careful* and *cautious* are the two most important words to remember when you use this technique.

BROWNING

Can you brown in a microwave oven? This question is asked more than any other and the answer is yes, you can. But how? you ask. Anything with a high sugar and/or fat content cooking in the microwave uninterrupted for 10 minutes or more will begin to brown, but if you want to brown foods that require only a very short cooking time, you need to use a micro-safe browning dish.

The browning dish will brown foods just as a frying pan on a regular stove top does. These browning dishes get extremely hot, reaching temperatures of 500 to 600 degrees, and they will burn you and your countertop if not properly handled with sturdy pot holders and placed on a trivet or board.

These are the most important *do*s and *don't*s to follow when using any type of micro-browner:

1. Be sure the inside of your microwave oven is clean. (See p. 9.) If you leave any grease residue on the top, floor, or sides of your oven, the high temperatures needed to make the browning device work can bake the grease spots permanently onto the surface of your oven.
2. Always follow the manufacturer's instructions for the amount of preheating time necessary for your browner. Failing to preheat turns your browner into a regular microwave dish and your meat goes back to steaming instead of browning.
3. Slash the edges of steaks and large chops to prevent them from curling.
4. If the first step of your recipe is to melt butter, do so in the last minute of preheat time.
5. Wipe out the browning dish between batches and preheat for one-half as long for the second and third batches as you did for the first.
6. Never use non-stick greasing sprays on your browner or they will scorch.
7. Never try to cover a browning skillet with plastic wrap, paper towels, wax paper, or another plastic microwave cover. These items will melt or possibly ignite from the high heat of the browner.
8. The browning device is the only piece of microwave equipment that gets hot from the microwave itself. Regular microwave cookware allows the microwaves to pass through the dish to the food enclosed. The browning dish is coated with a material that absorbs microwave energy, causing it to get very hot during preheat time. If any dish other than a browner is hot when it comes out of the microwave (see p. 6), it is not safe for microwave use. There may be hot spots where the food has transferred heat, but the handles and area where there is no food should not be warm.

MICROWAVE MAGIC

There are a lot of little tricks the microwave can perform that you may not know. Do you know that you can:

Warm brandy right in its snifter in about 20 seconds on HIGH power.

Open fresh clams by placing them in a circle on a plate and covering with plastic wrap for 40 to 50 seconds on HIGH or just until they start to open.

Warm your liquid body lotion in winter by removing the dispenser top and microwaving on HIGH for 12 to 25 seconds until just warm.

Soften ice cream in its container on 50 percent or MEDIUM for 25 to 35 seconds; watch closely to prevent melting.

Soften peanut butter for easier spreading or mixing in recipes by microwaving the glass jar (with top removed) for 30 to 45 seconds on HIGH or until the consistency is smooth.

Double a recipe and increase cooking time by about two-thirds rather than double the time.

Make your own baby food, purée it, freeze it in ice cube trays, defrost and heat in a custard cup for 25 to 55 seconds on HIGH.

Toast shredded coconut by laying one layer flat in a round pan and microwave on HIGH for 3 to 6 minutes; stir every minute.

Crisp soft soggy potato chips, crackers, or cereal by placing one layer on a paper plate and microwaving for 45 to 60 seconds on HIGH.

Reheat a dinner plate of food, and serve when the bottom of the dish is hot to your touch.

Thaw frozen whipped topping for immediate use by placing the unopened container in microwave on LOW or 30 percent power for 1 to 2 minutes, depending on size. Be sure to stir container well before using.

Place a raw hotdog in a bun, wrap it in a paper napkin, and microwave for 35 to 40 seconds on HIGH and serve. Two take about one minute and four take about two minutes.

Grill extra hamburgers and hot dogs, freeze, defrost, then heat on MEDIUM or 50 percent for 1 to 3 minutes.

Eggs and Bacon

Eggs and bacon are a good place to begin—not only for breakfast, but because they cook differently from any other foods in the microwave, and they're both very successful. Once you've tried them in the microwave, I think you'll always cook them that way. Just learn the tricks first and you'll cook them like a pro.

EGGS

DANGER First, some words of caution: Never try to cook a whole egg in its shell in your microwave oven. The steam that builds up inside the egg will cause it to explode. There have been cases where such an explosion caused severe damage to a microwave. Please, do not reheat whole, conventionally cooked and peeled hardboiled eggs either, without first slicing or quartering them—they have been known to explode with a great force.

Along with not microwaving an egg in its shell, you can't poach, bake, or fry an egg in your microwave without first piercing the yolk with a toothpick. The egg yolk has a thin covering that must be vented to allow the steam to escape, or it will explode all over the inside of your oven. (If this happens to you, see p. 9 for oven-cleaning directions.)

Poaching an egg in the microwave is a snap. Place 2 tablespoons of water and ¼ teaspoon of vinegar in a custard cup. Cover with vented plastic wrap (see Covering and Venting, p. 7) and microwave on HIGH for 2 to 3 minutes or until the water boils. Then break one large egg into the custard cup, pierce the yolk with a toothpick, and recover with vented plastic wrap. Microwave on 50 percent or MEDIUM for 1½ to 2 minutes or until most of the white of the egg is opaque but not set. Let the covered egg stand for 2 to 3 minutes before serving, and shake the cup gently during standing time to help set the white. If you're cooking more than one egg, multiply the cooking time accordingly.

Eggs cook differently in the microwave from a conventional stove. The yolk cooks first because the fat content attracts and absorbs more energy than the white. When egg yolks and whites are mixed together for cooking, they microwave more evenly. Therefore, omelets, scrambled eggs, and custards need less stirring than they would if conventionally cooked.

The only way to fry an egg in the microwave is to use a browning dish. (See Browning, p. 11.) You treat the dish as you would a frying pan on your stove top. Add butter, the egg, seasonings, then cover and microwave on HIGH for 30 to 90 seconds, depending on the degree of doneness you wish. Remember, eggs finish cooking while standing for 1 to 2 minutes.

Scrambled Eggs

Equipment:	1-quart casserole dish
Cooking time:	5 minutes
Standing time:	1 to 2 minutes
Serves:	2

1 tablespoon butter
4 eggs
¼ cup milk
dash of salt and pepper

Place butter in casserole dish and microwave on HIGH for 35 to 45 seconds.

Add eggs, milk, salt, and pepper, and beat with a fork or whisk until well scrambled. If you're using a flat-bottomed container, **elevate** on an inverted saucer. Microwave on HIGH for 2½ to 3 minutes, until eggs are almost set, **stirring** after the first 2 minutes.

When almost set and microwaving is finished, stir and let **stand** for 1 to 2 minutes before serving.

FOR 2 EGGS: 2 tablespoons milk, 1 tablespoon butter, bake for 1 to 2 minutes until almost set. Let stand 1 to 2 minutes.

FOR 6 EGGS: ⅓ cup milk, 2 tablespoons butter, bake 3 to 4½ minutes until almost set. Let stand 1 to 2 minutes.

FOR 8 EGGS: ½ cup milk, 2 tablespoons butter, bake 4 to 5½ minutes until almost set. Let stand 1 to 2 minutes.

Troubleshooting: Eggs get very tough if overcooked. Do not bake until completely set, or they will overcook during standing time. Be sure the center of the dish is still a bit runny.

Suggestions: To add a little different zip to your eggs, try adding one or two of the following: ½ cup grated cheese, 1 small can of drained mushrooms, ¼ cup finely chopped green pepper and onion, 1 tablespoon parsley flakes, 2 strips bacon cooked and crumbled, ¼ cup cubed ham or salami, or garlic or onion powder to taste.

Filled Omelet

Equipment:	4- or 6-cup glass measure, 9-inch glass pie plate
Cooking time:	10 to 18 minutes
Standing time:	1 minute
Serves:	2

FILLING
4 strips bacon, diced
½ medium green pepper, diced
1 small onion, minced
¼ teaspoon garlic powder
2 fresh or canned tomatoes, cut in eighths
½ cup canned or frozen peas*
salt and pepper to taste
1 cup shredded monterey jack or sharp cheddar cheese

*If using frozen peas, microwave with bacon and vegetables and add an extra 2 to 3 minutes to microwaving time.

OMELET
  1 **tablespoon butter**
  4 **eggs**
  4 **tablespoons milk**
     dash of salt and pepper

In the glass measure, place bacon, green pepper, onion, and garlic powder. Microwave **uncovered** on HIGH for 4 to 6 minutes until vegetables are crisp-tender, breaking up bacon every 2 minutes. Drain off fat and add tomatoes, peas, salt, and pepper to taste. Set aside.

Melt butter in pie plate on HIGH for 35 to 45 seconds. Whisk together eggs, milk, and a dash of salt and pepper. Pour into pie plate and spread out evenly.

Microwave uncovered on 50 percent power or MEDIUM for 3 to 4 minutes until eggs have just begun to set. Using a flat turner or spatula, lift edges of omelet to gently spread the unset portion of eggs evenly over the set portions.

Continue microwaving on 50 percent power or MEDIUM for 2 to 3 minutes until center is almost set.

Let **stand** for 1 minute, to completely set the center, while heating filling on HIGH. Place hot filling in center of omelet, fold in half, sprinkle shredded cheese on top, and serve.

Troubleshooting: Omelets are usually not stirred, so be sure to lift edges gently and distribute the uncooked portion of eggs over the cooked portion. This will help the finished product to be evenly cooked.

When serving, lift the edges carefully and slide onto a serving platter, being careful not to crack.

If omelet is not hot enough to melt shredded cheese, microwave for 45 to 50 seconds on HIGH on serving plate.

Bacon

Let's talk bacon! How many times have I heard, "I can't get my bacon crisp"? Well, cheer up, I'm here to help—it's incredibly easy to cook delicious, crisp bacon, with much less fat, in the microwave.

You can either cook your bacon between layers of paper towels or on a meat rack; the method you use will determine how crisp it gets. The fat and sugar content in the particular bacon you use also helps determine crispness, but it's the method of microwaving that makes the real difference.

Don't waste the entire package of bacon trying to figure out just how long to cook it, to get it just "your way." Microwave 1 slice in short takes and time it until it is perfect. Multiply the time it took by the number of slices you want to cook—and like magic they will all be perfect.

Remember, once the microwave shuts off, the bacon continues to cook and brown—and sometimes burn—so be sure to let your test slice stand for 2 minutes before you decide it's perfect.

If after standing time you find it still isn't quite crispy-crunchy to your satisfaction, pop it back in the microwave at 15-second intervals until you are pleased. Once you determine the time and method that's perfect for you, cooking bacon will be as easy as snapping the crisp slice in half.

Equipment: white paper towels (see Box p. 19) and/or a meat rack
Cooking time: 40 to 60 seconds per slice
Standing time: 2 to 3 minutes per batch

PAPER TOWEL METHOD

For very crisp bacon: Arrange 1 to 8 strips of bacon, side by side but not overlapping, on a paper plate **covered** with 3 layers of white paper towels. Place 2 layers of paper towels on top of the slices and pat gently. (See Box p. 19.)

Microwave on HIGH for 40 to 60 seconds per slice of bacon.

Let **stand** covered, for 2 to 3 minutes before serving to finish crisping and browning.

MEAT RACK METHOD

Note: This is the best method to use when microwaving extra-lean beef or pork strips.

For less crisp bacon and to collect the drippings: Place 1 to 8 strips of bacon across a micro-safe meat rack, side by side but not overlapping—if your meat rack has no well to catch fat, set it into a larger casserole dish to catch the drippings.

To keep your oven from collecting the spatters, **cover** the strips with 2 layers of white paper towels, patting gently. (See Box below.) Cook on HIGH for 40 to 60 seconds per slice of bacon.

Let **stand** for 2 to 3 minutes before serving.

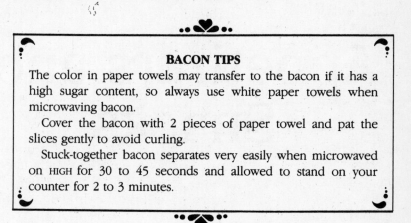

BACON TIPS

The color in paper towels may transfer to the bacon if it has a high sugar content, so always use white paper towels when microwaving bacon.

Cover the bacon with 2 pieces of paper towel and pat the slices gently to avoid curling.

Stuck-together bacon separates very easily when microwaved on HIGH for 30 to 45 seconds and allowed to stand on your counter for 2 to 3 minutes.

Troubleshooting: If brown spots appear on paper towels or bacon sticks to the towels, the bacon has a very high sugar content. If this happens to your test slice, use a meat rack to avoid sticking problems. Cover with 2 paper towels.

Unevenly cooked bacon results from excessive drippings when you try to cook more than 8 slices at once.

Appetizers and Snacks

Hot Holiday Dip

I happen to be crazy about progressive dinners. If you have to provide the appetizers, though, it can be difficult, because there are so many dishes involved. For the center of your tidbit table I suggest you start with a relish tray. Select a large tray and purchase a small pumpkin, large grapefruit, or pineapple just the right size for the center of the tray.

Here are some suggestions for finger foods to be placed in rows around the centerpiece: pitted black and green olives, pineapple chunks, rose radishes, dill pickle spears, stuffed celery, deviled eggs, marinated mushrooms, artichoke hearts, and sweet mixed pickles.

Carefully insert toothpicks all over the pumpkin or other centerpiece and alternate different kinds of cheese chunks on the picks. You may also want to alternate ½-inch cubes of salami, which you have spread with cream cheese and then rolled in toasted sesame seeds or chopped parsley.

Little shrimp cocktail crackers are always popular. On your favorite cracker place a small lettuce leaf, a shrimp, and a bit of cocktail sauce. For your hot finger food I suggest some attractive chafing dishes, a fondue bowl for a hot dip, or an insulated dish.

Equipment: 4-cup glass measure, chafing dish
Cooking time: 14 to 18 minutes
Standing time: none required.
Makes: enough for 1 large box of crackers

1 10-ounce frozen chopped broccoli
2 tablespoons butter
2 celery stalks, chopped
1 small onion, chopped
1 4-ounce can sliced mushrooms, drained
1 10¾-ounce can cream of mushroom soup, undiluted
1 small jar cheese spread
1 tablespoon garlic salt
¼ teaspoon oregano

Place paper-covered box of frozen broccoli on 2 layers of paper towels on the floor of your microwave. (Be sure there is no metal wrapping on the box.) Microwave on HIGH for 7 to 9 minutes or until hot and steaming, then drain and set aside.

To glass measure add butter, celery, onion, and mushrooms. Cook **uncovered** for 4 to 5 minutes on HIGH until vegetables are crisp-tender. Mix in drained broccoli, soup, cheese spread, garlic salt, and oregano.

Microwave on HIGH for 3 to 4 minutes until everything is soft and hot, stirring every 90 seconds. Place in chafing dish and serve with crackers.

Chili Beef Dip

Equipment: colander and casserole dish to catch drippings, 2-quart casserole dish
Cooking time: 14 to 17 minutes
Standing time: none required
Makes: enough for 1 to 1½ large bags of dip-size corn chips, about 12 ounces.

1 **pound ground beef**
1 **clove garlic, minced**
¼ **cup finely chopped, green pepper**
1 **8-ounce can tomato sauce**
¼ **cup ketchup**
¾ **teaspoon oregano**
½ **teaspoon red wine vinegar**
2 **to 3 teaspoons chili powder, to taste**
1 **8-ounce package cream cheese**
⅓ **cup grated Parmesan cheese**
1 **large bag dip-size corn chips**

Place colander in casserole dish to catch drippings. Crumble ground beef into colander and cook on HIGH for 3 minutes. Break up meat with a fork and add garlic, onions, and green pepper. Microwave on HIGH for 3 to 4 minutes more until meat is no longer pink and vegetables are crisp-tender.

In casserole dish place beef, vegetables, tomato sauce, ketchup, oregano, vinegar, and chili powder. Mix well, then **cover** with vented plastic wrap and cook on 80 percent power or MEDIUM-HIGH for 7 to 9 minutes.

Place cream cheese in a bowl and microwave on HIGH for 45 to 50 seconds until soft. Add softened cream cheese and Parmesan to hot meat and vegetables. Stir until cream cheese has melted, and serve with large corn chips for dipping.

Cheeseball Surprise

Equipment: turntable
Cooking time: 4 to 6 minutes
Standing time: 2 minutes
Makes: 36 to 40 meatballs

1 **pound lean ground beef**
½ **cup seasoned breadcrumbs**
1 **egg**
⅓ **cup white wine**

 4 **tablespoons finely minced onion**
 ½ **teaspoon seasoned salt**
 ⅛ **teaspoon pepper**
 1 **pound chunk blue cheese**

Combine all ingredients except blue cheese.

Cut blue cheese into 36 to 40 chunks and **cover** with hamburger mixture to form a ball. Place cheese balls in a circle around the outside edge of a plate and **elevate** on an inverted saucer. If you have a turntable, place saucer and dish on top and **rotate** dish while cooking.

Cook on HIGH for 4 to 6 minutes, turning meatballs over halfway through cooking. If you don't have a turntable, rotate the dish manually several times during cooking period.

Let **stand** for 2 minutes. Serve on toothpicks.

Little Party Chicken Legettes

My house has always been full of children, and it seems they are always ready for lunch. My children were never sandwich eaters, so Mom always had to come up with new main-dish ideas. Enter chicken legettes. I started using these little wing portions when my children were too young to eat the leg but loved the idea of eating meat off the bone.

As the years passed and the kids started eating a whole chicken each, my little legettes became an appetizer rather than a main dish. By dipping the meat in butter before rolling in the crumbs you get a fried effect. By mixing spices with dark-colored corn flake crumbs the finished product has the texture and look of fried chicken rather than the crumb coating just sitting on the outside—the usual result when you crumb-coat chicken or chops in the microwave.

You can prepare the legettes and freeze them for later use or bread them in advance of your party and keep them tightly covered in the fridge until you're ready to microwave. They cook so fast that you can constantly have a hot tray ready to pass.

COOKING CHICKEN PIECES

When placing pieces of chicken on a meat rack, be sure to place the meatiest portion to the outside of the dish and the bony section to the inside of the dish. The parts to the outside of the dish get more cooking time than the parts near the center. Be sure to turn over chicken pieces halfway through cooking to help in achieving evenly cooked meat.

Equipment: meat rack
Cooking time: 4 to 7 minutes
Standing time: 5 minutes
Serves: 6 to 8

20 chicken wings
¼ cup butter
1 teaspoon garlic powder
¾ cup cornflake crumbs
⅓ cup grated sharp Italian cheese, Parmesan or Romano work well
½ teaspoon dried parsley flakes
½ teaspoon oregano
½ teaspoon basil
¼ teaspoon paprika
½ teaspoon seasoned salt
pinch of pepper

If you're using whole chicken wings, cut off the section with one bone. Freeze the tip sections for soup or stock. (My husband uses them for crab bait.)

Starting at narrow end of bone, scrape meat away from bone with knife and pull the meat and skin down over the large end, forming a ball of meat at the bottom with a built-in "toothpick." This is really quite easy and can be done with your fingers once you have done a few and see how quickly it goes. You can also get your butcher to do it for you.

Place butter in custard cup, **cover** with paper towel to avoid spattering, and microwave on HIGH for 45 to 55 seconds or until melted. Add garlic powder. Place cornflake crumbs, cheese, and remaining spices in a small bowl and mix together.

Dip meat end of chicken into butter, then into dry ingredients, coating well. Press crumbs onto meat if necessary. Place legettes on meat rack in a circle and **cover** with wax paper. You may need to cook several batches, depending on the size of your meat rack.

Cook on HIGH for 4 to 7 minutes or until meat is no longer pink and juices are running clear. Turn legettes over halfway through cooking.

Let **stand**, covered, for 5 minutes before serving.

Troubleshooting: Legettes will be tough and hard if you overcook. Be sure to remember that they continue to cook during standing time after they are removed from the microwave and very often will overcook and dry out.

Since wings are not always the same size, try to use equally proportioned pieces in each batch to assure even cooking.

If you forget to cover with wax paper, the cornflake crumbs will pop all over the inside of your oven.

Suggestions: Try this same coating for pieces of cut-up chicken: follow the same instructions, just microwave 7 minutes per pound of chicken on HIGH power until juices no longer run pink when chicken is pierced with a fork. (See Box p. 94.)

COOKING MEATBALLS

Meatballs "fry" best when placed in a circle in a glass pie plate or casserole dish. You can also form a circle inside a square casserole dish. An oval glass baking dish works wonderfully with meatballs, since there are no square corners where the microwaves tend to overcook. If you have to use a square-cornered container, rotate the meatballs from the center of the dish to the outside edges and the ones along the edges to the center of the dish. Watch the ones in the corners so they don't overcook.

Uniform-sized meatballs will all cook in the same length of time, so be careful to make them as equal in size and shape as possible. To aid the "frying" process, elevate your flat-bottom cooking container on a simple inverted saucer.

MEATBALLS

Everybody loves meatballs! One of my readers wrote, "I have a big family gathering coming up and I need some new ideas for preparing my old standby meatballs for the buffet table—can you help?"

Meatballs are a favorite party dish for me and I like to make a variety of sauces for them. Try your family's favorite meatball recipe combined with one of my sauces to produce something new and different.

Meatballs in Mushroom Sauce

Equipment: 4-cup glass measure, glass pie plate, 2-quart casserole dish or 8 × 12-inch baking dish.
Cooking time: 20 to 27 minutes
Standing time: 5 minutes
Serves: 4 to 5 as appetizers or 2 as a main course

- 2 **tablespoons butter**
- 2 **medium onions, 1 chopped and 1 sliced**
- ⅔ **cup flavored breadcrumbs**
- ½ **cup milk**
- 2 **tablespoons A-1 Sauce**
- 1 **pound hamburger (or half beef and half pork)**
- 1 **egg**
- 1 **teaspoon seasoned salt**
- ¼ **teaspoon pepper**
- 1 **cup sliced fresh mushrooms, or 1 medium can of sliced mushrooms, drained**
- 1 **tablespoon flour**
- ½ **cup water**
- ⅓ **cup white wine**
- 1 **tablespoon beef bouillon**

In glass measure, place butter and the chopped onion. Microwave on HIGH for 3 to 4½ minutes or until onion is soft.

In a medium bowl combine breadcrumbs, milk, and 1 tablespoon A-1 Sauce. Blend together well. Add meat, egg, salt, pepper, and cooked onion to breadcrumb mixture. Mix together completely and form into 15 to 20 uniformly sized meatballs.

Place meatballs around the edge of a glass pie plate or round casserole dish (see Box, p. 26) and microwave **uncovered** on HIGH for 6½ to 9½ minutes or until no pink color remains and they are firm to the touch. Repeat until all meatballs are cooked. Do not overcook, as they will continue cooking for 2 to 3 minutes after being removed from the oven.

Place finished meatballs in the casserole or baking dish and **cover** with mushrooms and onion slices. In the glass measure combine flour, water, white wine, bouillon, and 1 tablespoon A-1 Sauce, and **whisk** until smooth. Pour sauce over meatballs and cover with wax paper. **Elevate** flat-bottomed container on an inverted saucer and place on a turntable if available.

Microwave on HIGH for 3 minutes, then reduce to 50 percent power or MEDIUM for 7 to 10 minutes or until sauce mixture has thickened, **stirring** carefully during cooking so as not to break up meatballs. (**Rotate** dish ½ turn after 4 minutes if not on a turntable.)

Let **stand** for 5 minutes before serving.

Suggestions: Triple the sauce and serve it over rice or noodles for a luscious main course.

Barbecued Meatballs

Equipment: 2- or 3-quart casserole dish and a 4-cup glass measure
Cooking time: 35 to 45 minutes
Standing time: 5 to 10 minutes
Serves: 10 to 15 as appetizers, 3 to 4 as a main course

MEATBALLS
1½ **cups breadcrumbs**
¾ **cup milk**
1 **egg**
1½ **pounds ground beef or 1 pound ground beef and**
½ **pound ground pork**
1 **teaspoon seasoned salt**
pepper to taste

SAUCE
- ¾ **cup ketchup**
- ¾ **cup water**
- ¾ **cup chopped onion**
- ¾ **cup chopped green pepper**
- ⅓ **cup cider vinegar**
- 4½ **tablespoons sugar**
- 2¼ **tablespoons Worcestershire Sauce**

Moisten breadcrumbs with milk. Add egg, meat, salt, and pepper to crumbs.

Shape beef mixture into small, ¾-inch, appetizer-size balls and place in casserole dish. Combine remaining ingredients in glass measure and pour over meatballs. Cook **uncovered** for 35 to 45 minutes on 70 percent power or MEDIUM-HIGH until sauce thickens and meatballs are brown. For best results **elevate** flat-bottomed container on an inverted saucer and use a turntable if one is available or rotate dish ½ turn every 10 minutes.

Do not **stir** until mixture has cooked for 10 to 15 minutes, as meatballs are very soft and will fall apart.

Let **stand,** 5 to 10 minutes before serving.

Suggestions: Double the sauce and serve over broad noodles for a main-course dish.

Party Dip Stuffed Bread

If you have never attended a food show put on by one of your local food store chains, you are really missing some good snacking. You can walk from one aisle to another just tasting various meats, pizzas, popcorn, drinks, yogurts, ice cream, etc., and then pick up some household cleaners and beauty supplies. People walk through the show filling plastic bags with goodies and really have a good time.

I frequently demonstrate microwave techniques at these shows, and this recipe is always a big hit, so I thought I would pass it on to you. I keep round pumpernickel breads in the freezer and a package or two of cream cheese in the fridge, so that I am always ready for unexpected company. You may have had a similar dip cold, but wait till you taste it hot.

Cooking time: 12 to 14 minutes
Standing time: none required
Serves: 15 to 20

    1 16-ounce round crusty pumpernickel bread
    2 packages (10-ounce boxes) frozen chopped spinach or broccoli, in their paper wrappers
    2 packages (8-ounces each) cream cheese
    2 teaspoons fresh lemon juice (see Box p. 227)
    1 tablespoon chopped scallions
  ⅛ teaspoon pepper
      crackers for dipping

Place frozen spinach or broccoli packages on 2 layers of paper towels on the floor of your microwave. Cook on HIGH for 9 to 11 minutes or until hot. Drain, pressing out excess liquid. Place cream cheese in a medium bowl. Microwave on HIGH for 40 to 55 seconds or until softened.

Cut a 1½- to 2-inch slice from top of bread. Remove center chunks of bread, leaving at least 2 inches of bread on the bottom. Cut center and top into pieces for dipping.

Add spinach and remaining dip ingredients to cream cheese and spoon into bread shell. Place filled bread on a paper-towel-lined paper plate and cook on HIGH for 45 to 60 seconds or until bread is warm.

Serve with bread pieces and assorted crackers for dipping. As you are serving, when dip starts to firm up, just place bread back on paper towels and reheat in your microwave for 45 to 60 seconds and stir dip before serving.

Suggestions: Try adding an envelope of onion or vegetable soup mix without the noodles for a different flavor.

To use half a recipe, I have my local bakery divide the pumpernickel dough in half and bake two small rounds breads instead of one large one. These breads freeze well, and when you keep a few on hand you are always ready to defrost and serve.

STUFFED MUSHROOMS

Mushrooms are an appetizer I always stayed away from because they are so soft that holding them with just a napkin at a party was impossible. But after microwaving them just once and seeing how fast and easy it is, and how beautifully they hold their shape, I now serve them all the time.

Because mushrooms have a high moisture content they become very soft when conventionally cooked but hold their shape when microwaved. They appear firm on the outside, but when you bite into them they're very soft. An entire plate of mushroom caps cooks in 2 to 3 minutes.

The largest mushroom caps go on the outside of the dish; that way they have a longer cooking period than the small caps in the center of the dish. Always place the caps in circles around the dish.

To soften cream cheese, unwrap and place it in a micro-safe bowl. Cook on HIGH for 45 to 60 seconds until soft or on 50 percent power or MEDIUM for 60 to 90 seconds. Check the texture after 45 seconds to be sure you don't melt it.

Cheese and Bacon Caps

Equipment: 2- and 4-cup glass measures
Cooking time: 2 to 3 minutes
Standing time: 2 minutes
Serves: 8 to 10, depending on the size of the caps

1 pound fresh mushrooms, caps and stems separated with stems chopped
4 bacon slices, diced
2 tablespoons minced green pepper
¼ teaspoon minced garlic
¼ cup minced onion
dash of salt
½ teaspoon A-1 Sauce
1 3-ounce package cream cheese at room temperature (see above)
1 tablespoon butter
½ cup breadcrumbs

In the 4-cup glass measure, combine mushroom stems, bacon, green pepper, garlic, and onion. **Cover** with paper towel and microwave on HIGH for 3½ to 4 minutes. Drain off fat and stir in salt, A-1 Sauce, and cream cheese. Fill wiped mushroom caps with bacon-cream cheese mixture and set aside.

In 2-cup glass measure, melt butter on HIGH for 45 to 55 seconds

and add breadcrumbs. Press breadcrumbs evenly over tops of stuffed mushrooms. Cover a paper plate with two layers of paper towels, arrange mushrooms in a circle on the plate, and cook on HIGH for 2 to 3 minutes.
Let **stand** for 2 minutes before serving.

Troubleshooting: Never wash mushrooms with water as they act as a sponge and absorb it. Use a clean damp kitchen towel or paper towel and carefully wipe the caps. Be sure to cut off the bottom slice of the stem before chopping.

Suggestions: Prepare your stuffed mushrooms the day before, place in an airtight container, and refrigerate until ready to use. Microwave the stuffed mushrooms within 48 hours of preparation.

Nutty Stuffed Mushrooms

Equipment:	4-cup glass measure
Cooking time:	5 to 7 minutes
Standing time:	2 minutes
Serves:	8 to 10, depending on size of mushrooms

1 **pound fresh mushrooms, stems and caps separated with
   stems chopped**
4 **slices bacon**
¼ **cup chopped onion**
½ **teaspoon finely chopped, fresh garlic**
⅓ **cup seasoned breadcrumbs**
¼ **cup chopped pecans**
½ **teaspoon parsley flakes**
2 **tablespoons white wine**
  pecan halves

Dice bacon and place in glass measure along with the onions, mushroom stems and garlic. Cook on HIGH for 3 to 4 minutes or until bacon is crisp, **stirring** every minute to keep bacon from sticking together. Drain off all but 2 tablespoons of drippings and add breadcrumbs, chopped pecans, parsley, and white wine, and mix together.
Stuff into wiped mushroom caps, top with a pecan half, and arrange on a paper plate that has been **covered** with 2 layers of paper towels. Cook on HIGH for 2 to 3 minutes. Let **stand** for 2 minutes before serving.

Suggestions: Try substituting very lean salt pork for the bacon.

Seafood Stuffed Mushrooms

Equipment:	4-cup glass measure
Cooking time:	7 to 10 minutes
Standing time:	2 minutes
Serves:	8 to 10, depending on size of mushrooms

- **1 pound mushrooms, caps and stems separated with stems chopped**
- **¼ cup finely chopped onions**
- **1 clove garlic, finely minced**
- **¼ cup chopped crabmeat or shrimp**
- **2 tablespoons butter**
- **2 tablespoons white wine**
- **½ cup seasoned breadcrumbs**
- **pepper to taste**
- **1 egg**

In the glass measure place onions, mushroom stems, garlic, seafood, butter, and wine. Cook on HIGH for 5 to 7 minutes until vegetables are crisp-tender. Stir in breadcrumbs, pepper, and 1 slightly beaten egg. Mound stuffing into mushroom caps and arrange on a paper plate that has been **covered** with 2 layers of paper towels.

Cook on HIGH for 2 to 3 minutes until heated through.

Let **stand** for 2 minutes before serving.

Suggestions: Use any seafood you have on hand, or try sausage or diced pepperoni.

THE SOGGY-BOTTOM PROBLEM

The microwave does such a wonderful job of heating up, melting, and boiling, but it also softens the bottom of hard rolls and the bottoms of hot cracker appetizers. This can be a problem if you're trying to heat only the meat on crusty bread or the topping on a cracker and you wind up with soft bread or crackers.

I have a solution to this problem but it will work only if you are very careful and pay close attention to my instructions. As you should know by now, aluminum foil repels the microwaves and is used only when you want to shield something that you do not want to cook. The microwaves hit the aluminum foil and bounce off and away from the food it shields.

Using this principle, you can keep the bottom of crackers and bread crisp by placing a small flat piece of aluminum foil, shiny side up, on a paper plate. Remember, no crimps, folds, no touching itself in any way, or it will arch and possibly ignite. Place 2 paper towels over the foil to absorb the moisture that will form and you're ready to place the bread or crackers on the towels. The foil will keep the microwaves away and the bottom of the food will stay crisp. Forgetting to put paper towels or a paper napkin down will cause moisture to penetrate into the food and it will get soggy and eventually toughen.

Pizza Snacks

Try some of my pizza crackers, guaranteed not to have soggy bottoms. I always serve these when I need a quick finger food or the kids want pizza and I don't have any dough.

Cooking time: 30 to 35 seconds per dish
Standing time: 1 to 2 minutes
Serves: 5 to 8 crackers per person

> **crackers of your choice**
> 1   **small jar pizza or spaghetti sauce**
>   **thickly sliced mozzarella cheese, cut into squares smaller than the tops of the crackers**
> ¼   **pound pepperoni, sliced**

Place a flat square of aluminum foil on top of a paper plate, shiny side up. **Cover** with 2 layers of paper towels. Place crackers on paper in a circle and add a dab of sauce. Place a square of cheese on the sauce and cover with a slice of pepperoni.

Microwave **uncovered** on HIGH for 30 to 35 seconds until the cheese just begins to melt.

Let **stand** for 1 to 2 minutes before serving.

Troubleshooting: If the cheese square is too large, it may melt over the edge of the cracker, so try a sample before doing an entire plate.

Suggestions: You can omit the pepperoni or use a slice of cooked meatball, sausage, mushroom, or a small onion ring.

Bacon Poles

I started making this recipe for my boys when they were little. They love little finger snacks when watching a special television show on Saturday evenings. I prepare them in the afternoon, pop them in the fridge, and then microwave them when the boys announce they are hungry.

I find they also make good nibbles when you're sitting around the kitchen table playing cards and everyone wants a little something.

Cooking time: 4 ½ to 6 minutes
Standing time: 2 minutes
Serves: 3 to 4

   6 slices bacon
   12 sesame seed bread sticks
   ⅓ cup grated Parmesan cheese
   ¼ teaspoon parsley flakes
   ¼ teaspoon toasted sesame seeds

Halve bacon slices lengthwise and wrap, barber-pole style, around bread sticks. Place poles on a paper plate lined with 2 layers of paper towels and cook on HIGH for 4½ to 6 minutes.

While poles are cooking, mix cheese, parsley flakes, and sesame seeds together on a paper plate.

As soon as poles come out of the microwave, immediately roll in cheese mixture and place them standing up in a decorative coffee mug and let **stand** for 2 minutes before serving.

Suggestions: If you want to wrap bacon around precooked fillings such as olives or water chestnuts, precook bacon ½ normal cooking time and then wrap and complete cooking just before serving. Wrap raw bacon around chicken livers, place on a meat rack to keep the livers from absorbing the drippings, and cook the bacon and liver at the same time.

Soups

Aunt Lee's Vegetable Soup

Some of my fondest childhood memories are of the days I spent with my very special Uncle Gene. I always knew when fall was in full swing before I even opened the kitchen door, because Aunt Lee would have a pot of her famous vegetable soup simmering on the back burner of her very old-fashioned gas stove. Then, soup making was confined to fall, winter, and spring; now, however, with your cool-cooking microwave, you can have it anytime you have a craving.

When I was old enough to learn how to cook, my aunt shared her recipe with me and I have been making it ever since. I used to prepare it when my sons were babies—for them. I would put it through the blender, freeze it in ice cube trays, and defrost the cubes in the microwave.

I think the reason my sons will eat any vegetable you can think of is that their first solid food was the array of fresh and frozen vegetables in Aunt Lee's vegetable soup. Aunt Lee would be amazed if she could see how fast her soup now cooks in the microwave; she had to simmer her pot all day.

Try Aunt Lee's soup and don't be afraid to add your own special ingredients to make our family's favorite your own.

Equipment: deep 3- or 4-quart casserole dish.
Cooking time: 2¼ to 2½ hours
Standing time: 10 minutes
Serves: 4

1 pound beef shank, meat and bone
5 cups water
1 8-ounce can tomato sauce
1 medium onion, diced
1 medium potato, diced
1 celery stalk, thinly sliced
½ cup diced turnips (optional)
2 carrots, thinly sliced
1 28-ounce can whole tomatoes with the juice, broken up into small chunks
1 box frozen mixed vegetables
salt and pepper to taste

Place beef shank, water, and tomato sauce in casserole dish. Microwave **covered** with casserole cover or vented plastic wrap on HIGH for 8 to 10 minutes or until boiling. Reduce to 50 percent power or MEDIUM and simmer for 50 minutes. If you're using a flat-bottomed container, **elevate** on an inverted saucer and place it on turntable if available. (If not using turntable, **rotate** dish ¼ turn every 10 minutes.)

Allow soup base to sit covered for 20 minutes, then remove the meat from the bones, dice, and return to the soup.

Add all remaining ingredients and microwave on 80 percent power or MEDIUM-HIGH for 1 hour until all vegetables are tender.

Let **stand,** covered, for 10 minutes before serving.

Troubleshooting: If you find some of your vegetables are not tender enough, it may be that you did not dice them in uniform size. In order to cook in the same time they must be the same size.

Do not return the bones to the soup, as you may find there isn't enough liquid. They are great for the dog, however.

If you would like to turn your soup pot into a slow cooker, see Box p. 45.

Wonton Soup

To make one of my stir-fry recipes into an entire Chinese meal, I add Chinese-style barbecued spareribs (see p. 72) and wonton soup. My microwave version is very good made the day before and reheated before dinner, freeing your microwave for the rest of your Chinese feast. Add pretty lotus bowls to your table arrangement, chopsticks on your napkins, and hot towels (see Box p. 72) for everyone's hands, and you're ready for company.

Equipment:	deep 3- or 4-quart casserole dish
Cooking time:	31 to 39 minutes
Standing time:	5 minutes
Serves:	4 to 6

  1 10-ounce package frozen chopped spinach
  ¾ pound lean ground pork
  6 canned water chestnuts, finely minced
  ¼ teaspoon finely minced fresh ginger root
  ½ teaspoon salt
  ¼ teaspoon pepper
  4 teaspoons soy sauce
  1 teaspoon white wine
  1 package wonton wrappers
  6 cups chicken broth—fresh, canned, or from bouillon
  1 cup thinly sliced Chinese celery cabbage
  3 scallions, chopped

Microwave paper-covered box of frozen spinach on 2 layers of paper towels for 9 minutes on HIGH. Drain and squeeze dry, then chop and set aside.

Combine pork, water chestnuts, ginger, salt, pepper, sugar, soy sauce, and wine. Mix thoroughly, then add spinach and mix once more.

Roll the wontons as follows: Place 1 teaspoon filling in the center of the wrapper. Moisten the upper edges with water. Bring together two sides of the wrapper and pinch it all around to seal in the filling. Pull the two bottom edges together and pinch firmly to seal. As you work, cover wonton wrappers and finished wontons with a damp cloth to prevent drying out.

Place chicken broth, Chinese cabbage, scallions, and wontons in casserole dish. Microwave **covered** with wax paper on HIGH for 12 to 15 minutes until boiling.

Reduce to 60 percent power or MEDIUM and microwave **uncovered** for 10 to 15 minutes until wontons are soft.

Let **stand,** covered, for 5 minutes before serving.

Troubleshooting: If you have never worked with wonton wrappers before, be careful not to let them dry out. Most supermarkets carry wonton wrappers in their fresh produce section. If there are too many in a package for one recipe, just tightly wrap, label, and freeze the unused ones. They are very easy to work with and you'll be surprised what a nice touch they will add to your meal.

Suggestions: Soup is best when made the day before and chilled until ready to serve. Be sure to skim any congealed fat from the top of the soup before reheating.

Serve with fried Chinese noodles, hot mustard, and duck sauce.

Mushroom Vegetable Soup

When I was a child my mother made the greatest mushroom vegetable soup. It was always a lunch favorite, and, unknown to me, all the ingredients except the potatoes came from cans. She used to add a BLT sandwich, a great combination.

When I married and started cooking I was eager to learn about Mom's soup—was I surprised to find it so easy. This soup is wonderful in the microwave, and even though it almost all comes from cans it tastes like you simmered it for hours. The recipe can be doubled easily, and as long as you have potatoes in the house and the canned vegetables, you're always ready to make this soup.

Equipment:	6-cup glass measure and deep 2- or 3-quart casserole dish
Cooking time:	11 to 15 minutes
Standing time:	none required
Serves:	4

1 **medium potato, diced**
¼ **cup water**
2 **10¾-ounce cans cream of mushroom soup, undiluted**
2 **soup cans milk**
1 **16-ounce can peas and carrots, drained**
1 **16-ounce can creamed corn**
   salt and pepper to taste

Place potato in glass measure and add water. Microwave on HIGH for 4 to 5 minutes until potato is tender, then drain.

Whisk soup and milk together in casserole dish until smooth. Add potato, peas and carrots, and creamed corn to soup.

Microwave on 50 percent power or MEDIUM for 7 to 10 minutes until completely heated through, then add salt and pepper to taste.

Troubleshooting: If you microwave soup that contains milk on HIGH, it will boil and possibly curdle just as it would if you put it in a sauce pan on high heat on your range top. Milk products must be microwaved on MEDIUM or 50 percent power so they will heat more slowly.

If you feel it necessary to salt the potato before cooking, dissolve the salt in the ¼ cup of water before adding to potato. If you sprinkle it onto the potato it will leave little gray spots of dehydration where it touches.

Updated Turkey Noodle Soup

Do you get the turkey-carcass blues after the holidays? Here are some simple suggestions to free that shelf in the fridge, use up all that turkey the family is tired of, and put a smile back on your face.

First and most important, clean all the meat from the bones. If you have too much meat for soup and you are turkey salad lovers, freeze the meat in marked packages for easy defrosting. But if your family is like mine and loves soup, here are two variations I know you will enjoy.

Equipment: 3- or 4-quart casserole dish (with cover if available)
Cooking time: 14 to 18 minutes
Standing time: 5 minutes
Serves: 3 to 4

   2 **cups cooked cubed turkey**
   3 **cups chicken broth or 3 cups hot water with**
     1½ tablespoons chicken bouillon
1½ **cups fine egg noodles**
   1 **10-ounce package frozen mixed vegetables**
   2 **teaspoons minced scallions or onions**
   1 **tablespoon fresh chopped parsley, or ¼ teaspoon parsley**
     flakes
     salt and pepper to taste

Combine all ingredients in casserole dish. **Cover** with casserole cover or vented plastic wrap and microwave on HIGH for 14 to 18 minutes, or until the noodles are tender, **stirring** frequently during cooking.

Let **stand,** covered, for 5 minutes before serving.

Quick Turkey Rice Soup

Equipment: 4-quart casserole dish (with cover if available)
Cooking time: 55 to 60 minutes
Standing time: 10 minutes
Serves: 4 to 6

   1 **turkey carcass (if carcass has already been cleaned of its**
     meat, add 2 cups diced turkey)
   3 **quarts hot water**
   1 **large onion, finely chopped**
½ **cup finely chopped celery**
   1 **teaspoon salt**

½ teaspoon pepper
2 cups thinly sliced carrots
1 cup uncooked rice

Combine turkey carcass, water, onion, celery, salt, and pepper in casserole dish. Use casserole cover or vented plastic wrap to **cover** dish.

Microwave on HIGH for 35 to 40 minutes. Remove carcass from the pot and take all the meat off of the bones. Discard bones, strain the soup, and then return turkey meat to strained soup.

Add carrots and microwave, covered, on HIGH for 10 minutes, **stirring** once. Add rice and microwave, covered, 10 minutes more on HIGH, stirring once.

Let **stand,** covered, for 10 minutes before serving.

Old Fashioned
Split Pea and Ham Soup

I come from a family where Mom used to cook pea soup all day to extract that delectable ham and vegetable flavor. My husband the chef said, "I have an easier method that my mom used to make."

Since you can't fight the mother-in-law's old family recipe, I began making it their way. Even though I would never admit it to them, it really did taste the same and cooked in only a few hours instead of all day.

I know, using a canned soup as the base for this hearty soup makes you skeptical, but try it, because even an old cook like me can always learn a new trick.

Equipment: 3- or 4-quart casserole dish
Cooking time: 40 to 50 minutes
Standing time: 5 minutes
Serves: 4

2 10¾-ounce cans Campbell's Manhandlers Split Pea with
Ham soup
2 soup cans water
1 ham bone
1 cup diced ham from bone
2 small carrots, thinly sliced
1 large celery stalk, thinly sliced
1 medium onion, diced
1 large potato, diced
salt and pepper to taste

In casserole dish, combine soup and water, mixing well. Add bone, meat, and vegetables, stirring to dissolve soup mixture.

Microwave tightly **covered** (see Covering and Venting, p. 7) on HIGH for 10 minutes, then reduce to 50 percent power or MEDIUM and microwave covered for 30 to 40 minutes until vegetables are tender, **stirring** several times during cooking. Taste and adjust seasonings, adding salt and pepper to taste.

Let **stand,** covered, for 5 minutes before serving.

Suggestions: Grated Parmesan cheese sprinkled over the top just before serving adds a nice flavor.

Meat

STEWS

According to *Webster's* dictionary, to stew means to boil slowly or with simmering heat. By micro-cooking you accomplish this beautifully; a big bonus is that there's no frying pan to wash and no spatters all over the stove to wipe up.

The most important element of a good stew is the type of meat you use. Butchers usually sell cut-up round as stew beef. You are much better off buying beef chuck, in the form of a roast or a steak, and cutting it into uniform-sized pieces yourself. The marbling of the fat in the chuck makes it more tender and also cheaper than precut stew beef.

To make this stew a real time-saver, make a double batch and freeze half for another brisk night. The easiest way to freeze for later heating up in the microwave is to line a container with plastic wrap. Place your precooked food in the lined container, making a nicely fitting package.

Then put the container in the freezer. Once frozen, remove the package from the container and wrap it in freezer wrap. Mark the package with whatever size container you used, so when you're ready to defrost and heat you need only remove the freezer wrapping and the package will fit right back into the container.

The nice thing about stew is that once you have the meat and basic gravy, almost any vegetable will do and make it interesting.

Beef and Beer Stew

Equipment:	deep 3-quart casserole dish
Cooking time:	1 hour 15 minutes
Standing time:	15 minutes
Serves:	4 to 5

1½ **pounds chuck, cut into ¾-inch cubes**
  3 **tablespoons flour**
  3 **medium potatoes, cut into ½-inch cubes**
  2 **large carrots, cut into ¼-inch slices**
  2 **medium onions, sliced**
  ½ **cup sliced fresh mushrooms**
  1 **cup beer (any brand, light or dark)**
  1 **8-ounce can tomato sauce**
  1 **clove garlic, minced**
  1 **tablespoon beef bouillon**
  1 **tablespoon brown sugar**
1½ **teaspoons Worcestershire Sauce**
  ½ **teaspoon seasoned salt**
  ⅛ **teaspoon pepper**
  1 **package frozen string beans, peas, lima beans, or mixed vegetables**

In the casserole dish, mix chuck and flour, coating meat well. Add all remaining ingredients except the frozen vegetables. Mix together carefully, keeping meat under the liquid. Place a piece of flat aluminum foil over the top of the casserole dish (see Box p. 45) or **cover** tightly with vented plastic wrap.

Elevate flat-bottomed casserole on inverted saucer and microwave on HIGH for 5 minutes. I suggest using a turntable if one is available.

Change power setting to 50 percent or MEDIUM and cook for 60 minutes. **Stir** twice during cooking to evenly distribute the heat throughout the dish—if not using a turntable, **rotate** dish ½ turn each time you stir.

Add frozen vegetables and microwave another 10 minutes on 50 percent power.

Let **stand,** covered, for 15 minutes before serving.

Troubleshooting: If you find some pieces of meat that are tough and dried out, your problem could be that they were not fully covered by the liquid. Try to keep the meat under the liquid at all times.

If some of the meat and vegetables are not completely cooked after standing time, it is because you did not cut them uniformly in size and shape. This is a *must* for even cooking.

If after standing time you find your gravy is too thin, thicken it with 1 teaspoon of cornstarch dissolved in 2 teaspoons of water. Mix cornstarch mixture into gravy and microwave for 2 minutes on HIGH.

Suggestions: Serve over broad noodles.

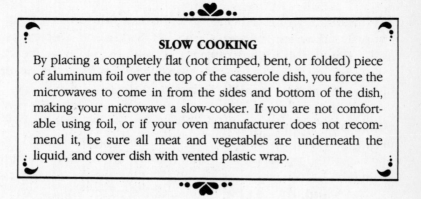

SLOW COOKING

By placing a completely flat (not crimped, bent, or folded) piece of aluminum foil over the top of the casserole dish, you force the microwaves to come in from the sides and bottom of the dish, making your microwave a slow-cooker. If you are not comfortable using foil, or if your oven manufacturer does not recommend it, be sure all meat and vegetables are underneath the liquid, and cover dish with vented plastic wrap.

Hearty Beef Stew

Equipment: 3- or 4-quart casserole dish (with cover if available)
Cooking time: 90 to 95 minutes
Standing time: 15 minutes
Serves: 4 to 6

2 **pounds chuck, cut into ¾-inch cubes**
⅓ **cup flour**
2 **cups water**
2 **tablespoons beef bouillon**
1 **bay leaf**
1 **teaspoon sugar**
1 **teaspoon seasoned salt**
¼ **teaspoon pepper**
1 **clove garlic, minced**
3 **tablespoons A-1 Sauce**
1 **tablespoon Worcestershire Sauce**
4 **medium potatoes, peeled and cut into eighths**
4 **medium carrots, thinly sliced**
2 **celery stalks, thinly sliced**
1 **large onion, thinly sliced**
1 **box frozen peas**

Toss meat and flour together in casserole dish. **Stir** in water, bouillon, bay leaf, sugar, salt, pepper, garlic, A-1 Sauce, and Worcestershire Sauce. **Cover** dish with aluminum foil (see Box p. 45), or the casserole cover, or vented plastic wrap. **Elevate** flat-bottomed casserole dish on an inverted saucer and place on a turntable, if available.

Microwave on HIGH for 5 minutes, then reduce to 50 percent power or MEDIUM and microwave for 40 minutes. Add all the remaining vegetables except the peas, stir, and cover. Microwave for 45 to 50 minutes on 50 percent power until meat is fork tender, adding peas during the last 10 minutes of cooking time.

Let **stand,** covered, for 15 minutes before serving.

Suggestions: If you aren't adding frozen peas, microwave for 70 minutes on 50 percent power.

Add your favorite hot rolls, salad, and brownies (see p. 201) to round out your meal.

Roast Beef

I suggest you micro-roast only tender cuts of beef. I find sirloin tip, top round, and eye round cuts roast very well and stay extremely juicy. The microwave extracts about one-third more fat from meat than conventional cooking does; however, it doesn't extract meat juices, therefore there are no drippings for gravy until you slice the meat. I suggest having a gravy base ready, and then once you begin slicing you can add the juices to the base.

Select as evenly shaped a roast as you can find for microwaving and be sure the fat is marbelized throughout the meat. If the meat is oddly shaped, you may find some areas overcooking while others are undercooked. Again, shape is an important factor in a perfect finished product.

You can estimate cooking time by weight, but the most accurate way is by using a thermometer made for microwaving or by using the temperature probe that comes with many ovens. When using your probe or thermometer, be sure to place it in the center of the roast, and be sure it is actually in meat, not fat or bone (see Box p. 68).

Regardless of what your oven manufacturer or other microwave cookbooks say, never micro-roast your beef or any red meat on HIGH—it cooks too quickly and doesn't allow the meat the time it needs to tenderize. I suggest starting the meat on HIGH for only the first 5 minutes, then reducing to 50 percent power or MEDIUM to allow more cooking and tenderizing time.

If your oven has only HIGH power, it will cook your roast too quickly, not giving it enough time to properly tenderize. To slow down the cooking power, place a small bowl of water alongside your roast. Some of the energy will be drawn to the water, decreasing the number of microwaves cooking the roast.

You need to elevate meat off the bottom of the flat cooking container to allow microwaves to get underneath as well as around the sides for more even cooking. If you do not have a meat or roasting rack made for the microwave, carefully balance your meat on top of two custard cups, an inverted saucer, or a small micro-safe bowl. Whatever you use, be sure it's set into a casserole dish to catch the fat that the microwaves will extract.

SALT IN THE MICROWAVE

Salt—in any form—can't be applied to any surface that is exposed to microwave energy or it will leave little tiny dehydration spots where it touches. Therefore, when microwaving do *not* use any product containing salt granules, such as garlic salt, onion salt, seasoned salt, or salt substitutes, unless they are combined in a sauce. Salt exposed food surfaces *after* they are microwaved, not before.

Equipment: meat rack
Cooking time: 8 to 12 minutes per pound, depending on degree of doneness
Standing time: 5-10 minutes
Serves: 6 to 9

2 to 4 pounds tender eye round, sirloin tip, or top round roast
garlic and/or onion powder
pepper
3 to 4 slices bacon

Rub your roast with garlic and/or onion powder and pepper, never salt (see above). Unless roast is very fatty, wrap it with slices of bacon and place it fat-side down on a meat rack set into a casserole dish to catch the fat.

Timetable for cooking by time and weight:

Rare—8 to 9 minutes per pound
Medium rare—9 to 11 minutes per pound
Well done—11 to 12 minutes per pound

Temperature guide for cooking with probe or thermometer:

INTERNAL TEMPERATURE

After Microwaving	*After Standing*
Rare—115 degrees	Rare—130 degrees
Medium rare—120 degrees	Medium rare—140 degrees
Medium—130 degrees	Medium—145 degrees
Well done—145 degrees	Well done—160 degrees

STANDING TIME

Standing time is one of the most important concepts to remember and understand when microwaving. Once the oven is shut off there are no microwaves entering the food; however, the molecules within the food are still vibrating—still causing heat—so the food is still cooking. Whenever you remove food from the microwave it is safe to assume that no matter what the food is, it will continue to cook for 5 to 10 minutes after the microwaves are shut off.

This can be seen best in meat because you can micro-cook a roast to 120 degrees, tent it in aluminum foil (see Box p. 69) and watch the temperature go up 15 to 20 degrees in the course of 5 to 10 minutes. Always slightly undercook food in the microwave and it will finish cooking during standing time. If you cook your food to the exact degree of doneness you want, it will overcook while it stands and you prepare to serve it. Standing time is one of the least understood and yet most important tips in microwave cooking. It can mean the difference between overcooked hard food and tender food cooked to the proper doneness.

If you're cooking by my guide to minutes per pound, begin by calculating cooking time, and if you're cooking by temperature, insert your probe (see Box p. 68) or microwave thermometer.

Regardless of the cooking method, start the meat on HIGH for the first 5 minutes and then reduce to 50 percent power or MEDIUM.

Turn the roast over halfway through cooking time, and when cooking time has finished or the internal temperature has been reached, remove the meat from the microwave, **tent** with aluminum foil, shiny side toward the meat, and let **stand** for 5 to 10 minutes before serving.

When slicing, be careful that you have a deep plate to catch the drippings; I have had them running all over the table before I realized what was happening.

Base for Roast Beef Gravy

Equipment: 6-cup glass measure
Cooking time: 8 to 12 minutes
Standing time: none required
Makes: 2¼ cups

½ **cup sliced fresh mushrooms**
2 **tablespoons butter**
⅓ **cup flour**
2 **tablespoons Burgundy wine (see Box p. 65)**
1½ **cups beef broth, canned or from bouillon**
⅓ **cup roast drippings**
salt and pepper to taste

Place mushrooms and butter in glass measure and microwave on HIGH for 4 to 6 minutes until soft. **Whisk** in flour and wine until smooth. Whisk in beef broth. Whisk in meat drippings and season to taste.

Cook on HIGH for 4 to 6 minutes until thick and smooth, whisking twice during cooking.

Troubleshooting: If your gravy is lumpy, you forgot to use your whisk.

Suggestions: Try freezing any leftover gravy in a marked container and add it to your next batch of fresh gravy. It will add flavor and color and will extend the amount.

Pot Roast

To bag or to pot ... a not-so-tender roast is just personal preference but you should try it both ways and see which you prefer. In microwaving, when you want something to braise, as you would a less tender cut of meat (see Box p. 51), it must be steamed with enough liquid to almost cover the meat.

For those of you with a touch of "old fashioned" still in you who feel that a pot is necessary for true pot roast, a good-sized casserole dish with a tight-fitting cover will do wonderfully (see Box below).

For those of you who want little to zero cleanup, the roasting bag is for you. Everything is sealed inside the bag, with no mess in the casserole dish that holds it (see Box below).

The basic method of preparation is the same whether using a bag or a casserole dish: the only thing that changes is the recipe. Since my family loves to experiment and doesn't care for things constantly prepared the same way, I want you to try some of our favorites.

Write down the ingredients of your favorite conventional recipe. By using my times and temperatures, and basic amount of liquid, you can convert it to a microwave recipe yourself. Experiment with your first try, but be sure to write down the quantities you use and the exact time it takes your oven to create a perfect pot roast with your own recipe.

POT ROASTING

When selecting meat for pot roasting; use less tender flat cuts such as chuck, brisket, or bottom round. To help tenderize these cuts, pierce both sides of the meat deeply with a fork before beginning the recipe and slash the fatty edges of the meat to help it remain flat during cooking.

To obtain a tight-fitting cover, place a piece of wax paper between the dish and the cover. This will make a tighter fit and ensure that whatever is inside is steaming.

When using a roasting bag be sure to tie it closed *loosely,* leaving room for the steam to escape. Never use a metal twist-tie to close a roasting bag. Use a piece of string, dental floss, or cut off the top rim of the bag and use it for a closure.

To allow meat to stand as long as possible without getting cold, place on serving platter and tent with aluminum foil, shiny side toward the meat. This will help keep meat hot while you are preparing the gravy.

Equipment:	large roasting bag with casserole dish to hold it, or a 3- or 4-quart casserole dish with cover
Cooking times:	65 to 75 minutes for meat and vegetables; 1 to 3 minutes for gravy
Standing time:	10 to 15 minutes
Serves:	4 to 6

2 to 3 pounds chuck or brisket roast
1 envelope dry onion soup mix, undiluted
1 10¾-ounce can cream of mushroom soup, undiluted
¼ cup white wine
1 cup sliced fresh mushrooms
1 onion, sliced
3 carrots, cut in half lengthwise and then into 1½-inch chunks
6 small red potatoes, cut in half

GRAVY
2 tablespoons flour or 1 tablespoon cornstarch
¼ cup water

Pierce both sides of meat deeply with a fork and slash fat edges. Place meat in casserole dish or roasting bag (see Box p. 51). Combine dry onion soup, mushroom soup, and wine, and spread over meat.

Cover casserole tightly and **elevate** flat-bottomed casserole on inverted saucer. Cook on HIGH for 10 minutes, using a turntable if available or **rotating** dish ½ turn every 3 minutes. (If you want your pot roast to cook as if in a slow-cooker, see Box p. 45.) Reduce to 50 percent power or MEDIUM and microwave for 25 minutes.

Turn roast over (turn over entire bag if using) and add vegetables. Cover tightly or secure loosely, if you're using a roasting bag— and microwave on 50 percent power for 30 to 45 minutes until vegetables and meat are fork tender, rotating dish ½ turn twice during cooking. (If you're using a larger roast and more vegetables, be sure to increase cooking time after vegetables are added.)

Let **stand,** tightly covered, for 10 to 15 minutes, then remove the meat to a platter and **tent** (see Box p. 69) with aluminum foil, shiny side toward meat, while making gravy. Slice meat across the grain to serve.

Gravy: Remove meat and vegetables to platter. If you're using a roasting bag, pour drippings into a bowl. Skim off fat. **Whisk** flour and water together and add to drippings. Cook on HIGH for 1 to 3 minutes or until thick, whisking several times.

Suggestions: Try using red potatoes; they hold their shape better than white baking potatoes.

Allow meat to sit in a marinade overnight to help tenderize it.

Pot Roast with Tomato Pan Gravy

Equipment: large roasting bag with casserole dish to hold it, or 4-quart casserole dish with cover
Cooking times: 65 to 80 minutes for meat and vegetables; 1 to 3 minutes for gravy
Standing time: 10 to 15 minutes
Serves: 4 to 6

2 to 3 pounds chuck roast, brisket, or bottom round
1 8-ounce can tomato sauce
1 clove garlic, minced
1 tablespoon beef bouillon
2 tablespoons A-1 Sauce
1 tablespoon Worcestershire sauce
¼ cup burgundy wine
½ cup water
2 celery stalks, sliced
2 large carrots, sliced
1 large onion, cut in eighths
1 small head broccoli, cut into bite-size pieces
6 small red potatoes, cut in half—or 4 medium baking potatoes, cut into fourths

GRAVY
2 tablespoons flour
¼ cup water

Pierce both sides of meat and slash edges. Place meat in casserole dish or large roasting bag set into a casserole dish. In a small bowl mix tomato sauce, garlic, bouillon, A-1 Sauce, Worcestershire Sauce, wine, and water together. Pour over meat and loosely close bag or tightly **cover** casserole dish.

Cook on HIGH for 10 minutes, using a turntable if you have one; if not **rotate** dish ½ turn every 5 minutes. Reduce to 50 percent power or MEDIUM and microwave for 25 minutes. Turn meat over and add vegetables, **stirring** gravy at the same time. Cook for another 30 to 45 minutes on MEDIUM or 50 percent power, turning dish ½ turn twice.

Let **stand** covered, for 10 to 15 minutes, then remove to platter and **tent** (see Box, p. 69) with aluminum foil, shiny side toward the meat, while making gravy. Slice meat across the grain to serve.

Gravy: If you're using a casserole, remove meat and vegetables. If you're using a roasting bag, pour drippings into a bowl. Skim off fat. **Whisk** flour and water together and add to drippings. Microwave on HIGH 1 to 3 minutes or until thick, whisking several times.

Stuffed Flank Roll-Up

If you buy your beef by the hind-quarter or side for the freezer, you always have a flank steak that you may not know how to prepare. Flank steak can be very tough if not prepared and sliced just right.

In the microwave, I feel it is best when cooked in some type of sauce. This is a favorite recipe of mine that can be served to company or just to the family. I once used this recipe for the main course of my Father's Day dinner in my newspaper column and received letters from several men who wrote, "I'm not a dad, but I microwaved your dinner for my girlfriend and she loved it."

But the best letter of all came from a gentleman who wrote, "For years I saw flank steak in my supermarket and was too embarrassed to ask what to do with it. You have not only satisfied my curiosity but taught this old dog a new trick."

TENDERIZING STEAKS

To tenderize steaks and flat cuts of meat, place meat on a cutting board and use a meat mallet or the edge of an unbreakable saucer to pound the meat. Start at one end and go over the entire piece, being sure to pound, not cut through the meat. Turn the meat over and repeat the process on the other side.

Equipment: meat mallet or unbreakable saucer, 4-cup glass measure, wooden skewers or string, 6-cup glass measure, meat rack or chopsticks, 8 × 12-inch casserole dish

Cooking time: 33½ to 40½ minutes

Standing time: 10 minutes

Serves: 3 to 4

1½ to 1¾ **pound flank steak**
2 **tablespoons butter**
2 **tablespoons white wine**
½ **cup diced onion**
½ **cup sliced fresh mushrooms**
¾ **cup seasoned stuffing crumbs**
1 **envelope brown gravy mix**
¼ **cup red wine**
1 **8-ounce can tomato sauce**
¼ **teaspoon garlic powder**

Start by tenderizing steak (see Box above).

In the 4-cup glass measure, combine butter, white wine, onion, and mushrooms and microwave uncovered on HIGH for 4 to 5 minutes or until vegetables are tender. Add stuffing crumbs and toss. Lay flank steak flat and spread stuffing evenly over steak. Roll up jelly-roll fashion and fasten with wooden skewers or tie with string to keep from unrolling.

In the 6-cup glass measure, add water to dry gravy mix according to package instructions. Microwave on HIGH for 4½ to 5½ minutes until slightly thickened. **Whisk** in wine, tomato sauce, and garlic powder.

Place meat, seam side up, on meat rack or chopsticks in casserole dish and pour gravy mixture over meat. **Cover** with vented plastic wrap and microwave on HIGH for 5 minutes. Reduce to 50 percent power or MEDIUM and microwave for 20 to 25 minutes or until meat is fork-tender. Baste and turn meat over halfway through cooking time.

Let **stand,** covered, for 10 minutes before serving. After standing time, remove skewers or string and slice across the grain, serving gravy on the side.

Suggestions: Always slice flank steak or any other meat across the grain, not with it, for tender meat slices that don't fall apart.

SHISH KABOBS

Have you ever been in the grocery store and found one of those sections of marked-down kitchen gadgets? Not long ago I found a container of 12 wooden skewers on sale for fifty cents. Into the shopping cart they went, and was I pleased with my bargain.

When I got home and took them out of the grocery bag I knew why they were so cheap. What can you use 12 wooden skewers for? You will never guess what we had for dinner for the next couple of nights.

Shish kabobs can be made out of almost any meat and vegetable combination. Since the heaviness of the meal is regulated by the number of skewers you consume, it is a meal adaptable to anyone's appetite and preference of meat, fish, and vegetables.

The three most important items to remember when microwaving shish kabobs: make sure you have uniformly sized pieces of meat and vegetables, elevate the skewers up off the flat cooking container, and be sure the skewers are made of wood or micro-safe plastic, not metal. You should microwave the kabobs on a meat rack, but two inverted saucers will also work.

Most people serve their shish kabobs on rice, which can be made in the microwave; however, there is no time saved, as it takes the exact same amount of time to microwave as it does to cook conventionally. I suggest that you cook the rice on your stove top while preparing and microwaving your skewers.

Marinated Beef Kabobs

Equipment: 6 to 8 wooden skewers and meat rack (or custard cups or large flat casserole dish with lips)
Cooking time: 7 to 10 minutes (after marinating)
Standing time: 2 to 3 minutes
Serves: 4

1 pound beef tenderloin or sirloin, cut into 1-inch cubes

MARINADE
¼ **cup apple cider vinegar**
¼ **cup red wine**
½ **bay leaf**
1 **teaspoon whole peppercorns**
1 **onion, diced**
1 **cup water**
½ **teaspoon dry mustard**
1 **clove garlic, minced**
pinch of basil, oregano, paprika, thyme, and pepper

VEGETABLES
1 **large green pepper, cut into 1-inch cubes**
½ **pound small white onions**
¼ **pound cauliflower florets**
1 **8-ounce can unsweetened pineapple chunks**
½ **pound whole small mushrooms**

Mix marinade ingredients together in small bowl. Add beef cubes and marinate several hours or overnight. Arrange drained cubes of meat, green pepper, onions, cauliflower, pineapple, and mushrooms on 10-inch skewers. Do not push meat and vegetables together too tightly.

Place skewers on meat rack (see Box p. 57) and microwave on HIGH, **covered** with wax paper, for 7 to 10 minutes or until meat is done nearly to your individual taste—standing time will finish it.

Let **stand,** covered, for 2 to 3 minutes before serving over rice.

Sweet and Sour Pork Kabobs

Equipment: 4 to 6 wooden skewers and meat rack (or custard cups, or flat casserole dish with lips)
Cooking time: 6 to 9 minutes (after marinating)
Standing time: 2 to 3 minutes
Serves: 4

1 **pound boneless pork, cut into 1-inch cubes**
1 **medium green pepper, cut into 1-inch cubes**
1 **16-ounce can unsweetened pineapple chunks, drained**
1 **cup frozen carrot slices**

MARINADE
1 **21-ounce can pineapple pie filling**
3 **tablespoons white vinegar**
3 **tablespoons soy sauce**
1 **clove garlic, minced**
 pinch of ground ginger

Mix marinade ingredients together well. Place pork in marinade and refrigerate for several hours or overnight.

Alternate cubes of marinated pork, green pepper, pineapple, and carrot slices on 4 10-inch skewers. Place filled skewers on meat rack (see Box p. 57).

Cover with wax paper and microwave for 6 to 9 minutes or until pork is no longer pink and done to your satisfaction.

Let **stand,** covered, for 2 to 3 minutes before serving over rice.

PORK

Have you been afraid to try a pork roast in your microwave because you thought it wouldn't brown? Well, you're in for a surprise. Anything that cooks in the microwave for more than 10 minutes begins to self-brown. Maybe not to the crisp degree it would if cooked conventionally, but it looks and tastes great, and you can always pop it under your broiler for 5 minutes at the end if crisp is what you want.

Pork dries out and becomes tough if overcooked, so the use of a probe or thermometer is helpful. Pork roasts, whether bone-in or boneless, cook at the same temperature for the same length of time. I suggest that you insert slivers of garlic into the pork and use either garlic powder or onion powder and a bit of pepper on the outside. Remember, never salt the exterior of foods exposed to microwaves (see Box p. 48).

Your pork roast must be elevated on a meat rack, inverted custard cup, or on an inverted saucer for even cooking. Start your pork with the fat side down for the first half of cooking time, then turn it over to finish cooking. When microwaving pork, all but the first 5 minutes is cooked at 50 percent power or MEDIUM to allow the meat to cook slower and have the time needed to completely tenderize.

Pork Roast

Equipment: meat rack, custard cups, or saucer
Cooking time: 27 to 44 minutes (depending on size)
Standing time: 5 to 10 minutes
Serves: 4 to 6

1 pork roast, 3 to 4 pounds
1 large clove garlic, sliced in thin slivers
garlic or onion powder
pepper

Cut little slits all over the meat and insert the garlic slices. Rub the outside of meat with seasonings and place it, fat-side down, on a meat rack or balanced on 2 custard cups or an inverted saucer. If you're using a microwave thermometer, insert it now into the end of the meat, as close to the center as possible but away from fat and bone. Pork cooks for 9 to 11 minutes per pound, or until it reaches 165 degress. Begin by calculating cooking time.

Start out on HIGH for the first 5 minutes and then reduce to 50 percent power or MEDIUM for the balance of the cooking time. Halfway through cooking time, turn roast over, and if you're using the probe that comes with many ovens, insert it now into the center of the meat away from fat and bone. Microwave for second half of cooking time or until the internal temperature reaches 165 degrees.

Tent (see Box p. 69) with aluminum foil, shiny side toward the meat, and let **stand** for 5 to 10 minutes, or until the internal temperature reaches 170 degrees, before serving.

Crown Roast of Pork
With Rice and Sausage Stuffing

Tired of roast beef or turkey for those holiday feasts? Why not stuff a crown roast of pork? Be sure to order it a few days in advance from your butcher, since he needs to form a pork loin into a circle and remove the backbone for easier carving.

You may use your favorite bread stuffing or my rice and sausage stuffing, or you can fill the cavity with mushrooms or apples microwaved in butter.

My Sausage Stuffed Crown Roast of Pork appeared in *Family Circle*'s "Great Ideas" in the January 1987 issue. The editor, Diane Hodges, couldn't believe how beautifully the recipe microwaved; her comment was, "This is the type of recipe people should realize their microwaves can do."

Equipment:	colander, 2- and 3-quart casseroles, meat rack or custard cups
Cooking time:	1½ to 2½ hours (depending on size)
Standing time:	5 to 10 minutes
Serves:	10 to 15

1   **crown roast pork, 6 to 10 pounds**
¾   **pound fresh hot or sweet sausage meat**
3   **tablespoons butter, sliced**
2   **celery stalks, minced**
½   **pound fresh mushrooms, sliced**
1   **large onion, minced**
2   **cloves garlic, minced**
2   **cups cooked rice**
1   **tablespoon parsley flakes**
    salt and pepper to taste
    garlic or onion powder
    spiced preserved peaches or spiced crab apples for garnish

Crumble sausage into a colander placed inside a larger casserole dish. Microwave on HIGH for 5 to 6 minutes or until sausage loses it pink color (see Box below). Once the meat is no longer pink, set aside, and discard drippings.

In the 2-quart casserole dish, place butter, celery, mushrooms, onion, and garlic. Microwave on HIGH for 5 to 6 minutes or until vegetables are crisp-tender. Stir in reserved sausage, rice, parsley flakes, and salt and pepper. Set aside.

Place roast on meat rack or balance on inverted custard cups, with crown ends down. Rub with garlic or onion powder and pepper, but no salt.

Pork needs to cook for 9 to 11 minutes per pound. Estimate total cooking time and divide in half. Microwave the first 5 minutes on HIGH, then reduce to 50 percent power or MEDIUM for the remainder of the first half of cooking time.

COOKING HAMBURGER AND SAUSAGE

When cooking crumbled sausage or hamburger in a colander, you will see the outside edges beginning to cook while the inside remains pink. Use a fork to break up the chunks and bring the pink inside sections to the outside of the colander and the cooked outside sections to the inside of the dish. This will help the meat to cook much more evenly.

Be sure the colander is dishwasher-safe plastic, so it won't melt in the microwave.

Turn roast over, crown up. Start microwaving on 50 percent power the second half of cooking time until approximately 35 minutes of cooking time remains. At this point, fill cavity with whatever stuffing you have chosen.

Cover just the stuffing in the cavity with wax paper to prevent excess browning. Any leftover stuffing can be placed in a casserole dish and warmed during the roast's standing time.

Microwave remaining time or until internal temperature reaches 165 degrees. If your oven has a probe, you may want to insert it now to make sure you have reached the proper internal temperature.

Tent with aluminum foil, shiny side toward the meat, and let **stand** for 5 to 10 minutes, or until the internal temperature reaches 170 degrees, before serving.

Transfer meat to a serving dish and place paper frills over the crown tips. Decorate with spiced peach halves or spiced crab apples. To serve, carve down between the bones and serve with stuffing.

PORK CHOPS

Have you ever overcooked a pork chop in the microwave? Would *bricklike* be the right adjective? Pork chops need some kind of coating to hold in the juices or to be added to ingredients that will provide moisture. Never cook pork chops on HIGH; they must be cooked on 50 or 60 percent power or MEDIUM, covered, to keep them moist.

If you just want to brown your chops you can use your browning dish, but I *do not* recommend trying to cook them alone, just browned. If this is your preference for serving, do them on your regular stove. However, there are many prepackaged crumb-coating mixes for pork that work well even though they do not crisp as they would if fried on your stove top.

To prepare chops with a crumb coating, start by slashing the edges to prevent curling. Moisten 4 chops with milk or water and toss with crumbs. Arrange in a baking dish with the meatiest parts to the outside edges of the dish. Cover with wax paper and microwave on 50 percent power or MEDIUM for 16 to 18 minutes per pound. Halfway through cooking, rearrange the chops so that the less-cooked areas are to the outside of the dish and remove the wax paper.

Using a coating does not produce as moist a pork chop as putting chops in a sauce does.

You might want to sear the pork chops on an outdoor grill and then quickly freeze them for a future meal. If you are careful to use a very hot grill and sear only the outside, they will microwave very quickly—60 to 90 seconds per chop, once defrosted—and have beautiful color and barbecue flavor.

REMOVING EXTRA FAT FROM MEAT

The microwave extracts one-third more fat from meat than conventional cooking does, yet it seals the juices inside the meat. Even if you are using very lean pork chops you will see some fat floating on the surface, so remove it before serving.

Be sure to skim off any fat in your recipes unless you need some calories. Rather than trying to spoon it out, lay a lettuce leaf or slice of bread on top of the area where the grease has collected. Remove and discard the lettuce or bread as soon as the grease has been absorbed.

Microwaving is an excellent way to cook meat for those on diets or having a cholesterol problem.

Saucy Pork Chops

Equipment: 9 × 13-inch flat casserole dish
Cooking time: 24 to 27 minutes
Standing time: 10 minutes
Serves: 2

    4 pork chops about ½ inch thick
    ½ teaspoon garlic powder
    ⅛ teaspoon pepper
    1 medium onion, sliced, rings separated
    ¼ pound fresh mushrooms, sliced
    1 10¾-ounce can cream of mushroom soup, undiluted
    ½ envelope dry onion soup mix

Sprinkle chops with garlic powder and pepper and place in casserole dish with meatiest portions to the outside of the dish. Place onion rings and mushrooms over the chops. Mix together mushroom and onion soups and pour over chops. **Cover** with plastic wrap, venting back one corner, and microwave on 50 percent power or MEDIUM for 16 to 18 minutes per pound, rearranging and turning chops over halfway through cooking.

Pork chops are done when they have no pink color when cut in the center.

Let **stand,** covered, for 10 minutes, and skim off any fat before serving (see Box p. 63).

Troubleshooting: If your chops are overcooking on the outside edges, be sure you place those edges to the inside of the cooking container when rearranging.

Suggestions: Serve over rice, mashed potatoes, or noodles, and add Dressed-Up Corn (see p. 139) for a quick, easy-clean-up meal.

Wine-Braised Pork Chops

If you want to use your browning dish, this is a tasty recipe that my family enjoys. Be sure to review the section on browning, on p. 11, before using yours.

If you have a family favorite you want to try, use the times and temperatures from one of my pork chop recipes and try your skills. Remember, you can always cook it some more, but once it is bricklike, supper is over, whether you have eaten it or not. Be sure to record how long you cooked my recipe in your oven, making the next time you use this recipe a snap.

Equipment:	browning dish with cover
Browner preheat time:	5 to 7 minutes (depending on brand)
Cooking time:	27 to 31 minutes
Standing time:	5 minutes
Serves:	2 to 4

4 1-inch-thick pork chops
1 tablespoon oil
1 medium green pepper, sliced crosswise
1 clove garlic, minced
½ pound fresh mushrooms, sliced, or 1 6-ounce can, drained
1 teaspoon salt
¼ teaspoon pepper
2 to 3 medium tomatoes (more if you like a richer gravy)
⅓ cup white wine

Preheat your browning dish for 5 to 7 minutes on HIGH or time recommended by the manufacturer.

Wipe the chops with a damp paper towel. Add oil and chops to hot browning dish. Microwave for 2 minutes on HIGH. Turn chops over and microwave other side for 4 minutes more on HIGH. Remove chops. Drain all but ½ tablespoon of fat from browning dish and add green pepper, garlic, and mushrooms. Microwave 2 minutes 25 seconds on HIGH, **stirring** once.

Place chops on peppers, sprinkle with salt and pepper, and top with tomatoes and wine. **Cover.** Microwave for 18 to 22 minutes on 60 percent power or MEDIUM.

Let **stand,** covered, for 5 minutes before serving.

Troubleshooting: If your pork chops are very tough and hard, they are overcooked. I try not to use the thinly sliced chops in the microwave as they overcook quickly.

If your browning dish doesn't have a cover, be very careful to make sure it isn't hot when covering with any plastic material.

Suggestions: If you don't have a browning dish, just brown on the stove top and place chops in a 9 × 13-inch casserole dish and go on with the recipe.

This dish is excellent served over noodles or rice.

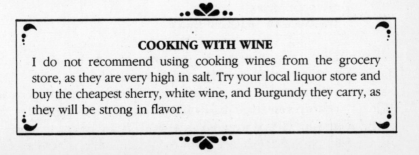

COOKING WITH WINE

I do not recommend using cooking wines from the grocery store, as they are very high in salt. Try your local liquor store and buy the cheapest sherry, white wine, and Burgundy they carry, as they will be strong in flavor.

Italian Sausage and Peppers

This favorite combination is a popular buffet dish—it also makes great quick suppers when stuffed into Italian bread or hero rolls. Cooked on top of the stove, the sausages spit and the grease flies while you are frying them, and then you have to stand over the peppers to keep them moving so they don't burn. In the microwave you can do the peppers and sausages at the same time and there's no mess.

Sausages, potatoes, squash, egg yolks, hot dogs, tomatoes, and some fruits have casings that will burst in the microwave if not vented. The tines of a fork inserted into the food two or three times before cooking will properly vent the steam and keep your food in one piece. With sausages, piercing the skin also helps to rid the meat of all the fat inside the casing.

If you have never cleaned your oven after an exploding potato or egg, you are in for a real experience (see oven-cleaning directions, p. 9). There are more nooks and crannies in those square ovens than you can imagine, and each of them has something stuck to it when food explodes.

Equipment:	casserole dish large enough to lay sausages flat
Cooking time:	12 to 16 minutes
Standing time:	5 minutes
Serves:	4 to 6

1½ **pounds hot or sweet sausage**
3 **large green peppers (or include one red one for color)**
1 **large onion, sliced**
1 **cup sliced fresh mushrooms (optional)**
⅛ **teaspoon oregano**
⅛ **teaspoon dried basil**
1 **16-ounce jar spaghetti sauce**

Pierce sausage casings well with the tines of a fork and set aside. Slice peppers into uniform strips and lay in the bottom of casserole dish. Place onion slices and mushrooms, if using, over peppers and sprinkle with oregano and basil. Lay sausages over vegetables and **cover** with vented plastic wrap, **elevate** on an inverted saucer if using a flat-bottomed dish, and **rotate** on a turntable, if available.

Microwave on HIGH for 4 minutes. Turn sausages over, pricking each piece again to allow fat to drain, **stir** vegetables, recover, rotate dish ½ turn, and microwave another 4 to 6 minutes until sausage is no longer pink.

Completely drain fat from casserole, slice sausages, and lay over peppers. Add spaghetti sauce, cover, rotate dish ½ turn, and microwave for 4 to 6 minutes on 80 percent power until sausage is completely cooked and sauce is hot.

Let **stand,** covered, for 5 minutes before serving.

Troubleshooting: If some of your peppers have black spots, it means they have overcooked. This can happen if the peppers stay too long in the corners of square-cornered pans or from a microwave that does not cook evenly enough. If you have problems with your oven always overcooking in certain spots, you need a turntable to help distribute the microwaves. If you don't have one, be sure to rotate your cooking dishes quite often.

Suggestions: If you're using a square-cornered container, be sure to keep food out of the corners or it will overcook. Substitute home-made spaghetti sauce for jar sauce, adding your own signature to the recipe.

HAM

Remember my first microwave disaster, the Christmas ham that I wrote about in the Introduction)? Since that first ham dinner I have learned, through much experimentation, how to perfectly microwave ham, so have no fear, The Microwhiz will have your next ham perfect, even if you have never tried it before.

Shield any of the cut ends your ham may have with flat pieces of aluminum foil and secure with wooden toothpicks to keep those cut ends from overcooking.

CANNED HAMS: Place a 5-pound canned ham in a casserole dish, pour 1½ cups of pineapple juice over the ham, and **cover** with vented plastic wrap. If you're using a meat thermometer or probe, insert through the plastic wrap so that tip is in the center of the meat (see Box p. 68).

Microwave the ham on HIGH for the first 10 minutes, then reduce

GLAZING HAM

When glazing, always remove any coverings and paint the glaze on during the last 3 to 5 minutes of cooking time, because the outside layers of meat tend to overcook and dry out from the added sugar. Be very careful not to get glaze on your meat probe or thermometer (if you're using one) because the hot sugar will affect the way the thermometer registers.

USING A MEAT PROBE

If your microwave comes with a probe, which is really a thermometer, take care with it. Never leave it in your oven unless it is inserted into some type of food. Insert the probe into the center of the food at a horizontal angle, if possible, being sure that at least one-half of the probe is inside the food.

Be careful not to set the probe near fat or bone, as they conduct heat and will cause the probe to register an incorrect temperature. Once inserted into the food, you can program your microwave to cook the food to the desired temperature. The microwave will automatically shut off when this temperature is reached. Many newer ovens will *hold* the food at the temperature you program.

to 50 percent power or MEDIUM and cook for 6 to 8 minutes per pound. Turn ham over halfway through cooking.

If you're using a probe or thermometer, ham is done at 130 degrees.

To glaze the ham, remove plastic wrap and glaze during the last 5 minutes of cooking time (see Box above).

When cooking time has finished, remove ham from oven and **tent** in aluminum foil, shiny side toward the meat, and let **stand** 5 to 10 minutes. The internal temperature will rise 5 to 10 degrees during standing time.

BONE-IN HAM PORTION: Begin by turning the ham around in your oven. If any part of the ham is closer than 3 inches from the top or sides of your oven, the ham is too big to microwave. If the ham fits, place it on a meat rack or elevated on inverted custard cups, and

---

TENTING

Tenting food is the process of covering food completely with aluminum foil, shiny side of the foil facing the food, after the food has been removed from the microwave. This tenting during standing time helps to keep the heat in the food as it finishes cooking. Many meats also finish the tenderizing process during their standing time.

---

cover the cut side with a flat piece of aluminum foil to keep it from drying out. If the edges start to dry out during cooking, **shield** with aluminum foil (see Arching and Shielding, p. 10). Remove from oven, **tent** with aluminum foil, shiny side toward the meat, and let **stand** for 10 minutes before serving.

SMOKED BONELESS PORK SHOULDER ROLL: Remove all packaging and place meat in a floured roasting bag. Add enough ginger ale or water to cover the meat. Close bag loosely with string, leaving a 2-inch opening to allow the steam to escape. Place in a casserole dish and microwave on HIGH for 10 minutes. Reduce power to 50 percent or MEDIUM and cook for 15½ to 18½ minutes per pound, or until meat is tender and heated through. Let **stand,** in bag, for 5 to 10 minutes before serving.

Ham cooks so beautifully in the microwave that it no longer has to be a special-occasion dinner. Next time they are on sale, buy an extra one for your freezer, and be sure to save the bone for pea soup—what a treat!

Glazes

Equipment: 4-cup glass measure
Cooking time: 1 to 3 minutes
Standing time: none required
Makes: enough to glaze a good-sized ham

Troubleshooting: Be sure to follow the tips in the Box on p. 68 when using any of the following glazes for your ham.

Suggestions: Any of these glazes can be spooned over corned beef that is completely cooked and placed on a meat rack. Once glazed, microwave for 5 minutes on HIGH for a really different buffet dish.

Dice any leftover ham and place in plastic bag along with ham bone. Freeze until ready to make pea soup (see p. 41).

CHERRY GLAZE
   2 tablespoons white wine
   2 tablespoons white raisins
   1 cup cherry pie filling
   1 tablespoon brown sugar
      dash of both cinnamon and ground cloves

Sprinkle wine over raisins and let **stand** for 15 minutes. Combine all ingredients and mix well. Spread over ham during last 5 to 10 minutes of cooking time.

STRAWBERRY OR RASPBERRY GLAZE
   1 10-ounce package frozen strawberries or raspberries, defrosted
   1 tablespoon cornstarch
      dash of both cinnamon and ground cloves

Combine all ingredients in glass measure and stir. Microwave on HIGH for 3 minutes or until clear and thickened. Spoon over ham during last 5 minutes of cooking time.

TRADITIONAL MUSTARD GLAZE
   1 8-ounce can crushed pineapple in heavy syrup, drained
   ¾ cup dark brown sugar
   3 tablespoons Dijon mustard
   ⅛ teaspoon ground cloves
   6 maraschino cherries, diced

Combine all ingredients and mix well. Spoon over ham during last 5 minutes of cooking time.

APRICOT GLAZE
- ½ **cup apricot preserves**
- 1½ **teaspoons cornstarch**
- 1 **teaspoon finely shredded orange zest**
- 3 **tablespoons orange juice**
- ⅛ **teaspoon ground cinnamon**
- **dash of ground cloves**

Combine all ingredients in a 4-cup measure and mix well. Microwave on HIGH for 2 to 3 minutes until thick and bubbly. Spoon over ham during last 5 minutes of cooking time.

SPARERIBS

The word *sparerib* usually refers to pork ribs closely trimmed of their meat. As a rule of thumb, it takes ¾ to 1 pound of spareribs per person for one to realize he has consumed any meat. This is a good guide to use when purchasing ribs.

Cut your sparerib slabs into two-rib portions to make cooking and eating easier. I prefer using a meat rack set into a casserole dish, but if you do not have a meat rack and dish big enough, and are using just a casserole dish, be sure to turn and rearrange ribs frequently.

The most important microwave hint I can give you is to start the meatiest sections to the outside of the dish and overlap them slightly, with the boniest sections toward the center of the dish. Rearrange them frequently by bringing the center pieces to the outside of the dish and the outside pieces to the center.

There are various methods for microwaving ribs, but I prefer using the same principle I use for all red meat. Determine your cooking time and start the first 5 minutes on HIGH, then reduce to 50 percent power or MEDIUM for the balance of time. Because of the uneven distribution of meat and bone, spareribs tend to dry out and toughen if cooked too quickly on too high a power setting.

Because of the high fat content, they will continue to cook and very likely overcook during standing time. Be sure to undercook just slightly, then let the dish stand, tented with aluminum foil, shiny side towards ribs, for 5 minutes. Remember, you can always put them back in the oven if you are not satisfied with their doneness, but once they have charred and overcooked, forget it.

I use the marinated Chinese-style spareribs as an appetizer when making a stir-fry dinner, but you could add a salad and hot finger towels (see Box below) for a complete dinner. Feel free to substitute your own favorite barbecue sauce for mine in the barbecue recipe; just use my recipe for a time and temperature guide.

HOT FINGER TOWELS

Serve fragrant hot towels to your family or guests right from your microwave. Completely dampen white or colored wash cloths with water, sprinkle with lemon or lime juice, and roll up. Place side by side in either a dish or a small wicker basket. Place a slice of lemon or lime on top of each roll and microwave for 20 to 25 seconds per towel. Check to make sure rolls are not too hot before serving. These are great any time you're serving finger food. (Yes. This is an exception to my rule of no fabrics in the microwave.)

Chinese-Style Barbecued Spareribs

Equipment: container for marinating, meat rack, large casserole dish or baking sheet
Cooking time: 35 to 40 minutes (after marinating)
Standing time: 5 minutes
Serves: 3 to 4

2½ to 3 pounds pork spareribs cut into 2-rib portions

MARINADE
¼ cup soy sauce
2 tablespoons honey
2 tablespoons hoisin sauce
2 tablespoons white vinegar
2 tablespoons chicken stock
1 tablespoon white wine
1 tablespoon chopped garlic (about 3 to 4 cloves)
1 tablespoon Chinese black bean sauce
1 teaspoon sugar

Combine all marinade ingredients in container large enough to hold ribs. Pour marinade over ribs and marinate at least overnight, but 24 to 48 hours is better.

Place ribs on meat rack, if you have one, set into the largest casserole or baking sheet you have. If you do not have a meat rack, be sure to turn and rearrange ribs often. Place the meatiest part of the ribs to the outside edges of the dish and **cover** with wax paper to prevent spatters. Microwave on HIGH for 5 minutes and then drain off any excess fat.

Reduce to 50 percent power or MEDIUM and microwave for 30 to 35 minutes or until fork-tender, being sure to rearrange and turn over several times during cooking. Cooking time is 10-12 minutes per pound. (See Spareribs, p. 71.)

Tent, (see Box p. 69) with aluminum foil shiny side toward meat, and let **stand** for 5 minutes before serving.

Suggestions: Combine these with one of my stir-fry recipes for a great Chinese dinner. Add a hot finger towel, chopsticks, and hot mustard, and a Chinese feast awaits your guests.

Barbecued Spareribs

Equipment: bowl for sauce, meat rack, or large casserole dish
Cooking time: 40 to 50 minutes
Standing time: 5 minutes
Serves: 3 to 4

2½ to 3 pounds pork spareribs cut into 2-rib portions

SAUCE
  1 bottle barbecue sauce

or make mine:
  ¾ cup ketchup
  2 tablespoons cider vinegar
  2 tablespoons brown sugar
  1 tablespoon Worcestershire sauce
  1 tablespoon A-1 Sauce
  1 teaspoon dry mustard
  ½ teaspoon garlic powder

Combine all sauce ingredients and blend well. Place meatiest portion of ribs to outside of the largest casserole or baking sheet you have. If you have a meat rack, place it in your casserole dish and place ribs on top. Lightly cover with sauce mixture.

There are two methods of cooking: for roasted ribs, **cover** with wax paper; for braised ribs, cover with vented plastic wrap. Braised ribs are softer and the meat nearly falls off the bone. Microwave your ribs for 10 to 12 minutes per pound. Figure cooking time and microwave on HIGH for the first 5 minutes. Reduce to 50 percent power or MEDIUM for balance of cooking time. Turn, drain any excess liquid, and rearrange ribs every ten minutes, basting on more sauce each time until fork-tender.

Tent with aluminum foil (see Box p. 69) shiny side toward meat, and let **stand** for 5 minutes before serving.

Troubleshooting: If your spareribs burned, you overcooked them or cut them too thin. Because of the high fat content in the meat, they continue to do a lot of cooking during standing time, and if you microwave them to perfection they will char while they stand.

Mess: Forgetting to cover with wax paper will give you an oven full of spatters. If this happens, see p. 9 for directions on how to clean and deodorize your microwave oven.

CHILI

Even when it's hot outside there can still be chili in the microwave! Yes, chili! Everyone's finished product may taste different, but the basic preparation is the same.

The most common main ingredient in chili is the meat, which is usually either ground or cubed. If you're going to use ground beef and/or pork, you want to cook it in a colander. If you don't have one that's made for the microwave, you can substitute a plastic one that is dishwasher-safe, doesn't have any metal on it, and has been tested for micro-safeness (see Box p. 75).

Once you have a micro-safe colander in hand, place it in a casserole dish to catch the drippings. Crumble your ground beef into the colander and microwave on HIGH for 4 to 6 minutes until meat is no longer pink, breaking up meat chunks every 2 minutes. Drain fat from casserole dish and continue with your recipe.

Should your recipe call for chunks of chuck, be sure to cut the meat into uniform-sized pieces so that they will cook evenly. As with a stew, the meat and vegetables will cook together, without your having to precook the meat.

Here are a few variations on the theme, but feel free to use the basic preparation method with your own spices and various vegetables. Unless your family loves real "hot stuff," be careful with the chili powder: add it slowly until you reach the edge of your tolerance.

TESTING FOR MICRO-SAFETY

If you question whether any dish or utensil is micro-safe, use this easy test to double-check. Take a glass measure and fill it with 1 cup of water. Place the glass measure in or next to the piece of equipment you wish to test and microwave on HIGH for 90 seconds. If your test piece is warm, it is *not* safe to use in the microwave.

South of the Border Chili

Equipment:	3- or 4-quart casserole dish
Cooking time:	55 to 65 minutes
Standing time:	10 minutes
Serves:	4

1½ **pounds chuck cut into uniform ½-inch cubes**
1 **medium onion, diced**
1 **medium green pepper, diced**
1 **12- or 16-ounce can Mexican corn (corn with red and green peppers)**
1 **clove garlic, minced**
2 **16-ounce cans red kidney beans, drained and rinsed**
2 **16-ounce cans whole tomatoes, cut up**
1 **6-ounce can tomato paste**
1 **tablespoon brown sugar**
1 **to 2 teaspoons chili powder**
1 **teaspoon salt**
½ **teaspoon oregano**
2 **teaspoons red wine vinegar**
¼ **teaspoon pepper**

In casserole dish, combine all the ingredients and **cover** with lid from casserole dish or vented plastic wrap. **Elevate** flat-bottomed dish on an inverted saucer, and place on turntable if available. Microwave on HIGH for 5 minutes.

Reduce to 50 percent power or MEDIUM and microwave **uncovered** for 50 to 60 miuntes or until meat is fork-tender, stirring two or three times during cooking time and **rotating** the dish ½ turn every 20 minutes. Adjust chili powder to taste during this cooking period.

Let **stand,** covered, for 10 minutes before serving.

Troubleshooting: If meat chunks dry out it is because they were sticking out of the liquid. To avoid this, keep them covered with liquid during microwaving.

Chili-Con-Carne

Equipment: colander and 3-quart casserole dish
Cooking time: 48 to 56 minutes
Standing time: 5 minutes
Serves: 3 to 4

1 **pound ground beef or pork**
1 **medium onion, chopped**
1 **medium green pepper, chopped**
1 **clove garlic, minced**
2 **to 4 teaspoons chili powder**
1 **teaspoon salt**
½ **teaspoon dried oregano**
1 **28-ounce can whole tomatoes, undrained**
1 **6-ounce can tomato sauce**
2 **16-ounce cans red kidney beans, drained and rinsed**
1 **tablespoon red wine vinegar**
tortilla chips or crackers

Crumble meat into colander (see Box p. 61) and set into casserole dish. Microwave **uncovered** on HIGH until meat is no longer pink, 4 to 6 minutes. **Stir** with a fork to break up meat every 2 minutes. Discard fat and transfer meat to casserole dish, breaking up meat chunks with a fork. Stir in onion, green pepper, and garlic. Microwave uncovered on HIGH until onion and pepper are tender, 4 to 5 minutes.

Add chili powder, salt, and oregano to casserole and mix well. Drain tomato liquid into casserole. Chop tomatoes and add to casserole. Add tomato sauce and kidney beans and mix well. **Elevate** flat-bottomed dish on an inverted saucer, and place on turntable if available. Microwave covered on HIGH for 5 minutes.

Add vinegar to chili and stir well. Microwave uncovered on 50 percent power or MEDIUM for 35 to 40 minutes until slightly thickened, stirring twice during cooking and **rotating** dish ½ turn every 20 minutes.

Adjust chili powder to taste and let **stand** for 5 minutes before serving.

Rocking Horse Ranch Texas Chili

This recipe, which comes from a Catskills dude ranch, has a wonderful way with spices that I know you lovers of "hot stuff" will enjoy. On the other hand, if you love only slightly warm things, tone down the amount of spices you use and taste as you add them. The key is taste, taste, taste—and keep in mind my motto: Skinny cooks can't be trusted.

This recipe freezes beautifully. For easy defrosting, line the container you will use to reheat in with plastic wrap. Ladle in the chili and freeze. Once frozen, remove the block from the container, wrap in freezer wrap, then label with contents, date, and the container it was frozen in. When you're ready to defrost and heat, just unwrap the block, pop it into the appropriate container, and you're ready to go.

Equipment:	colander with a casserole dish, deep 3- or 4-quart casserole dish
Cooking time:	46 to 56 minutes
Standing time:	5 minutes
Serves:	4 to 6

2 pounds hamburger
2 cloves garlic, minced
2 medium onions, diced
1 green pepper, diced
1 cup sliced fresh mushrooms, or 1 8-ounce can sliced mushrooms, drained
2 16-ounce cans red kidney beans, drained and rinsed
5 to 8 tablespoons chili powder
¼ teaspoon crushed red pepper
⅛ teaspoon oregano
⅛ teaspoon basil
1 teaspoon Tabasco Sauce
¼ teaspoon salt
⅛ teaspoon pepper
2 medium fresh tomatoes, peeled and diced into small chunks
1 28-ounce can peeled crushed tomatoes
dash of thyme

Crumble hamburger into colander set into casserole dish. Microwave on HIGH for 3 minutes. Break meat up with a fork and add garlic, onions, and green pepper.

Microwave on HIGH for another 3 minutes, break up meat, and discard fat.

In deep casserole dish, combine meat, mushrooms, drained kidney beans, and spices to taste, mixing together well. Add fresh and canned tomatoes and **cover** with vented plastic wrap. If using a flat-bottomed container, **elevate** on an inverted saucer—it would help to use a turntable if available.

Microwave on HIGH for 5 minutes, remove the plastic wrap, and continue microwaving on 50 percent power or MEDIUM for 35 to 45 minutes, until slightly thickened and flavors blend, **stirring** several times. (If not using a turntable, **rotate** dish ¼ turn each time you stir.)

Let **stand,** covered, for 5 minutes before serving. Dish into bowls, or serve with large corn chips for an appetizer.

Troubleshooting: If you use a square-cornered container you may find that whatever sits in the corners will be dried out, so stir frequently.

If you don't have fresh tomatoes substitute whole canned ones.

Lasagna

One of my adult education students was a physician in his sixties who had just lost his wife. Since she had always done the cooking, he had a lot to learn. One of his first questions was whether it was possible to make lasagna in the microwave.

He thought lasagna was a great dish to fix when his children visited, but in his first attempt at preparing it he had followed the directions on the box of noodles and found it very messy.

It seems the instructions told him to boil the noodles, drain them, and to be sure the noodles were dry before continuing with the recipe. Carefully he laid them all over his living room rug on paper towels to dry, but then his rug got wet.

Trying to control a very wide grin, I handed him my no-cook noodle recipe for lasagna. He went home, tried it, and sent me a beautiful plant for saving his rug.

ELEVATING

By elevating a flat-bottomed cooking container on an inverted saucer, custard cup, meat rack, or bowl, you allow the center of the container to cook as evenly as the outside edges. If the container sits flat on the bottom of the oven, the microwaves can enter only from the top and sides; however, if the dish is elevated, they can also get in from underneath.

Equipment: colander and 2- or 3-quart casserole dish to catch the fat, 8 × 12 or 9 × 13-inch baking dish or 2-quart flat casserole dish
Cooking time: 39 to 46 minutes
Standing time: none required
Serves: 6

    1 pound ground beef
    4 cups spaghetti sauce
    1 pound ricotta cheese or cottage cheese
    2 eggs
    1 tablespoon chopped fresh parsley
    ½ teaspoon garlic powder
    2 tablespoons grated Parmesan cheese
    8 to 10 uncooked lasagna noodles
    2 cups shredded mozzarella cheese
    ½ cup grated Parmesan cheese

Set colander inside 2- or 3-quart casserole dish. Add crumbled ground beef and cook on HIGH for 4 to 6 minutes. Meat will be light pink. Transfer meat to a bowl and break it up with a fork, then add spaghetti sauce.

Combine ricotta, eggs, parsley, garlic powder, and 2 tablespoons of Parmesan in a bowl. Mix well and set aside.

Pour cup of sauce mixture into 9 × 13-inch baking dish or 2-quart flat casserole dish and place 4 to 5 uncooked noodles evenly over sauce, overlapping noodles if necessary.

Cover noodles with another cup of sauce, spread half of cheese mixture over noodles and sprinkle with 1 cup of mozzarella cheese.

Cover mozzarella with another cup of sauce and remaining noodles. For the top layer, add the mozzarella first, then the sauce and the remaining ricotta cheese mixture. The mozzarella must not be exposed to the microwaves or it will toughen. Cover tightly with plastic wrap, **venting** back one corner, and microwave on HIGH for 15 minutes, **rotating** dish ½ turn after 7 minutes.

Reset your microwave for 60 percent power or MEDIUM for 20 to 25 minutes or until noodles are tender, rotating the dish ½ turn every 10 minutes.

Sprinkle top with Parmesan and microwave **uncovered** on HIGH for 1 to 2 minutes until cheese melts.

Let **stand,** covered, for 10 minutes before serving.

Troubleshooting: When you need to change power setting to MEDIUM and your microwave has only HIGH, follow these directions: After the initial 15 minutes cooking, cook for 4 minutes and let rest for 2 minutes. Repeat this twice more and let stand on a hard, heat-proof surface for 10 minutes. Check doneness of noodles and if necessary microwave for 2 to 4 minutes more. Once noodles are done, go on with the last step of melting the Parmesan cheese.

If sauce is overcooking in spots, you need to rotate the dish more often, as your oven is not evenly distributing the microwaves.

If noodles are overcooked in the corners and if you are using a square-cornered dish, try not to fill up the corners, as the microwaves overcook things in square corners.

If the center noodles are not done, you used a flat-bottomed dish and did not elevate it on an inverted saucer.

Suggestions: Try spreading cooked, drained, chopped spinach on top of your sauce for a Florentine-type lasagna. It is very colorful and adds a different flair to the taste.

Instead of using ground beef, try slicing uncooked Polish kielbasa and placing the slices evenly over the sauce in each layer.

Stuffed Cabbage

My father's side of the family always gathered at my grandmother's house on Sundays. As a little girl I remember the stove being full of simmering pots as the family gathered. Of course I had my favorites, and some of them I have carried over to my children, and they have become dishes they will associate with their childhood.

When I would rush into Grandma's kitchen and catch the aroma of that wonderful sweet-and-sour sauce mixed with cabbage, I knew dinner would be stuffed cabbage as only Grandma and Aunt Lee could make it. After a little experimenting, I was able to convert our family recipe for all of you to make without any problems. The secret to perfectly cooked cabbage rolls is to leave the center of the dish empty and to elevate it if it is flat-bottomed.

By leaving an opening, the microwaves can come up through the center of the dish and cook far more evenly than if the dish were packed full and they could cook only from the sides and top. If you have your own filling recipe, go ahead and use it; just follow my instructions for baking.

This recipe is wonderful for potluck suppers or for a buffet table. If you are going to make the dish for a crowd, be sure to select a cabbage with small leaves; this way you can prepare a large dish of small rolls that will stretch farther.

Equipment:	deep 3- or 4-quart casserole dish, 9 × 13 or 8 × 12-inch baking dish
Cooking time:	48 to 60 minutes
Standing time:	5 to 10 minutes
Serves:	6 to 8

  1 **large-leafed cabbage (3 to 5 pounds)**
  ¼ **cup water**

  FILLING
  1½ **pounds ground beef**
  1 **egg**
  1 **cup cooked rice**
     salt and pepper to taste
  ¼ **cup flavored breadcrumbs**
  1 **tablespoon A-1 Sauce or ketchup**

2 tablespoons milk
1 tablespoon parsley flakes
1 medium onion, minced

SAUCE
1 8-ounce can tomato sauce
1 28-ounce can whole tomatoes, broken up
1 medium onion, chopped
2 tablespoons brown sugar
1 tablespoon vinegar or lemon juice
2 tablespoons raisins (optional)

Remove any damaged outer leaves from the cabbage. Make 4 deep cuts all around the core into the cabbage. Place cabbage, core down, in the deep 3- or 4-quart casserole dish. Add ¼ cup of water and **cover** tightly with plastic wrap, venting back one corner. Microwave on HIGH for 8 to 10 minutes. Place in a colander and flush with cold water. Once cool enough to touch, separate the leaves.

Combine the filling ingredients and blend together well. Place a mound of filling (1 to 2 heaping tablespoons, depending on the size of the leaf) in the center of each cabbage leaf, bring the top of the leaf over the meat, fold in the sides of the leaf, and bring the bottom of the leaf up and tuck it into the sides, forming a little package. Distribute all the filling among the leaves and then shred any leftover cabbage. Place a glass in the center of your baking dish, then line the bottom with the shredded cabbage. Place your cabbage rolls on top, largest rolls to the outside of the dish, smallest rolls to the inside. Once rolls are all in the dish remove the glass but leave that space open. Combine sauce ingredients and pour over cabbage rolls. Cover dish with vented plastic wrap and **elevate** flat-bottomed dish on an inverted saucer. Bake on HIGH for 5 minutes.

Reduce to 80 percent power or MEDIUM-HIGH and bake for 35 to 45 minutes or until cabbage rolls are tender and filling is completely cooked, basting and **rotating** dish ½ turn every 20 minutes. If your oven is large enough, you might want to place the dish on a turntable if one is available.

Let **stand,** covered, for 5 to 10 minutes before serving.

Troubleshooting: Keep rolls basted with sauce to prevent them from drying out.

Suggestions: I always add baked or boiled potatoes and a salad for a complete meal.

Traditional Moussaka

To raise money for their new church, the New Haven Greek community held a festival complete with food and entertainment from their homeland. I, of course, headed right for the food to see what would go best in the microwave. This moussaka was the winner; Helen Proestakis supplied her family recipe.

Greek cooking is noted for its use of phyllo dough, which can't be done in the microwave. But fear not; my moussaka, using the old traditional recipe, converted to the microwave beautifully. The festival was a unique opportunity in this day and age to see people join together to make a reality of their beliefs.

Equipment:	colander and casserole dish, 9 × 13 or 12 × 8-inch baking dish, 4- or 6-cup glass measure
Cooking time:	45 to 70 minutes
Standing time:	15 to 20 minutes
Serves:	6 to 8

>   2 **medium eggplants, sliced into ¼-inch slices**
>   4 **tablespoons olive oil**
>   4 **tablespoons grated Parmesan cheese or any other good dry Italian cheese, grated**

FILLING
> 1½ **pounds ground beef**
>   1 **medium onion, minced**
>   1 **tablespoon chopped parsley**
>   3 **to 4 tablespoons tomato paste**
>   ¼ **teaspoon cinnamon**
>   **dash of nutmeg**
>   **dash of salt and pepper**

TOPPING
>   2 **tablespoons butter**
>   2 **tablespoons flour**
> 1¾ **cups milk**
>   ½ **cup grated Parmesan cheese**
>   2 **eggs, beaten**
>   **dash of cinnamon**
>   **dash of paprika**

Place eggplant slices in a circle around the outside edges of a dinner plate, overlapping if necessary. Microwave **covered** with vented plastic wrap on HIGH for 4 to 6 minutes or until soft. Repeat process until all eggplant slices are cooked.

Place ground beef in a colander set into a casserole dish to catch the fat. Cook on HIGH for 3 minutes. Break up meat with a fork and add onion. Microwave on HIGH for 3 to 4 minutes more until the meat loses its pink color. Place beef in a bowl and add parsley, tomato paste, cinnamon, nutmeg, salt, and pepper (mixture will be on the dry side).

Using the baking dish, add 1 to 2 tablespoons of olive oil and distribute evenly over bottom of dish. Place ½ of eggplant slices over entire bottom of dish and sprinkle with 1 tablespoon olive oil and 1 tablespoon Parmesan. Cover eggplant slices with beef mixture and sprinkle with 2 tablespoons Parmesan. Cover meat with remaining eggplant slices, 1 tablespoon olive oil, and 1 tablespoon of Parmesan.

In the glass measure, melt butter on HIGH for 45 to 60 seconds or until melted. Whisk in flour and slowly add milk, **whisking** to prevent lumping. Add remaining ingredients, whisking well. Pour sauce mixture over top layer of eggplant and sprinkle top with cinnamon and paprika. Microwave **uncovered** on 80 percent power or MEDIUM-HIGH for 16 to 18 minutes or until custardlike top is set.

Let **stand** for 15 to 20 minutes, then cut into squares before serving.

Corned Beef

I grew up eating corned beef on a regular basis because my dad is a meat-and-potatoes man who loves corned beef and my mom makes it often. You usually take recipes you're used to eating into your marriage and now my two boys also love corned beef. They like it best served hot on rye bread with cabbage, carrots, hot potato salad, and kosher dill pickles on the side.

My husband, on the other hand, prefers it on his plate with boiled potatoes, cabbage, carrots, and onions. So what is a mother to do? Make a hot boiled New England dinner with a side dish of hot potato salad, and then everyone is happy.

In my experience, flat cuts of beef microwave best, so I suggest using the flat cut or brisket corned beef for best microwaving results. All the vegetables I use are unnecessary if your family doesn't eat them, but they are our favorites. Remember, when cooking vegetables in the microwave, be sure they are cut in uniform size and shape.

Equipment:	deep 3- or 4-quart casserole dish or largest one you have to fit in your microwave, with a cover if possible
Cooking time:	1½ to 1¾ hours
Standing time:	20 to 30 minutes
Serves:	6 to 8

2½ to 3 pounds flat corned brisket, about 1½ inches thick
4 to 6 cups water or enough to cover meat
1 tablespoon peppercorns
½ lemon
1 bay leaf
3 carrots, peeled and sliced in thin strips
2 medium onions, quartered
2 large potatoes, cut into eighths
1 medium head cabbage, cut into sixths

Place corned beef in casserole dish and add water, peppercorns, lemon, and bay leaf. **Cover** tightly (see Box p. 51) and microwave on HIGH for 10 minutes. Add carrot strips and onions and reduce to 50 percent power or MEDIUM and microwave for 40 minutes.

Turn meat over, add potatoes, top with cabbage, and **rotate** dish ½ turn. Recover tightly and continue cooking on 50 percent power for 40 to 50 minutes, until meat flakes with a fork and vegetables are tender.

Let **stand**, covered, for 20 to 30 minutes before serving.

Suggestions: For a different flavor, substitute ginger ale for the water in this recipe. You can also use a floured roasting bag. Cooking times are the same, just be sure to keep the meat covered with liquid and secure the tie loosely, so the steam can escape.

Troubleshooting: If your meat is tough, you may not have let it stand long enough. Meat tenderizes during standing time, not cooking time.

If your meat is stringy when you are cutting it, be sure you are cutting across the grain of the meat, not with it.

If the top of the meat is hard and dried out, you probably allowed it to sit above the liquid rather than in it.

Basic Meatloaf

A meatloaf is a meatloaf is a meatloaf! *"Wrong,"* wrote a microwaver in need of help. "I am a good cook but I can't seem to get a good moist meatloaf out of my microwave." Another letter said, "Help! I do my week's cooking on Sunday and during the week I just heat up in my microwave. I took my already cooked meatloaf, wrapped it in paper towels, and microwaved it. It came out hot and hard as a brick. What did I do wrong?"

To begin with, let's figure out how to make that perfect meatloaf, and then I'll tell you how to reheat it. The shape of the meatloaf rather than the recipe is the key. I find that when you form your meatloaf into a round shape with a hole in the center, it cooks and browns far more evenly. I know most people think of the loaf shape for a meatloaf, but by making it round with the center open you are supplying yourself with a natural bowl for vegetables and eliminating yet another dish to wash.

You can form this round shape by using a gelatin mold, bundt pan, tube pan, or by forming the meat around a drinking glass. To ensure that the meat doesn't fry on the bottom, use a meat rack to elevate it up off the flat cooking container. The microwave extracts about one-third more fat than conventional baking does, and even if you use the best possible grade of hamburger you will still have fat around the meat if you don't elevate it.

If you don't have a meat rack and are placing your meatloaf flat on the cooking container, be sure to drain off the fat several times during microwaving. Meatloaf cooks in 7 minutes per pound; be sure you don't overcook, as it will continue to cook during standing time.

For my reader whose meatloaf turned into a brick, I send my regrets and ask that you read carefully Covering and Venting on p. 7. Plastic wrap will steam whatever is inside it and keep in the moisture. Wax paper also causes steaming but allows some of the moisture to escape, while paper towels will absorb the moisture and keep in the spatters. By wrapping the meatloaf in paper towels, all the moisture from the meat was absorbed by the paper, leaving it hard as a brick. She should have wrapped it in plastic wrap to keep it moist.

MEATLOAF TIPS

Spray shortenings can't be used in the microwave because they don't dissolve; however, if you spray your meat rack lightly before placing the molded meatloaf on it, you will find it much easier to remove the finished product. The ingredients in the meatloaf are not as important as the technique for forming and baking it. Feel free to use your own recipe and follow my instructions for preparation.

Equipment: gelatin mold with open center, bundt pan, tube pan, or drinking glass to form a round shape with an open center, meat rack
Cooking time: 13 to 14 minutes
Standing time: 5 minutes
Serves: 4 to 6

   2 **pounds ground beef or a combination of beef and ground pork**
   1 **egg**
   ¼ **cup ketchup**
   1½ **cups seasoned or plain breadcrumbs**
   ½ **cup diced celery**
   ½ **cup diced onion**
   ⅓ **cup milk or water**
   3 **teaspoons A-1 Sauce**
   1 **teaspoon Worcestershire Sauce**
   ½ **teaspoon thyme**

a shake or two of all or any of these spices:
   oregano
   basil
   dry mustard
   powdered onion soup mix
   parsley flakes
   garlic or onion powder
   salt and pepper

Mix all ingredients together, making sure everything is completely blended. Mold mixture in a ring shape, using a tube pan, gelatin mold, bundt pan, or a round drinking glass, packing tightly, and invert onto a meat rack (see Box p. 88). If you're not using a meat rack, be sure to drain fat periodically. Microwave **uncovered** on HIGH for 13 to 14 minutes or until meat is brown, **rotating** dish ½ turn every 5 minutes. Be careful not to overcook, as meatloaf cooks in 7 minutes per pound.

Tent (see Box p. 69) with aluminum foil and let **stand** for 5 minutes. Remove to serving platter and garnish.

Troubleshooting: Overcooking occurs during standing time if you microwave the meatloaf to the exact degree of doneness you wish. Be sure to undercook slightly and allow the meat to finish cooking while tented in foil.

Suggestions: You may want to microwave 2 or 3 slices of bacon on 2 paper towels for 1 minute, then slice them in thirds and place all around meatloaf top. You can also drizzle ketchup over the top for decoration before microwaving.

Garnishing suggestions: Fill the center with mashed potatoes surrounded by a ring of peas and carrots, corn, string beans, limas, or your favorite veggie. Dot the outside of the meatloaf with cherry tomatoes, and you have an entire meal on one plate.

Roast Chicken

One of the very first people to whom I passed my microwaving recipes is my friend Mary Ann. I had successfully roasted my first chicken and of course I called Mary Ann to brag. We hung up and she went grocery shopping. Upon her return, with a chicken of course, she called to say, "Teach me!"

I gave her all the instructions, explaining that she must elevate the chicken, preferably on a meat rack. I explained that in order to get the chicken to cook completely, you must elevate it off the bottom of the flat cooking container. Since she didn't have a meat rack, I suggested using an inverted custard cup, saucer, or bowl. Any of these will raise the bottom of the chicken enough to allow the microwaves to get underneath as well as around the top and sides of the chicken.

Halfway through our dinner that evening, the phone rang; frantic, Mary Ann had put her lovely-looking chicken on the table, started carving, and found the bottom raw. "What happened?" she screamed into the phone. Being new to this, I really didn't know.

Mary Ann was so busy trying to follow the cooking times and glaze recipe that she forgot to elevate the chicken, so the top portion cooked beautifully but the bottom, which sat flat on the cooking container, didn't.

To save calories and help with cholesterol problems, you may want to skin your chicken before microwaving. When cooking chicken in your conventional oven you must keep the skin on so that the meat will not stick to the pan and dry out, but this will not happen in the microwave. Your chicken will microwave just as well without the skin.

The microwave extracts one-third more fat from meat than conventional cooking does, but it holds the juices inside, making a very moist chicken. Once the skin is removed, the chicken will microwave with the same results as if it were boiled—the meat won't be dry or crisp.

Our eyes are used to the lovely caramel color on conventionally cooked chicken. If chicken is just placed into the microwave with nothing on it, you'll get a naked-looking boiled chicken. The simple glaze recipe that follows will help add brown color and a bit of crunch.

If you are stuffing your chicken, you may want just to brush the skin with butter and sprinkle on paprika. The addition of butter to the skin will not crisp it, but it will give it a bit of color. I use a honey base for my glaze; the high sugar content in the honey is what crisps the skin.

Chicken microwaves for 7 minutes per pound or until it reaches an internal temperature of 180 degrees, so be sure to check the weight before discarding the wrapping. Some roasting chickens come with a pop-up thermometer already inserted; however, most manufacturers do not recommend their accuracy in the microwave.

The best way to tell if your chicken has finished microwaving is to check the cavity juices. When raw, they turn red; as the chicken cooks, they turn pink; when the chicken is done, they run completely clear. You can also pierce the area between the leg and the breast. The juices will gather there and will be clear when the chicken is done.

When finished, remove the chicken from the microwave, tent it in aluminum foil (see Box p. 69), shiny side toward the chicken, and let it stand, covered, for 5 to 10 minutes before serving.

At this point, if the outside is still not crisp enough for your taste, pop it under your conventional broiler for a few minutes, but watch it so that it doesn't burn and dry out. This method should produce a perfectly cooked whole chicken each and every time.

Watch the sales on 3-pound whole frying chickens, freeze them, and teach your teenagers how to make an inexpensive healthy snack for themselves instead of using the meat you planned for dinner. Remember, 7 minutes per pound, elevate, and tent with foil during standing time.

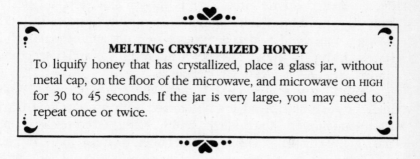

MELTING CRYSTALLIZED HONEY

To liquify honey that has crystallized, place a glass jar, without metal cap, on the floor of the microwave, and microwave on HIGH for 30 to 45 seconds. If the jar is very large, you may need to repeat once or twice.

Equipment:	meat rack
Cooking time:	7 minutes per pound
Standing time:	5 to 10 minutes
Serves:	3 to 4

3-pound whole frying chicken

GLAZE
- 1 tablespoon Dijon mustard
- 1 tablespoon apricot preserves
- 2 tablespoons soy sauce
- 2 tablespoons honey

Remove giblets, neck, and livers from chicken, then wash well with cold water. Place chicken, breast side up, on a meat rack or balanced on an inverted custard cup, bowl, or saucer placed in a casserole dish. Mix glaze ingredients together and brush all over chicken.

Microwave **uncovered** on HIGH for 20 to 25 minutes (7 minutes per pound), or until the meat cut near the bone is no longer pink. If using a probe or thermometer, the internal temperature should be

180 degrees, and regardless of your cooking method, the inside cavity juices should run clear, not pink.

Tent (see Box p. 69) with aluminum foil, shiny side toward the chicken, and let **stand** for 5 to 10 minutes before serving.

OVEN-FRIED CHICKEN

The ultimate dream of many microwavers is to fry chicken. Classic fried chicken, deep-fried in oil as it is on your stove top, just can't be done—but oven-fried chicken can be done very successfully. The coating you use will help to determine the color and crispness of the chicken. Using just a flour coating will not work; egg and breadcrumbs will not give an eye-pleasing appearance.

Instead, try something different, like crushed canned onion rings, or seasoned bread crumbs mixed with an envelope of dry onion soup mix, crushed stuffing crumbs, or crushed cornflake crumbs. First dip the chicken pieces in melted butter, then roll in the crumbs.

Prepackaged coating mixes for chicken will also work, but the breading does not get crusty; it stays soft and similar in appearance to being freshly breaded. Do some experimenting and I'm sure you can come up with your own combination of flavors for personalized micro-fried chicken.

Regardless of your method of breading, it all still cooks the same. You need a meat rack so that your chicken pieces will be elevated off the flat cooking surface. If you don't have a meat rack, try chopsticks spaced across the bottom of your dish. Since the microwaves begin the cooking from the outside of the food to the center, place the meatiest part of the chicken pieces to the outside of the dish and the boniest sections toward the center. When using just legs or thighs, place them in a circle like the spokes of a wagon wheel, boniest part toward the center of the dish. Covering chicken will give you a less crisp effect; however, if you find it decorating the inside of your oven, loosely place a piece of wax paper over the dish to hold in the spatters.

Chicken microwaves for 7 minutes per pound on HIGH. After the first 10 minutes of cooking time, rearrange the more cooked portions of the chicken to the inside of the dish and the less cooked pieces to the outside of the dish. Do not turn the pieces over, just rearrange them.

Continue cooking chicken on HIGH until the juices run clear when you pierce the pieces with a fork and the meat near the bone is no longer pink. If you have various-size pieces, such as wings, legs, thighs, and breasts, you may find the smaller pieces get done first. Remove the pieces as they finish cooking and let them stand under a piece of wax paper while the balance of the chicken cooks.

Basic Barbecued Chicken

This barbecued chicken is dry and burnt; my chicken is raw in the center; the gas grill ran out of gas; last but not least, we're out of charcoal. Do the old chicken barbecue problems sound familiar?

You can use your microwave to partially cook your chicken before grilling to ensure its doneness. By using the same barbecue sauce as you would use on the grill, you can ensure moist, juicy, tender chicken with no burnt, dried out, or undercooked spots right from your microwave.

When buying chickens be sure to choose plump ones with light-colored skin, as those with dark yellow skin or large pores will not be as tender and moist.

You may also want to add a sauce for color and flavor. Before coating your chicken with any color, brush lightly with melted butter to help keep the sauce from beading up.

Whether skinned or painted with a glaze, the most important factor to remember when microwaving chicken is to always elevate it off the flat surface of the cooking container you are using, preferably with a meat rack (see Box p. 94).

To ensure that your grilled chicken is completely cooked, microwave for at least one-half the time given in the recipe and finish on your outside grill. If microwaved chicken is still not brown or crisp enough for you, place it under your conventional broiler set at 450 degrees for just a few minutes.

Try my basic cooking method with your favorite barbecue sauce and see if you don't agree that a micro-barbecue is the next best thing when the tank on the gas grill is empty or there isn't quite enough charcoal left for one more fire.

COOKING CHICKEN

The trick of evenly cooked chicken is to elevate it off the flat cooking container. There are several ways to do this, but the best one is to use a meat rack made for the microwave. If you don't have one, balance a whole chicken on top of an inverted custard cup, bowl, or saucer set into a casserole dish to catch the drippings. (However, bowls and custard cups can become too crowded.)

Another way to elevate chicken pieces without a meat rack is a bit more difficult but will work: chopsticks evenly spaced in a large casserole dish will elevate the pieces off the flat container.

When cooking chicken breasts, you will notice that the outside edges are cooking while the centers are still pink. Turn the chicken over and bring the pink side to the outside of the dish— the cooked edge should be facing the center of the dish. Because the microwaves cook from the outside of the dish to the center, this rearrangement is necessary to achieve evenly cooked chicken.

Equipment: meat rack or chopsticks
Cooking time: 18 to 25 minutes
Standing time: 5 to 10 minutes
Serves: 3 to 4

2 to 3 pounds cut-up fryer parts
¼ cup butter, melted
1½ cups barbecue sauce (see recipe below, or use bottled or your own recipe)

Arrange chicken pieces on a meat rack (see Box above) in a circle with the meatiest pieces toward the outside of the dish. Brush each piece lightly with melted butter and cover with barbecue sauce.

Cover dish with wax paper and microwave on HIGH for 18 to 25 minutes or until chicken is tender and no longer pink near the bone. Halfway through cooking, turn chicken over, **rotate** dish ½ turn, and baste with sauce.

If completely cooking in microwave, let **stand** for 5 to 10 minutes before serving. If partially cooking to finish on grill, cook for 12 to 15 minutes and finish on your grill.

Suggestions: Try using the same glaze as in the recipe for Roast Chicken (see p. 91) for something different.

Basic Barbecue Sauce

Equipment: 1-quart bowl
Cooking time: 5 minutes
Standing time: none required
Makes: enough to cover and baste a 5- to 6-pound chicken or 3 to 4 pounds of cut-up chicken

- 1 **cup ketchup**
- ¼ **cup cider vinegar**
- 1 **tablespoon Worcestershire Sauce**
- 1 **tablespoon A-1 Sauce**
- 1 **small clove garlic, finely minced**
- 3 **tablespoons minced onion**
- 3 **tablespoons packed brown sugar**
- 1 **teaspoon prepared brown mustard**
  salt and pepper to taste

Combine all ingredients in bowl and mix well. Microwave on HIGH for 5 minutes or until sauce is hot and thick, **stirring** after 2 minutes.

Chicken Bundles

Equipment: meat rack
Cooking time: 8 to 12 minutes
Standing time: 3 minutes
Serves: 4

- 2 **whole chicken breasts, halved, skinned, and pounded thin**
- 4 **slices Muenster cheese (or other sliced mild cheese)**
- 12 **asparagus spears, cooked**
- 3 **tablespoons butter**
- 1 **teaspoon garlic powder or ½ teaspoon fresh minced garlic**
- 2 **tablespoons grated Parmesan cheese**
- ¼ **teaspoon oregano**
- ½ **cup cornflake crumbs**

On top of each chicken-breast quarter lay a piece of cheese, folded so as not to extend beyond edges of chicken. On top of cheese place 4 asparagus spears and fold edges of chicken around asparagus. If necessary, secure with a round-edge toothpick.

In small bowl, melt butter on HIGH for 45 to 55 seconds and mix in garlic powder. On a paper plate or in a wide-top bowl, mix Parmesan and oregano into cornflake crumbs. Dip only the top of each chicken roll into the butter and garlic and then into the cornflake crumbs.

Place chicken rolls in a circle on the meat rack in a wheel-spoke arrangement. Microwave on HIGH for 7 to 11 minutes or until chicken is no longer pink and is tender. You may want to loosely **cover** meat rack with wax paper during cooking to prevent chicken grease from popping all over the oven.

Tent with aluminum foil, shiny side toward the meat, and let **stand** 3 minutes before serving.

Troubleshooting: Don't turn bundles over during cooking, as the coating will fall off.

Suggestions: You can substitute cooked broccoli spears for asparagus.

Maresca's Chicken Bolognese

If you want to prepare something really special that is elegant yet easy, try my very favorite recipe. I put this together whenever I am short on time and need a dish that looks fussed over. The dish originated in Maresca's, a little northern Italian restaurant in New Haven, Connecticut.

Chef Frank Califano had never used a microwave and was a bit skeptical that I could reproduce his superb dish in one. My converted recipe is as close to perfect as you can get without traveling to Maresca's and having Chef Frank prepare it for you. Serve this dish with rice or linguine; no one will ever believe you spent less than 30 minutes in the kitchen.

Equipment: 9 × 13-inch baking dish, 4-cup glass measure, tenderizing mallet
Cooking time: 17 to 23 minutes
Standing time: 2 minutes
Serves: 2

2 boneless chicken breasts, skinned
3 tablespoons butter
2 cups sliced fresh mushrooms
1 cup fresh or frozen peas
2 tablespoons flour
½ cup dry white wine
1 cup chicken stock
salt and pepper to taste
4 slices prosciutto ham
4 slices mozzarella cheese

Cut the chicken breasts in half and pound them with the tenderizing mallet to flatten. Melt 1 tablespoon of butter in the baking dish on HIGH for 45 to 55 seconds or until melted. Roll flattened breasts in melted butter and lay flat in the dish.

Cover dish with wax paper, **elevate** on an inverted saucer if dish is flat-bottomed, and microwave on HIGH for 3 minutes. Turn chicken breasts over and rearrange (see Box p. 94), then cook for 3 minutes more on HIGH.

Arrange mushrooms and peas around the chicken in the baking dish. In the glass measure, microwave 2 tablespoons of butter on HIGH for 45 to 55 seconds, then whisk in flour. Add wine, chicken stock, salt, and pepper, **whisking** until well blended.

Pour wine mixture over chicken and vegetables and microwave **uncovered** on HIGH 8 to 14 minutes until sauce is thickened and chicken is tender. Rearrange chicken and **stir** sauce every 2 to 3 minutes.

Once chicken is tender, add a slice of prosciutto topped by a slice of mozzarella to top of each chicken piece. Microwave on HIGH for 60 to 80 seconds until the cheese just starts to melt—if it cooks longer, it will toughen.

Let **stand** for 2 minutes before serving.

Strands of Chicken

Whenever I make Maresca's Chicken Bolognese (see p. 97) I take turns serving it on linguine or rice. One day when I was preparing Spaghetti Squash Sauté (see p. 143), the idea of using strands of spaghetti squash instead of linguine or rice sounded like it had possibilities. I changed the green vegetable and didn't add the ham and mozzarella cheese, but the sauce is the same.

We love it, and I bet you will too. I heap it onto a serving platter and everyone just digs in. I brought it to a carry-in supper one night and amazed many who had never tried, and some who had never even heard of, spaghetti squash.

COOKING FROZEN VEGETABLES

It is much easier to cook frozen vegetables in the containers you purchase them in, even though their instructions call for you to place them in another container and add water. Because you don't add any extra liquid, you aren't forced to drain away precious vitamins and minerals. If vegetables are in a plastic bag, be sure to cut a large X in the bag to act as a vent for the steam to escape. If the box is covered with a foil label, *remove* it; otherwise, just put the box or bag of frozen vegetables right onto paper towels. To eliminate unevenly cooked frozen vegetables, halfway through cooking time shake the box or bag and make sure there are no ice crystals clinging to the vegetables. You might also want to rotate them on a turntable if you have one.

Equipment: 2-quart casserole dish, 4-cup glass measure
Cooking time: 23 to 29 minutes
Standing time: 5 to 10 minutes
Serves: 4 to 5

1 **large or 2 small spaghetti squash**
1 **box frozen chopped broccoli**
2 **tablespoons butter**
2 **tablespoons flour**

½ **cup white wine**
1 **cup chicken stock**
    salt and pepper to taste
2 **boneless, skinless chicken breasts, cut into strips**
4 **ounces fresh mushrooms, sliced**

Wash and pierce the skin of the squash. Place on 2 paper towels on the floor of your microwave and cook on HIGH for 4 to 7 minutes per pound or until squash is soft when the tines of a large fork are inserted.

Let **stand**, **covered**, for 5 to 10 minutes. Then cut crosswise, scoop out seeds and fiber, and carefully twist out the strands of squash. Place on paper towels to drain, and set aside.

Follow microwave time instructions on box of broccoli but place entire box on 2 paper towels (see Box p. 98). Cook, drain, and set aside.

In the glass measure, microwave butter on HIGH for 45 to 55 seconds or until melted. **Whisk** in flour, then add wine, chicken stock, salt, and pepper, **whisking** until well blended. Place chicken strips and mushrooms in the casserole dish and cover with chicken stock mixture. Cook **uncovered** on HIGH for 8 to 14 minutes until sauce is thickened and chicken is tender, rearranging strips every 2 to 3 minutes. Once tender, mix in reserved broccoli and spaghetti squash. Microwave uncovered for 2 to 3 minutes until hot.

Roast Turkey

Are you ready to microwave your first turkey? If you find a whole turkey too much, or want to cut down on leftovers, ask your butcher to cut it in half. Use half of the turkey tonight and freeze the other half for another dinner.

The largest turkey I suggest microwaving is 12 to 14 pounds. Before microwaving, place the turkey in your microwave and turn it around on all four sides to be sure there is a 2- to 3-inch space between the bird and the top and sides of your oven. If the turkey is too close to the top or sides of the microwave, cook it in a conventional oven.

Start with a fresh or defrosted turkey from which you have removed the neck, giblets, and any metal wire. Rinse the inside cavity and pat dry. At this point you are ready to go on with either stuffing the turkey or just preparing it for microwaving. Remember, in the microwave, stuffed or unstuffed turkey and chicken cook in the same length of time. When you cook a turkey in a conventional oven you must increase the cooking time when the bird is stuffed, but not in the microwave—what a time saver!

Equipment:	meat rack or several custard cups and a large flat casserole dish
Cooking time:	1½ to 3½ hours
Standing time:	20 to 30 minutes
Serves:	12 to 14

12- to 14-pound turkey, depending on oven size
¼ cup butter
1 tablespoon fresh minced garlic, or 1 teaspoon garlic powder (*not garlic salt*)
2 tablespoons soy sauce (optional)
2 tablespoons honey (optional)

Rinse cavity of turkey and pat dry. Place butter and garlic in a small bowl and microwave on HIGH for 45 to 55 seconds or until melted. Add soy sauce and honey (if using) and mix well. Baste turkey with honey or butter-and-garlic mixture and place, breast-side down, on the meat rack or balanced on top of several inverted custard cups set into the large casserole dish to catch the drippings. Do not use a thermometer or probe, as hot fat can run down the probe and turn off the oven before the turkey is done.

There are two different cooking methods you can follow:

1. If your oven has only HIGH and LOW settings, you want to bake the turkey on HIGH for 7 to 8 minutes per pound. Calculate the approximate cooking time and divide it into quarters. Start the turkey breast-side down for the first quarter of cooking time, then turn it left-wing down for second quarter, right-wing down for third quarter, and breast-side up for final quarter.

2. If your microwave has variable power settings, bake the turkey on 50 percent power or MEDIUM for 12 to 15 minutes per pound. Calculate cooking time and divide it into quarters. Start the

turkey breast-side down on HIGH for the first 10 minutes of the initial quarter of roasting time.

After the first 10 minutes on HIGH, reduce to 50 percent or MEDIUM and finish the balance of the first quarter's cooking time. Turn the turkey onto its left-wing side and cook for the second quarter of time, right-wing side for the third quarter of cooking time, and breast-side up for the last quarter of cooking time. You minimize the need for shielding tender parts by using the lower power setting.

Please be sure to baste often and **shield** turkey parts carefully with small pieces of aluminum foil, if your oven allows (see Arching and Shielding, p. 10), should they begin to overbrown or become dry. You may find it necessary to drain off some of the juices at various stages of cooking.

When the cavity juices run clear with no trace of pink color, or when the leg moves freely at the joint, and the flesh feels very soft when pressed, your turkey is done. If the turkey is stuffed, the juices should run clear when the breast meat under the wing is pierced with a fork or skewer.

Tent with aluminum foil, shiny side toward the meat and let **stand** for 20 to 30 minutes before serving. The internal temperature of the meatiest part of the thigh should register 185 degrees after inserting a meat thermometer or probe for 1 minute.

Suggestions: If you are cooking only half the turkey, be sure to elevate it off the flat cooking surface and follow either of the cooking methods listed above, but you don't have to turn over the turkey half.

Turkey Stuffing

Equipment:	2-quart casserole dish
Cooking time:	6 to 7 minutes
Standing time:	none required
Serves:	10 to 12

½ **cup butter**
½ **cup chopped onion**
½ **cup chopped celery**
½ **cup chopped mushrooms**
2 **cloves garlic, finely minced**
1 **teaspoon poultry seasoning**
½ **teaspoon seasoned salt**
⅛ **teaspoon pepper**
1 **cup chicken broth or water**
8 **to 10 cups bread cubes—if using prepackaged seasoned ones, omit seasoned salt**

In casserole dish place butter, onion, celery, mushrooms, and garlic. Microwave on HIGH for 3 minutes, then **stir**. Microwave for 3 to 4 minutes more on HIGH until vegetables are tender. Add poultry seasoning and salt and pepper; mix well. Add chicken broth and bread cubes, mixing very well to coat bread cubes.

Stuff turkey cavity and either sew it closed or push the heel from a loaf of bread over the stuffing to keep it from falling out of the cavity. Do not overstuff, as you must be able to turn the turkey four times during microwaving and you don't want to loose your stuffing in the process. Follow instructions for microwaving turkey.

Suggestions: You can add crumbled cooked sausage (see Box p. 61) to stuffing when you add bread cubes.

POTATO TOPPERS

My family can eat leftover holiday dinners for only just so long. I have come up with one more way to disguise leftover meat that may please your family as much as it does mine.

The classic baked potato is a favorite with us and I use various leftover meats to create tempting toppers. I just add a salad and dessert and no one guesses I'm really using up leftovers.

These toppings are also great for buffet tables. You can have your potatoes individually wrapped in foil in a basket lined with a pretty cloth napkin to help keep them hot, then several dishes of different toppings for folks to fix their own.

Turkey Divan Fixings

Equipment: 4-cup glass measure
Cooking time: 14 to 17 minutes
Standing time: none required
Serves: 4

1 10-ounce package frozen chopped broccoli
1 cup turkey cut into ¼-inch cubes
2 tablespoons butter
⅓ cup chopped onion
⅓ cup sliced fresh mushrooms
1 teaspoon chicken bouillon
¼ teaspoon dry mustard
4 teaspoons all-purpose flour
¾ cup milk
4 hot baked potatoes
4 ounces shredded cheddar cheese

If the box of frozen broccoli is paper-covered, microwave the entire box on 2 thicknesses of paper towels for 5 to 6 minutes on HIGH and drain. (See Box p. 98.) Combine turkey cubes with broccoli and set aside.

In the glass measure, microwave butter, onions, and mushrooms on HIGH for 4 to 5 minutes or until soft, **stirring** once. Add bouillon, mustard, and flour to mushroom mixture, stirring well. Add milk slowly, using a whisk to eliminate lumps. Microwave for 4 to 5 minutes on HIGH or until thick, **whisking** every minute. Fold in broccoli and turkey mixture.

Cut 4 baked potatoes in half, flake centers, and place on a paper plate. Mound turkey mixture over potato halves and cover with cheese. Microwave on HIGH for 45 to 60 seconds until cheese melts.

Confetti Ham Fixings

Equipment: 4-cup glass measure
Cooking time: 7½ to 9½ minutes
Standing time: none required
Serves: 4

  2 **tablespoons white wine**
  1 **tablespoon butter**
 ¼ **cup chopped green pepper**
 ¼ **cup chopped celery**
 ¼ **cup sliced fresh mushrooms**
  1 **onion, thinly sliced**
  1 **clove garlic, finely minced, or 1 teaspoon garlic powder**
  1 **cup ham, cut into ½-inch cubes**
  1 **8-ounce can of tomato sauce**
 ⅛ **teaspoon oregano**
 ⅛ **teaspoon pepper**
  4 **ounces shredded mozzarella cheese**
  4 **hot baked potatoes**

In the glass measure combine wine, butter, green pepper, celery, mushrooms, onion, and garlic. Microwave on HIGH for 5 to 6 minutes until vegetables are transparent. Add ham, tomato sauce, oregano, and pepper. Microwave on HIGH for 2 to 3 minutes or until mixture is hot.

Cut potatoes in half and flake centers. Place potatoes on paper plate and mound hot ham mixture over potatoes and sprinkle with mozzarella. Microwave on HIGH for 25 to 35 seconds, just until mozzarella begins to melt or it will toughen.

Leg of Lamb

Lamb is not a favorite in my house, and when it came time to do a perfect microwaved leg of lamb I consulted my friends the Jubinskys. Sandy Jubinsky produces a juicy, perfect-looking, perfect-tasting leg of lamb in the microwave and was eager to share the recipe if it would help others enjoy one of her family's favorite dishes.

> ### SOLVING MOISTURE PROBLEMS
>
> Paper towels, paper napkins, or paper plates can be used to absorb moisture when microwaving. Anything that sits directly on the floor of the microwave will collect moisture if you do not put it on 2 paper towels, paper napkins, or even a paper plate lined with a napkin or piece of paper towel. Paper under food sitting alone in the microwave is a *must*. Bread must be completely wrapped in a napkin or paper towel, especially if it is frozen. If there isn't something to collect moisture, it will be absorbed into the food ... and later it will be hard as a brick.

Equipment:	meat rack or custard cups
Cooking time:	55 to 65 minutes
Standing time:	10 minutes
Serves:	4 to 6

4 pounds leg of lamb, bone-in
2 to 3 cloves garlic, sliced thin
1 tablespoon rosemary
1 teaspoon thyme
¼ teaspoon sage
¼ cup olive oil

Cut several small slits into the surface of the lamb, about ½ inch deep. Insert a slice of garlic into each slit. Mix the remaining ingredients and rub half of the mixture over the entire leg of lamb.

Place lamb, fat-side down, on a meat rack or—if your meat rack has no well for drippings—balanced on two inverted custard cups, and microwave on HIGH for 10 minutes. Reduce to 50 percent power or MEDIUM and cook for 20 minutes. Turn lamb over and rub the remaining herb mixture over the lamb and cook on 50 percent power or MEDIUM for 25 to 35 minutes.

Tent with aluminum foil, shiny side toward the meat, and let **stand** for 10 minutes before serving. These times will produce medium doneness; a minute or so less for medium rare per pound, a minute or two more for well-done.

Fish

If you haven't discovered it yet, the microwave is the perfect place to cook fish. Because fish is very tender to begin with, it can be cooked on HIGH in most recipes. You can scallop, steam, poach, bread, brown, stuff, or put your fish in a sauce, and still have it moist and tender.

Fish should be cooked just until it flakes; overcooking will cause it to be dry and tough. Uniformly shaped fillets are hard to find, so to prevent overcooking the tips or pointed ends of a fillet, fold the tips under the fillet and they will cook much more evenly.

Seafood does not keep well and should be cooked just before serving. Should you have to cook it ahead, slightly undercook so it can finish cooking during the time you allow for reheating. However, fish without a sauce does not reheat well, for the reheat time is almost as long as the original cooking time. Standing time for fish is very short and can be the time it takes to remove it from the microwave and serve.

Butter-based sauces tend to hold their flavor better with fish, for as the fish cooks it produces juices that may dilute the flavor of some sauces. Here are two different butter-based sauces for you to try on your taste buds.

COOKING FISH FILLETS

If you place fish fillets flat in the cooking container, the narrow tips of the fillet will overcook before the center of the fillet completely cooks. I recommend that you tuck the tips under the fillet before microwaving, making a little bundle as if it were stuffed. This technique will allow the fillets to cook evenly.

Fish and Mushrooms in Wine Sauce

Equipment: 8 × 12 or 9 × 13-inch casserole dish
Cooking time: 7 to 9½ minutes
Standing time: 1 to 2 minutes
Serves: 4

1 **pound fish fillets of your choice (sole and flounder work well)**
2 **tablespoons butter**
2 **tablespoons chopped scallions**
¼ **teaspoon seasoned salt**
¼ **cup dry white wine**
1 **tablespoon parsley flakes**
¼ **teaspoon dried crushed basil**
dash of pepper
½ **pound fresh mushrooms, sliced**

Place butter and scallions in casserole dish. Microwave on HIGH, **uncovered**, for 1 to 1½ minutes. Add seasoned salt, wine, parsley, basil, and pepper, and **stir**. Arrange fish in dish, turning over to coat both sides with sauce. Place mushrooms on top of fillets and **cover** with plastic wrap, venting back one corner.

Elevate flat-bottomed dish on an inverted saucer and place on a turntable if available. (**Rotate** dish ½ turn after 3 minutes if not using turntable.) Microwave on HIGH for 6 to 8 minutes, basting sauce over fish twice during cooking. Cook until fish flakes easily.

Let **stand** 1 to 2 minutes before serving.

Seafarer's Dream

Equipment: 2- or 4-cup glass measure, 8 × 12-inch casserole dish, custard cup or small bowl
Cooking time: 8 to 10 minutes
Standing time: 1 minute
Serves: 4

1 pound fish fillets of your choice (sole and flounder work well)
2 tablespoons butter
¼ cup slivered almonds
3 tablespoons butter
2 tablespoons fresh lemon juice
¼ teaspoon dill weed
½ teaspoon onion powder
2 tablespoons dry white wine
1 tablespoon minced fresh parsley

In the glass measure, combine 2 tablespoons butter and almonds. Microwave on HIGH for 2 to 3 minutes or until brown. Set aside. In the casserole dish, arrange fillets (see Box p. 107).

Melt 3 tablespoons butter in a custard cup or small bowl on HIGH for 45 to 60 seconds. Add lemon juice, dill, onion powder, and wine to butter and spread over fillets. Sprinkle with parsley.

Cover dish with plastic wrap, venting back one corner, and **elevate** flat-bottomed dish on an inverted saucer. Place on turntable if available. Microwave for 5–6 minutes on HIGH or until fish flakes easily with fork. (**Rotate** dish ½ turn after 3 minutes if not on turntable.)

Let **stand** for 1 minute, then sprinkle with toasted almonds before serving.

Hawaiian Delight

How about a little bit more zip to your sauce? If you like a sweet-and-sour flavor this recipe is worth trying. Keep experimenting, and don't forget to note the time it took your oven to create these fork-tender dishes so that when you try them again you will know just how long to cook them.

Equipment: 8 × 12-inch flat and 1-quart casserole dishes
Cooking time: 6½ to 10 minutes
Standing time: none required
Serves: 4

1 pound fish fillets of your choice (sole and flounder work well)
¼ cup light brown sugar
3 teaspoons cornstarch
1 teaspoon chives
1 teaspoon minced garlic
¼ teaspoon dry mustard
1 8-ounce can pineapple chunks, drained and juice reserved
¼ cup white or cider vinegar
1 small green pepper, cut into strips
1 tablespoon ketchup
8 whole maraschino cherries, drained
¼ cup cashews

Place fish fillets in the 8 × 12-inch casserole dish (see Box p. 107). **Cover** with vented plastic wrap and **elevate** flat-bottomed dish on an inverted saucer. Microwave on HIGH for 4 to 6 minutes or until fish flakes easily. Set aside.

In the 1-quart casserole dish, combine brown sugar, cornstarch, chives, garlic, and dry mustard. Stir in drained pineapple juice, vinegar, green pepper strips, and ketchup. Microwave on HIGH for 1½ minutes, **stirring** every minute until thickened. Stir in pineapple chunks, cherries, and cashews.

Drain fish well and place back in clean 8 × 12-inch casserole dish. Spoon sauce over fish and microwave **uncovered** on HIGH for 1 to 2 minutes or until heated through just before serving.

Stuffed Fish Roll-Ups

For those of you who like your fillets stuffed, have I got a recipe for you. You can just poach these fillets in wine and serve them plain, or you can try my lovely Lemon Sauce, which adds a finishing touch for a perfect presentation.

Equipment: 1-quart bowl, round glass baking dish or pie plate, 2-cup glass measure
Cooking time: fish—25 to 30 minutes; sauce—10 minutes
Standing time: none required
Serves: 4 to 5

8 2-ounce fish fillets of your choice (sole and flounder work well)
2 tablespoons butter
2 cloves garlic, minced
½ cup chopped celery
¼ cup chopped fresh mushrooms
½ cup chopped onion
4 ounces fresh small or medium-size shrimp, chopped
1½ cups flavored breadcrumbs
1 tablespoon fresh lemon juice (see Box p. 227)
½ teaspoon seasoned salt
⅛ teaspoon pepper
1 egg, slightly beaten
¼ cup white wine

Place butter, garlic, celery, mushrooms, onion, and shrimp in bowl. Microwave on HIGH for 3 minutes. **Stir**, microwave on HIGH another 3 minutes. Stir in breadcrumbs, lemon juice, seasoned salt, pepper, and egg. Mix lightly but well. Place 1 heaping tablespoon of crumb mixture on the center of each fillet. Bring ends over stuffing, pushing gently into stuffing to hold.

In the baking dish or pie plate, arrange fish pointing toward the center of the dish in a wheel-spoke design. Add wine, **cover** with wax paper, and **elevate** flat-bottomed dish on an inverted saucer. Place on a turntable if available. Microwave on HIGH for 7 minutes. (If not using turntable, microwave for 3 minutes, then **rotate** ¼ turn, microwave for another 3 minutes on HIGH, rotating dish another ¼ turn, and microwave 1 final minute on HIGH until fish flakes easily with the tines of a fork.)

Suggestions: Try adding clams, lobster, or crabmeat to the stuffing in place of the shrimp or in addition to it.

LEMON SAUCE
Makes 1¼ cups

> 2 **tablespoons butter**
> ¼ **cup chopped scallions**
> 1 **tablespoon cornstarch**
> 1 **cup chicken broth**
> 2 **teaspoons fresh lemon juice (see Box p. 227)**
> ¼ **teaspoon grated lemon zest**

Place butter and scallions in the glass measure and microwave on HIGH for 1 minute. **Whisk** and microwave on HIGH for 2 minutes more. Add cornstarch and broth. Whisk until smooth and microwave on HIGH for 4 minutes, **whisking** each minute.

Stir in lemon juice and zest. Microwave 1 minute more on HIGH and serve over fish rolls.

Seafood Stuffed Sole

Equipment:	4-cup glass measure, glass pie plate or round 1-quart casserole dish, custard cup
Cooking time:	12 to 14 minutes
Standing time:	none required
Serves:	4 to 6

> 1 **pound of sole fillets**
> 1 **cup cooked flaked seafood (crab, shrimp, lobster, and/or scrod)**
> 1 **cup plain breadcrumbs**
> 5 **tablespoons butter**
> 2 **tablespoons all-purpose flour**
>   **dash of salt and pepper**
> 2 **tablespoons minced onion**
> ½ **cup plus 2 tablespoons white wine**
> 1 **cup milk**
>   **dash of paprika**

Combine flaked seafood with breadcrumbs, mixing well. In the glass measure, melt 1 tablespoon butter on HIGH for 35 to 45 seconds. Whisk the flour into the melted butter and add salt, pepper, onion, and 1 tablespoon white wine. Gradually add milk **whisking** until smooth.

Microwave this white sauce **uncovered** on HIGH for 4 to 6 minutes, whisking every minute until it thickens and coats a spoon. Blend white sauce into breadcrumb mixture, mixing well. Add 2 tablespoons butter to a custard cup, **covered** with a paper napkin, and microwave on HIGH for 35 to 45 seconds until melted. Add melted butter and 1 tablespoon wine to breadcrumb mixture. Lay 1 fillet flat and place 1 heaping tablespoon of stuffing in the center. Bring both ends to the center, folding over stuffing, and place on a thin slice of butter in the glass pie plate or casserole dish. Stuff remaining fillets and place them all in the dish in a wheel-spoke design. When all the fish are rolled, carefully pour ½ cup wine around the fillets. **Cover** with vented plastic wrap and **elevate** flat-bottomed dish on an inverted saucer or turntable if available.

Microwave on HIGH for 7 minutes. (**Rotate** dish ¼ turn after 3 minutes if not using turntable. Rotate ¼ turn again after the next 3 minutes.) Transfer to serving dish and sprinkle with paprika.

Fish Combo Kabobs

Equipment:	meat rack, custard cups, or flat casserole dish with lips, 6 wooden skewers
Cooking time:	4 to 7 minutes
Standing time:	none required
Serves:	4 to 6

  1 **pound large sea scallops, about 1 inch each**
  ½ **pound medium-sized shrimp**
  8 **small white onions**
  1 **medium green pepper, cut into 1-inch cubes**
  4 **lemon wedges**
  8 **cherry tomatoes**

BASTING SAUCE
- ½ **cup butter**
- 2 **tablespoons white wine**
- ¼ **teaspoon dry mustard**
  pinch of pepper

Starting at the bottom of the first of six 10-inch skewers, place a small onion, followed by alternating pieces of green pepper, scallop, and shrimp. Once skewer is almost filled, add another onion and a lemon wedge. Leave a small space at each end of the skewer for a cherry tomato. Repeat until all skewers are filled. Place filled skewers on meat rack or balanced on the lips of a casserole dish, or balanced between custard cups. (See Box p. 57.)

In small bowl place butter, wine, mustard, and pepper. Microwave on HIGH until butter is melted, 50 to 60 seconds. Mix butter mixture together and brush over kabobs.

Cover kabobs with wax paper and microwave on HIGH for 3 to 6 minutes until scallops flake easily. Baste with butter mixture every minute. Place cherry tomato on each end of skewer after third basting. Reheat butter sauce just before serving.

Salmon Supreme

This is my family's favorite salmon loaf, which I have converted to the microwave. I don't like the way conventional loaf shapes cook in the microwave, so I have turned this into a ring-shaped loaf.

Because salmon and tuna do not give off any fat or juices when cooking, you can use your regular recipe in the microwave, changing only the shape and cooking times. You don't need to elevate it on a meat rack; instead prepare it in a glass pie plate or right on a serving dish.

Equipment: glass pie plate or 9-inch round serving dish
Cooking time: 15 to 22 minutes
Standing time: 5 minutes
Serves: 4

1 16-ounce can salmon, drained, flaked, bones and skin
   removed
1 10½-ounce can cream of mushroom soup, undiluted
2 eggs, slightly beaten
1 cup breadcrumbs
1 medium onion, minced
1 tablespoon fresh lemon juice (see Box p. 227)
¼ teaspoon dill weed
½ teaspoon prepared mustard
   dash of salt and pepper
1 box frozen chopped broccoli
   Sour Cream Sauce (recipe follows)

In a medium bowl combine salmon, soup, eggs, breadcrumbs, and spices. Blend the ingredients together well. Place a drinking glass in the center of a pie plate or serving dish. Form salmon mixture into a ring-shaped loaf around the glass, packing tightly. Once shaped, remove the glass and elevate the flat-bottomed dish on an inverted saucer on top of a turntable if available. (If not using a turntable, **rotate** dish ½ turn every 8 minutes.)

Cover dish with vented plastic wrap and microwave on 50 percent power or MEDIUM for 15 to 22 minutes or until firm.

Let dish **stand**, covered, while preparing the broccoli.

Place paper-covered box of broccoli on 2 thicknesses of paper towels. Microwave on HIGH for 6 to 8 minutes and place in the center of the salmon ring. Drizzle Sour Cream Sauce over entire ring and serve.

SOUR CREAM SAUCE
Makes 1 cup

1 cup sour cream
2 tablespoons white horseradish
1 teaspoon prepared mustard
1 tablespoon chopped chives

Mix all ingredients together.

TROUT

Trout, no doubt, is an angler's dream! Trout can be cleaned, dressed, and prepared whole, or skinned and boned into fillets. To prepare it I suggest poaching in a fish broth made with wine, vegetables, and spices. In conventional oven cooking this broth is needed to keep the fish moist and to add flavor. In the microwave we can poach with little or no liquid; as long as the dish is tightly covered with plastic wrap and vented, it will hold in the moisture. Since using a broth helps to add flavor, I suggest using one in the microwave also.

When poaching fish fillets, be sure to place the thickest part to the outside of the dish and to fold the thin-tipped ends under the fillet. If you allow these thin tips to lie flat, they will overcook before the center of the fillet is flaky.

If you are cooking only one fish at a time, be sure to align the backbone of the fish against the side of the baking dish. If you are cooking two fish, have both backbones to the outsides of the dish, with the head of one and the tail of the other at one end. When cooking three fish, have them form a triangle; four fish, a square. By leaving the center of the dish empty you allow the microwave to cook the fish from all sides. Be sure to elevate the dish on a inverted saucer to allow the microwaves to get underneath as well.

Whether poached or stuffed, a whole dressed fish takes 6 to 9 minutes per pound on HIGH, while fillets take 4 to 6 minutes per pound on HIGH.

All right, you anglers, the cook has all the necessary instructions for cooking, now it's up to you!

Poached Trout

Equipment: casserole dish large enough to hold your fish
Cooking time: 12 to 15 minutes
Standing time: none required
Serves: 1 to 2

1 to 2 pounds cleaned and dressed trout

BROTH
¼ **cup white wine or water**
1 **medium onion, sliced**
1 **medium carrot, sliced**
1 **celery stalk, sliced**
1 **clove garlic, minced**
½ **lemon, sliced**
1 **bay leaf**
6 **peppercorns**

Place all broth ingredients in the casserole dish and **cover** tightly with vented plastic wrap. Microwave on HIGH for 5 minutes.

Uncover and lay fish, backbone toward the side of the dish, on top of broth. Cover with plastic wrap again, venting one corner. Microwave on HIGH for 7 to 10 minutes or until fish flakes easily at thickest portion.

POACHED TROUT FILLETS
1 **pound trout fillets**
Poaching broth (see above)

Place broth in a casserole dish large enough to accommodate fillets and microwave on HIGH for 5 minutes **covered** tightly with vented plastic wrap.

Place fillets over broth, making sure to tuck thin-tipped edges under the fillets and keep the thickest pieces toward the outside of the dish. Cover with vented plastic wrap.

Cook on HIGH for 4 to 6 minutes until thickest pieces of fish flake easily. Halfway through cooking, rearrange fillets, bringing the center ones to the outside of the dish and the ones on the outside to the center.

Stuffed Trout

Equipment: casserole dish large enough to hold fish, 4-cup glass measure, custard cup
Cooking time: 8 to 11 minutes
Standing time: none required
Serves: 2

   2 6- to 8-ounce trout
  ¼ cup chopped onion
  ¼ cup chopped celery
  ¼ cup chopped fresh mushrooms
  1 clove garlic, minced
  ¼ cup flaked crabmeat or diced shrimp (optional)
  2 tablespoons white wine
  3 tablespoons butter
  ½ cup seasoned breadcrumbs
  3 teaspoons fresh lemon juice

In the glass measure combine vegetables, garlic, 1 tablespoon wine, seafood if using, and 2 tablespoons butter. Microwave **uncovered** on HIGH for 3 to 4 minutes until tender.

Mix in breadcrumbs and 1 teaspoon lemon juice. (If too wet, add a bit more breadcrumbs.) Pack half of mixture into each fish and place in a casserole dish with backbones facing outside edges and head to tail.

In a custard cup microwave 1 tablespoon butter, 1 tablespoon white wine, and 2 teaspoons lemon juice for 35 to 45 seconds until melted. Brush fish with butter mixture, **cover** with vented plastic wrap, and **elevate** on an inverted saucer. Microwave on HIGH for 4 to 6 minutes until fish flakes easily.

Troubleshooting: If fish is dry, you have overcooked it, or you forgot to cover with plastic wrap. Covering with paper towel or wax paper will not do—the fish must steam and only plastic wrap or a tight cover will accomplish this.

Suggestions: If you are in a real hurry, try a packaged stuffing mix that can be put together very quickly, and use any leftover stuffing in mushroom caps (see recipe p. 29).

STEAMED CLAMS

Living near the shore, we have always been shellfish lovers. My husband's idea of steamed clams does not fit in with my idea of no mess and cleanup in the kitchen. The stove top is covered with spatters when he steams clams and he usually decorates the countertop and floor when draining the hot pot of excess broth.

The introduction of the microwave oven into our kitchen made the old clam pot obsolete, but best of all cleanup takes only a sheet of paper towel and hardly any elbow grease.

There are three different methods you can use to steam clams in your microwave, depending on how many you have, and whether or not you want the broth for drinking, dipping, or dunking garlic bread.

Try all three methods and pick your favorite and see if you don't also agree that a micro-clam bake is less work and mess than using that old clam pot.

Troubleshooting: Do not overcook or the clams will toughen. If some shells remain closed after longest cooking time in the recipe, remove the open ones and microwave the remaining clams on HIGH for 30 seconds. Repeat this only once and if some clams are still not open discard them, as they may be spoiled.

Roasting Bag Method

Equipment:	roasting bag, casserole dish large enough to hold bag filled with clams, string to close bag
Cooking time:	10 to 12 minutes
Standing time:	none required
Serves:	1 to 2

24 **clams**
1 **tablespoon flour**
1 **roasting bag**
1 **cup hot water**
1 **celery stalk, cut in thirds**
1 **teaspoon garlic powder**
1 **teaspoon seasoned salt**

Lightly flour the inside of the roasting bag and place it in the casserole dish. Scrub clams very well and place them inside the bag along with the hot water, celery, garlic powder, and seasoned salt. Tie the bag loosely with string, leaving a space for the steam to **vent**, and microwave on HIGH for 10 to 12 minutes or until the clams are opened. (Discard any unopened clams as they may be spoiled.)

Steamed Clams with Broth

Equipment: deep 3- or 4-quart casserole dish
Cooking time: 10 to 12 minutes
Standing time: none required
Serves: 1 to 2

2 dozen clams
1 clove garlic, minced
¼ pound butter
½ cup white wine

Scrub clams well and place in the casserole dish. Add garlic, butter, and wine, then **cover** with vented plastic wrap.

Microwave on HIGH for 10 to 12 minutes until all shells are open. (Discard any clams that have not opened as they may be spoiled.)

This method makes a fine broth for dunking and dipping.

Steamed Clams without Broth

Equipment: large flat plate
Cooking time: 3 to 5 minutes
Standing time: none required
Serves: 1

12 to 14 clams

Scrub clams well and place them in a circle on a large flat plate. **Cover** loosely with plastic wrap, venting back one corner to allow the steam to escape.

Microwave on HIGH for 3 to 5 minutes or until shells pop open. (Discard any clams that have not opened as they may be spoiled.)

Seafood Cocktail Sauce

Do you have a favorite recipe for the red cocktail sauce that goes on steamed clams? Mine doesn't need to be microwaved, but I thought you might like to have it.

> **1 cup ketchup**
> **2 to 3 tablespoons white horseradish (to taste)**
> **1 to 2 tablespoons fresh lemon juice**
>   **salt and pepper to taste**
> **1 teaspoon Worcestershire Sauce**
> **½ teaspoon Tabasco Sauce (to taste)**

Mix all ingredients together to your individual degree of hotness. Chill. Serve over lettuce for shrimp cocktails, or to accompany raw or cooked clams or other seafood.

Steamed Lobster

Is there a particular type of food that is special to only you in your household? Mine is lobster! No one else in our house can be bothered picking it apart. I give it my complete attention; when I finish, the red shell holds nothing but the pile of rubble. My husband's philosophy is, "I worked for my supper once and I'm not going to work through eating it." His loss means more for me!

Unless you are skilled at working with the live variety, have your seafood market clean and cut open the lobster for you. To keep the tail section flat during microwaving, insert a wooden skewer or chopstick under the shell from the tail to the head. This is especially helpful when you are stuffing your treat; however, this isn't necessary if you don't mind the tail curling up during cooking.

Microwaving lobster saves a great deal of mess on your stove, as there is no pot of steaming water to clean up and your cooking container doubles as your serving dish.

Equipment: casserole dish large enough to hold lobster flat, wooden skewer or chopstick.
Cooking time: 8 to 10 minutes
Standing time: 5 minutes
Serves: 1 to 2, 1 lobster per person

1 or 2 1- to 1½-pound cleaned lobsters
¼ cup dry white wine

Starting at the tail end of the cleaned lobster, insert a wooden skewer or chopstick between the meat and the shell all the way to the head.

Place the lobster in the casserole dish and add wine. **Cover** with vented plastic wrap and microwave on HIGH for 8 to 10 minutes, **elevating** the flat-bottomed dish on an inverted saucer.

Let **stand, covered,** for 5 minutes before serving with melted butter and lemon wedges.

Scallops and Mushrooms in Wine Sauce

Another shellfish love of ours is scallops. Our favorite recipe has a not-too-heavy cheese and wine sauce that is quick and very elegant when served in large seashells.

Equipment: 2-quart casserole dish, strainer, 4-cup glass measure, 2-cup glass measure
Cooking time: 15 to 21 minutes
Standing time: none required
Serves: 2 to 3

1 pound scallops
1 cup dry white wine
2 tablespoons butter
2 scallions, chopped
1 cup sliced fresh mushrooms

SAUCE
- 5 **tablespoons butter**
- 3 **tablespoons flour**
- ½ **cup milk**
- ½ **cup shredded sharp cheddar cheese**
- **salt and pepper to taste**
- 1 **cup soft breadcrumbs**
- **minced parsley for garnish**

Place scallops in bottom of the casserole dish. Add wine and micro-wave **covered** (vent plastic wrap if using) for 4 to 6 minutes on 80 percent power or MEDIUM-HIGH until scallops are tender. Strain when tender and reserve liquid. Do not overcook.

Place 2 tablespoons butter in the 2-cup glass measure and add scallions and mushrooms. Microwave on HIGH for 3 to 5 minutes or until soft.

Now make the sauce: Melt 3 tablespoons of the butter in the 4-cup glass measure on HIGH for 45 to 50 seconds. Add reserved wine liquid and flour to butter and **whisk** together well. Microwave on HIGH for 2 minutes, then add milk, cheese, salt and pepper, whisking well.

Microwave on HIGH for 2 to 4 minutes more until thick enough to coat a spoon, whisking every 2 minutes. Add scallions, mushrooms, and scallops to cheese sauce and heat for 2 minutes on 80 percent power or MEDIUM-HIGH until piping hot.

Melt the remaining 2 tablespoons of butter in a small bowl on HIGH for 45 to 55 seconds and add breadcrumbs until combined. Sprinkle this over the top of the scallop mixture and garnish with parsley.

Troubleshooting: If your sauce is lumpy, you didn't use a whisk, or you didn't whisk it long enough. Whisking rather than stirring with a spoon produces a much smoother lump-free sauce, and since you stir only occasionally in the microwave, a smooth sauce is important.

Your scallops will be very tough if overcooked, so be sure to allow for standing time when deciding if they are done. Remember, you can always put it back into the microwave.

Suggestion: I serve this mixture over rice for a hearty main dish.

Tuna Casserole

When we first married, my husband taught me to make tuna noodle casserole, so I have to give him complete credit for this recipe.

Equipment:	6-cup glass measure, 4-cup glass measure, 8 × 12-inch or 2-quart casserole dish
Cooking time:	17 to 25 minutes
Standing time:	2 to 3 minutes
Serves:	4

   5 tablespoons butter
   ½ cup diced red peppers
   1 cup frozen peas
   2 tablespoons flour
1½ cups milk
   1 cup shredded sharp cheddar cheese
   2 teaspoons Worcestershire Sauce
   2 6½-ounce cans tuna in water, drained and flaked
   8 ounces medium or wide noodles, cooked and drained
      black pepper to taste
   1 cup cornflake crumbs

To the 4-cup glass measure, add 1 tablespoon butter, red peppers, and peas. Microwave **covered** with vented plastic wrap on HIGH for 4 to 6 minutes or until peppers are crisp-tender. Drain and set aside.

To the 6-cup glass measure, add 2 tablespoons butter and microwave on HIGH for 45 to 55 seconds or until melted. **Whisk** in flour, then milk. Microwave **uncovered** on HIGH for 4 to 6 minutes, **whisking** every minute until thick enough to coat a spoon. Whisk in cheese and microwave for 1 minute more until melted. Whisk in Worcestershire Sauce and set aside.

Place noodles in casserole dish and mix in the drained peas, peppers, and tuna. Fold the cheese sauce into the noodle mixture, combining well and adding black pepper to taste.

Elevate the flat-bottomed container on an inverted saucer and place on a turntable if available. Microwave for 8 to 12 minutes on HIGH until hot, **stirring** every 3 minutes. (**Rotate** dish ¼ turn with each stirring if not using turntable.)

Let **stand** for 2 to 3 minutes before serving. While dish stands, melt the remaining 2 tablespoons of butter in a 4-cup glass measure. Mix in cornflake crumbs and blend well. Sprinkle over the top of the casserole and serve.

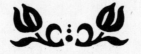

Stir-Fries

Whenever I mention stir-frying in the microwave, people look at me very strangely. Needless to say, the wok is the best utensil for Chinese cooking; however, stir-frying in the microwave requires far less of the cook's attention, with very little loss of traditional flavor.

Most stir-fry recipes require using a browning dish to obtain the best flavor. Many of you new microwavers may not be aware of the proper use and care of browning dishes, so pay careful attention to the basic information on page 11.

There are two types of browning devices made for the microwave. One has short sides and does not come with a cover, while the other has higher sides and does come with a cover. For our purposes, we need the covered browning dish so that we may steam our recipes once the browning has been accomplished.

Your microwaved stir-fry dishes need less attention than do ones cooked in a wok, but be sure not to overcook your vegetables—they should be crisp, not limp. Please feel free to experiment with various vegetables in the recipes that follow.

The most important part of these recipes is the marinade—once cooked, it will be the sauce for your dish. Most recipes tell you to marinate for at least 1 hour, but you may combine your meat and marinade before leaving for work in the morning and it will be ready for quick cooking when you arrive home.

Beef with Snow Peas

Equipment:	10-inch covered browning dish
Cooking time:	11 to 15 minutes, plus at least 1 hour to marinate
Standing time:	none required
Serves:	2 to 3

MARINADE

- 2 teaspoons sugar
- 4 tablespoons soy sauce
- 2 tablespoons sherry
- 4 teaspoons cornstarch
- 2 cloves garlic, minced
- ¼ teaspoon minced fresh ginger
- 1 pound London broil or sirloin steak, cut into ⅛- to ¼-inch strips, 1½ to 2 inches long
- 1 cup sliced fresh mushrooms
- 1 box frozen snow peas, defrosted in package on HIGH for 1 to 2 minutes
- ½ cup sliced bamboo shoots
- ½ cup sliced water chestnuts
- 3 scallions, chopped
- 2 tablespoons peanut oil

Mix the 6 marinade ingredients together and add meat. Allow meat to marinate at least 1 hour, but all afternoon is better.

Preheat browning dish for 5 to 7 minutes on HIGH or according to your manufacturer's instructions. Add oil and marinated meat. Using a wooden spoon, move meat around dish quickly to avoid sticking. Microwave **uncovered** on HIGH for 2 minutes. Add remaining ingredients, **cover**, and microwave on HIGH for 4 to 6 minutes more until vegetables are crisp-tender and meat is done. **Stir** twice during cooking. Serve with rice.

Suggestions: You may want to add an onion cut into eighths, with the pieces separated. Chinese mushrooms, both button and straw, substitute nicely for regular ones.

Chicken and Cashews

Equipment:	10-inch covered browning dish
Cooking time:	10½ to 14½ minutes, plus at least 45 minutes to marinate
Standing time:	none required
Serves:	2

1 pound boned chicken breasts cut into ¾ × 1½-inch strips

MARINADE
2 tablespoons soy sauce
1 tablespoon white wine or sherry
1 teaspoon sugar
1 teaspoon cornstarch
2 cloves garlic, minced
1 cup sliced fresh mushrooms
¼ cup roasted cashews
1 medium green pepper, cut in ¼- to ½-inch strips
2 scallions, minced
1 medium onion, thinly sliced with rings separated
2 tablespoons peanut oil

Mix the 5 marinade ingredients together and add chicken. Marinate in refrigerator for several hours or for 45 minutes at room temperature.

Preheat browning dish on HIGH for 5 to 7 minutes or according to manufacturer's instructions. Add oil and swirl around dish. Quickly add chicken and marinade, **stirring** with a wooden spoon to keep from sticking. Microwave **uncovered** on HIGH for 2 minutes. Add all remaining ingredients except cashews and microwave **covered** on HIGH for 3½ to 5½ minutes more until chicken is no longer pink and vegetables are crisp-tender. Add cashews and toss. Serve with rice.

Suggestions: You may want to add shredded spinach or small cuts of broccoli. If you don't have peanut oil, which adds flavor, use regular cooking oil.

Shrimp and Broccoli or Asparagus

Equipment: 10-inch covered browning dish
Cooking time: 15 to 17 minutes
Standing time: none required
Serves: 3 to 4

- 1 **pound raw shrimp, shelled**
- 1 **bunch broccoli or 1 pound asparagus, cut into uniform bite-sized pieces**
- 2 **tablespoons peanut oil (or cooking oil)**
- 2 **to 4 cloves garlic, minced**
- 8 **ounces fresh mushrooms, sliced**
- 1 **onion, sliced with rings separated**

SAUCE
- 1½ **tablespoons white wine**
- 2½ **tablespoons chicken broth**
- 2½ **tablespoons oyster sauce**
- ½ **teaspoon salt**
- ¼ **teaspoon sugar**
- ¼ **teaspoon sesame oil**
- 1 **tablespoon cornstarch**
  pinch of pepper

Lay cleaned shrimp flat on cutting board. Slice in half lengthwise, so that each half looks like a full shrimp.

Preheat browning dish on HIGH for 5 to 7 minutes or according to your manufacturer's instructions, and add oil, garlic, and shrimp. Move shrimp around with a wooden spoon to avoid sticking. Microwave on HIGH, **covered** with browning-dish cover for 3 minutes.

Add broccoli or asparagus, mushrooms, and onion. Cover and microwave on HIGH for 4 minutes or until vegetables are crisp-tender.

Blend sauce ingredients together well and stir sauce into shrimp and vegtables. Microwave **uncovered** for 3 minutes on HIGH until sauce thickens. Serve with rice.

Troubleshooting: Don't use spray shortenings; they will scorch.
Your browner may scratch if you try to stir the shrimp with a

metal spatula, so quickly move the shrimp around with a wooden spoon, not plastic, which might melt.

If you cover the browner with wax paper, plastic wrap, or a plastic cover, it will melt, so use the cover that comes with the browner or a glass one.

Suggestions: For a bit of the Orient, you might want to add ½ teaspoon of minced fresh ginger with the garlic.

Chinese Vegetables

When stir-frying vegetables, any combination of vegetables you have on hand will do. Be sure frozen vegetables are cooked in their package for 3 to 4 minutes on HIGH before stir-frying. If box is covered with aluminum foil, remove before microwaving. Also be sure that all your fresh vegetables are uniform in size for even cooking.

Equipment:	10-inch covered browning dish
Cooking time:	12½ to 17½ minutes
Standing time:	none required
Serves:	4

2 to 3 cups uniformly cut fresh or frozen vegetables of your choice
½ cup sliced fresh mushrooms
1 medium onion, sliced and rings separated
2 cloves garlic, minced
¼ teaspoon minced fresh ginger (optional)
½ cup fresh bean sprouts (optional)
2 tablespoons peanut oil

SAUCE
2 tablespoons chicken broth
1 tablespoon oyster sauce
1 tablespoon soy sauce
pinch of pepper
1 teaspoon sugar
¼ teaspoon sesame oil (optional)
1 teaspoon cornstarch

Preheat browning dish for 5 to 7 minutes or according to your manufacturer's instructions, then add oil, garlic, and ginger (if using). Add vegetables except for bean sprouts and stir with a wooden spoon to avoid sticking.

Microwave **covered** on HIGH for 4½ to 7½ minutes until vegetables are crisp-tender, **stirring** halfway through cooking. Add bean sprouts if using.

In a small bowl, blend all sauce ingredients together well and add to vegetables. Microwave **uncovered** for 3 minutes on HIGH until sauce coats vegetables.

Troubleshooting: If some of your vegetables are not evenly cooked it is because you did not cut them uniformly in size and shape. This is a necessity in microwave cooking.

Kung Pao Chicken

Now, for those of you who find these recipes too bland and like a little heat to your Chinese cooking, try Kung Pao Chicken. This dish was named for a high-ranking Chinese official, King Kung Pao, who fled to Szechwan as a political refugee a few hundred years ago during the Chin Dynasty. This dish is one of the best known and most often prepared Szechwanese foods.

Equipment:	cutting board and meat cleaver, covered 10-inch browning dish
Cooking time:	15 to 18 minutes, plus 30 minutes to marinate
Standing time:	none required
Serves:	3 to 4

  1 **pound boned and skinless chicken breast**
  1 **egg white**
  3 **teaspoons cornstarch**
  2 **tablespoons brown bean sauce**
  1 **tablespoon hoisin sauce**
  1 **tablespoon chili paste with garlic**
1½ **teaspoons sugar**
  1 **tablespoon white wine**

1 tablespoon wine vinegar
2 teaspoons minced garlic
6 tablespoons peanut oil
1½ teaspoons minced dried red pepper
1 scallion, chopped
½ cup roasted peanuts

Cut chicken into uniform ½-inch cubes. Combine with egg white and cornstarch and refrigerate for 30 minutes.

Combine brown bean sauce, hoisin sauce, chili paste, sugar, wine, vinegar, and garlic, mixing well. **Preheat** browning dish for 5 to 7 minutes or according to your manufacturer's instructions. Add 4 tablespoons of oil, completely coating bottom of browner. Add chicken and **stir**; very quickly move it around with a wooden spoon to avoid sticking and keep the pieces separated. Microwave **covered** for 3 minutes on HIGH until chicken is no longer pink. Remove from browner and drain.

Reheat browner for 3 minutes and add the remaining 2 tablespoons of oil. Cover bottom of dish with oil and add red pepper and scallions. Microwave uncovered for 2 to 3 minutes on HIGH until pepper darkens.

Return chicken to browner and add brown bean sauce mixture and peanuts. Microwave uncovered on HIGH for 2 minutes until heated through. Serve with rice.

Troubleshooting: If your chicken sticks to the browner or doesn't come apart in small cubes, you did not stir it enough. As soon as the chicken hits the hot browner and begins to sizzle, you must move it around.

Scallop and Vegetable Stir-Fry

Equipment:	10-inch covered browning dish
Cooking time:	14 to 21 minutes
Standing time:	3 minutes
Serves:	4

    1 **box frozen French-sliced green beans**
    1 **cup sliced fresh mushrooms, or 1 8-ounce can, drained**
    1 **pound fresh scallops, cut in fourths if large**
    1 **medium onion, cut into thin wedges and layers separated**
    1 **celery stalk, thinly sliced**
    2 **tablespoons peanut oil**
    2 **to 3 cloves garlic, minced**
    ¼ **teaspoon minced fresh ginger**

SAUCE
    2 **teaspoons cornstarch**
    ½ **cup water**
 1½ **tablespoons white wine**
    2 **teaspoons soy sauce**
    1 **teaspoon oyster sauce**
    1 **teaspoon sugar**
    1 **teaspoon instant chicken bouillon**

Place frozen box of green beans on 2 layers of paper towels on the floor of the microwave and cook for 6 to 8 minutes until crisp-tender.

Preheat browning dish for 5 to 7 minutes or according to your manufacturer's instructions. Once heated add oil, garlic, ginger, onion, celery and mushrooms. Microwave on HIGH for 2 to 4 minutes until crisp.

Place cornstarch in small bowl and blend in a few tablespoons of water and mix until smooth. Stir in remaining water and other sauce ingredients. Add to vegetables, stirring well.

Microwave **covered** on HIGH for 4 to 5 minutes until mixture boils. Add scallops and green beans and stir to coat with sauce.

Microwave covered on HIGH for 2 to 4 minutes until scallops are tender.

Let **stand**, covered, for 3 minutes and serve with rice.

Troubleshooting: Do not overcook the scallops, as they finish cooking during standing time.

Cook string beans to your personal degree of doneness in the box, as they will only heat when mixed with scallops.

Vegetables

ASPARAGUS

The day I received this letter it occurred to me that there are probably a great many people throwing away edible portions of asparagus. The letter read, "Can you tell me how to prepare asparagus in the microwave so that this costly vegetable will not be ruined? I end up with such a small stalk after cutting off the hard bottom that I hate to ruin it in cooking."

For years, I lost half of my asparagus to the trash until one day I cut off only the very dry bottom and peeled the stalk. Believe it or not, there is a soft, white, edible asparagus stem under that tough outside covering. By peeling the asparagus you lose a lot less of the vegetable, and once steamed in the microwave you have stalks of asparagus that are not only tender but long.

When microwaving asparagus, remember that the tip or bud area of the stalk must be pointed toward the center of the dish and the stalk end toward the outside of the dish. The ideal way to cook your asparagus is in a round container with all the tips in the center and the stalks fanned out all around the outside edge.

However, most people do not have a long enough round dish, so use an 8 × 12- or 9 × 13-inch baking dish. As long as all the tips are in the center of the dish and the stalks are to the outside, your asparagus will cook evenly. After arranging them in the baking dish, sprinkle ¼ cup of water evenly over the spears and cover tightly with vented plastic wrap, not wax paper, as they must steam to be tender. *Never* salt vegetables before microwaving or the salt will cause little gray dehydration spots wherever it touches.

For one pound of asparagus, microwave on HIGH for 4 minutes. Rearrange spears so that the ones that were in the middle of the dish are now to the outside of the dish, and vice versa.

Recover tightly with vented plastic wrap and microwave for 3 to 5 minutes more until spears are tender. Let stand, covered, for 2 minutes to finish cooking.

Once cooked, you can add a sauce or use in combination with other vegetables or meats to form the beginnings of a different main dish.

Asparagus Platter

Cooking time: 7 to 9 minutes, after marinating
Standing time: none required
Serves: 3 to 4

    1 pound asparagus, cooked

MARINADE
    2 medium tomatoes, diced
    1 medium onion, diced
    ¼ cup olive or vegetable oil
    2 tablespoons wine vinegar
    ¼ teaspoon crushed basil
    ¼ teaspoon oregano

Arrange cooked asparagus (see cooking directions on p. 133) on a round platter, with tips to the center and stalks fanned along the outside edge of the platter.

Combine remaining ingredients in a medium bowl and allow to marinate for at least 1 hour. Drain tomatoes and onion and place in a circle around the platter halfway down the stalk of asparagus, forming a circle around the tips.

Sprinkle leftover marinade over stalks and serve, hot or cold.

Brunch Roll-Ups

Equipment:	4-cup glass measure
Cooking time:	8 to 10 minutes
Standing time:	none required
Serves:	4

12 cooked asparagus spears (see cooking directions p. 133)
2 tablespoons butter
2 tablespoons all-purpose flour
¼ teaspoon salt
dash of pepper
2 tablespoons white wine
1 cup milk, minus 2 tablespoons
½ cup shredded sharp cheddar cheese
4 slices turkey breast
4 slices buttered toast
pimentos or parsley for garnish

Place butter in the glass measure and microwave on HIGH for 35 to 45 seconds, until melted. Add flour, salt, and pepper to butter. Whisk until smooth. Whisk in wine. Gradually add milk, whisking until smooth. Microwave this mixture on HIGH for 6 to 8 minutes, **whisking** every minute. When sauce thickens and coats a spoon, add cheese. Microwave 1 minute more and whisk until smooth.

Place 4 asparagus spears in center of slice of turkey and roll up.

Cut toast slice in half and place triangle points together. Place turkey roll-up on toast and pour ¼ of cheese sauce over top. Garnish with pimentos or parsley.

Suggestions: You may substitute boiled ham or roast beef slices for the turkey breast.

Old-Fashioned Baked Beans

With the cost of energy so high, I stopped baking beans in my regular oven years ago. Since baked beans are a picnic favorite with us, I tried making several extra batches while the weather was cool and freezing them. But the kids hated the mushy texture of frozen beans.

Since I couldn't afford 8 to 10 hours of cooking in my conventional oven, I went to simmering them overnight in my Crockpot. That was all right if I planned ahead, but I just couldn't always plan that far in advance.

Enter the microwave oven ... One of its many great advantages is that it sends no extra heat into your kitchen. You can microwave any of your picnic favorites in the heat of the summer and save time and energy, keeping your kitchen cool in the bargain.

Since anything that has a casing can explode in the microwave if not vented, and dried beans have a casing, I preboil them tightly covered (see Covering and Venting, p. 7) in the microwave until the skins split. If you are careful not to let the beans dry out you will never bake them any other way again, because they taste like they had been simmered all day in your conventional oven.

Equipment:	deep 4-quart casserole dish with cover
Cooking time:	3 to 3½ hours
Standing time:	none required
Serves:	4 to 6

1 **pound dried Great Northern Beans (or variety of your choice)**
2 **quarts water**
¼ **teaspoon baking soda**
6 **cups water**
1 **medium onion, chopped**
1 **teaspoon dry mustard**
2 **cups dark brown sugar (may add more to taste)**
⅛ **teaspoon pepper**
½ **cup ketchup**
½ **pound salt pork, scored (I prefer the meatier kind for added flavor)**

Sort and rinse beans and place in the casserole dish. Add 2 quarts of water and stir in baking soda. Cover and let **stand** overnight. Drain and rinse beans and return to casserole. Add 6 cups water. **Cover** tightly and microwave on HIGH for 18 to 20 minutes or until boiling.

Stir, cover again, and microwave at 30 percent power or low for 60 to 70 minutes until beans are tender and skins split. Drain, reserving liquid.

Stir in remaining ingredients and 1 cup reserved liquid. Cover with plastic wrap, venting back one corner, or with casserole lid and place on turntable if available. Microwave at 30 percent or low for 100 to 125 minutes, or until beans are very tender and flavors blend. (**Rotate** ¼ turn every 20 minutes if not using turntable.) Stir occasionally and add reserved liquid as needed, being sure not to let beans become dry. Sauce will thicken as beans cool.

Troubleshooting: If you let the beans dry out they will become parched and inedible. Just check them frequently and add liquid as soon as you see any dry beans showing through the liquid.

If salt pork is not pushed down into the beans when you begin cooking, it will not get completely soft.

Taste sauce halfway through cooking and if it's not sweet enough remove some of the hot liquid and add a few tablespoons of brown sugar. Dissolve sugar in hot liquid completely before adding to beans.

CORN

Whether you are picking corn on the cob from your backyard garden or your grocer's produce department, be sure you select ears with kernels that are plump, but not too large and dark yellow, as this usually indicates old corn. If the kernels break easily from the pressure of a finger pushing down on them and the husk is soft and bright green, it is safe to assume the ear is tender and fresh.

Once you have microwaved corn and find how easy it is, with no added heat in your kitchen and no pots to wash, you will never boil it again. Before placing the corn in your microwave, cover the floor of your oven with 2 layers of paper towels, as they will absorb any moisture formed while cooking and can be used to wipe out the oven after you remove the ears.

There are three methods you can use to prepare corn for micro-roasting:

1. Pull back the husks, remove the silks, and then soak the ears in your kitchen sink in enough water to cover them for about 5 minutes. Pull the husks back up. The ears will cook inside the husks.
2. Completely husk the ears and wrap them tightly in either wax paper or plastic wrap. You can butter the ears before roasting, but never salt them, as the salt will leave tiny gray dehydration spots wherever it touches.
3. Place the husked ears in a long flat casserole dish, add 1 tablespoon of water for each ear, and cover with vented plastic wrap.

Regardless of how you prepare the ears for roasting, they all microwave for 2 to 3 minutes per ear, and each batch must stand for 5 minutes before serving.

The placement in your microwave is important for even cooking.

Place 1 ear in the center of the oven
    2 ears go side by side;
    3 ears form a triangle;
    4 ears form a square;
    5 ears are 4 side by side with one over the top; and
    6 ears are 4 side by side with one over top and one over the bottom

But what do you do with the leftover ears that no one wanted to eat while they were hot? I have a few ideas for turning those leftovers into tomorrow night's side dish.

Confetti Relish

Equipment:	2-quart casserole dish
Cooking time:	3 to 5 minutes
Standing time:	none required
Makes:	4 cups

1 tablespoon cornstarch
¾ cup sugar
¼ teaspoon seasoned salt
¼ teaspoon pepper
¼ teaspoon dry mustard
⅓ cup cider vinegar
2 cups cooked corn kernels (about 4 ears)
½ green pepper, chopped
½ red pepper, chopped
1 medium onion, diced

In the casserole dish combine cornstarch, sugar, seasoned salt, pepper, and mustard. Whisk in vinegar, making sure all the dry ingredients are completely dissolved. Microwave on HIGH for 3 to 5 minutes or until mixture is boiling and has begun to thicken. Stir in the vegetables and cool. Refrigerate **covered** overnight.

Dressed-Up Corn

Equipment: 6-cup glass measure
Cooking time: 5 to 8 minutes
Standing time: none required
Serves: 4

1½ to 2 cups cooked corn kernels (about 4 ears)
2 tablespoons butter
1 medium onion, chopped
4 ounces fresh mushrooms, sliced

In the glass measure, combine butter, onion, and mushrooms. Microwave on HIGH for 4 to 6 minutes until vegetables are tender. Add corn and microwave 1 to 2 minutes more on HIGH until corn is heated. Serve.

CAULIFLOWER

Simple boiled vegetables just don't cut the mustard at our dinner table, and the day I received a letter asking me for ideas to zip up plain cauliflower, I got to work. The writer said she had several lovely heads of cauliflower that looked so perfect she hated to cut them up.

In the microwave a whole head of cauliflower cooks so quickly, with no prep time for the cook, that it seemed a perfect way to prepare it.

Whether in one piece or cut up, it still came out steamed, and since that won't do at my house, there was only one thing left to do—frost it! The soft cheesy sauce with Cauliflower Surprise can accompany anything from a simple steak to poached fish fillets, while Mushroom-Capped Cauliflower is not only tasty but is actually two vegetables in one.

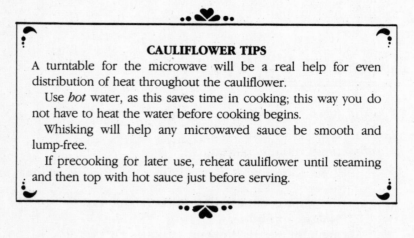

CAULIFLOWER TIPS

A turntable for the microwave will be a real help for even distribution of heat throughout the cauliflower.

Use *hot* water, as this saves time in cooking; this way you do not have to heat the water before cooking begins.

Whisking will help any microwaved sauce be smooth and lump-free.

If precooking for later use, reheat cauliflower until steaming and then top with hot sauce just before serving.

Cauliflower Surprise

Equipment:	2-quart casserole dish
Cooking time:	14 to 15 minutes
Standing time:	5 minutes
Serves:	4 to 6

1 **medium head cauliflower**
¼ **cup** *hot* **water**
2 **tablespoons butter**
2 **tablespoons flour**
½ **teaspoon seasoned salt**
1 **cup milk**
½ **cup grated sharp cheddar cheese**
2 **tablespoons white wine**
  salt and pepper to taste
1 **tablespoon chopped scallions**

Clean head of cauliflower and leave whole. With a sharp paring knife, remove hard core at stem end. Place head-up in the casserole dish.

Pour *hot* water (see Box p. 140) over cauliflower and **cover** with plastic wrap, turning back one corner to vent the steam. Cook on HIGH for 9 to 10 minutes, **elevating** flat-bottomed container on an inverted saucer, and placing on turntable if available. (If not using turntable, **rotate** dish ½ turn after 5 minutes.)

When cooking time is finished, but cauliflower is still crisp, remove to serving dish, cover with plastic wrap, and reserve liquid in casserole dish. Let **stand** 5 minutes.

To reserved liquid add butter and melt on HIGH for 30 to 45 seconds. Whisk in flour and seasoned salt. Whisk in milk and cook **uncovered** on HIGH for 2 minutes, **whisking** briskly after each minute. Add cheese and wine and whisk until blended.

Cook uncovered for 2 minutes more on HIGH, whisking after each minute until creamy. Add salt and pepper to taste and pour over hot cauliflower. Sprinkle with chopped scallions.

Troubleshooting: Be sure there is crispness to the cauliflower when microwaving finishes, as it continues to cook during standing time.

To avoid melted plastic wrap, see Covering and Venting, p. 7.

To avoid lumpy sauce, be sure to whisk several times during cooking.

Mushroom-Capped Cauliflower

Equipment: 2-quart casserole dish
Cooking time: 13 to 16 minutes
Standing time: 5 minutes
Serves: 4 to 6

1 medium head cauliflower
¼ cup *hot* water
½ cup water
2 tablespoons white wine
1 envelope instant brown gravy mix
1 small onion, minced
½ teaspoon garlic powder, or 1 clove fresh garlic, minced
8 ounces fresh mushrooms, sliced, or 1 8-ounce can, drained

Clean head of cauliflower and leave whole. With a sharp paring knife, remove hard core at stem end. Place head-up in the casserole dish, pour *hot* water over head, and **cover** with vented plastic wrap (see "Covering and Venting," p. 7).

Cook on HIGH for 9 to 10 minutes, **elevating** flat-bottomed container on an inverted saucer, and placing on turntable if available. (If not using turntable, **rotate** dish ½ turn after 5 minutes.)

When cooking time is finished, but cauliflower is still crisp, remove to serving dish, cover with plastic wrap, and reserve liquid in casserole. Let **stand** 5 minutes.

Add ½ cup water and white wine to reserved liquid. Whisk in gravy mix and when completely blended add onion, garlic powder, and mushrooms.

Microwave on HIGH for 2 to 4 minutes or until gravy is boiling and thickens, **whisking** every 2 minutes. Once boiling, reduce to 80 percent power or MEDIUM-HIGH and let cook for 2 minutes, whisking twice. Pour over hot cauliflower and serve.

Troubleshooting: If the gravy is too thick, add a little more water.

To avoid lumpy gravy, whisk very well.

If you have only HIGH power on your oven, instead of reducing power to 80 percent cook the gravy on HIGH for 1 minute 30 seconds, whisking after one minute.

SPAGHETTI SQUASH

The year after my husband bought his tractor from a dear old farmer in town he also came home with a bag of assorted squash seeds. Loving the idea of not knowing what the harvest would bring, he planted a handful all along the edges of our garden. What a surprise we had when besides all our regular summer squash we harvested spaghetti squash, which we had never cooked or eaten before.

I went to the cookbook shelf to find out how to prepare it so we could determine if we even liked it. Inside this yellow hard-skinned object are strands that resemble spaghetti, but with about one-eighth the calories. Since the answer to the question, "Are you on a diet this week?" is always "yes," this really intrigued me.

Together, farmer and cook worked with this great squash until we found just the right combination of flavors. I of course went one better and converted them to the microwave. They taste the same whether microwaved or cooked in a conventional oven, so why heat up your kitchen and all those dishes when it is so easy to microwave?

Spaghetti Squash Sauté

Equipment:	2-quart casserole dish
Cooking time:	20 to 33 minutes
Standing time:	5 to 10 minutes
Serves:	2 to 3

- 1 **medium spaghetti squash**
- 1 **small zucchini, cut into ½-inch pieces**
- 1 **small yellow squash, cut into ½-inch pieces**
- 2 **to 3 scallions, diced**
- 1 **clove fresh garlic, minced**
- 1 **teaspoon chopped fresh basil**
- 1 **tablespoon olive oil**
- ½ **pint cherry tomatoes, cut in half**
- 4 **ounces fresh mushrooms, sliced, or 1 4-ounce can sliced mushrooms, drained**
- 4 **slices boiled ham or turkey breast, cut into strips seasoned salt and pepper to taste parsley, cherry tomatoes and black olives, for garnish**

Wash and pierce the squash in several places. Place on 2 layers of paper towels and microwave for 4 to 7 minutes per pound, or until casing is soft when pierced with a fork. Wrap in plastic wrap and let **stand** for 5 to 10 minutes.

After standing time, cut squash lengthwise, remove fiber and seeds, and carefully twist out strands of squash. Remove all strands and place on paper towels to drain. Reserve 1 shell.

Combine zucchini, yellow squash, scallions, garlic, and basil in the casserole dish. Dribble olive oil over top and **cover** with vented plastic wrap.

Microwave on HIGH for 4 to 6 minutes or until vegetables are tender, **stirring** twice. Add all remaining ingredients, including reserved squash strands, and toss lightly.

Microwave on HIGH for 3 to 5 minutes until hot, add seasoned salt and pepper to taste, then mound into reserved shell and garnish with parsley, cherry tomatoes, and black olives.

Troubleshooting: Be sure the tines of a large fork can easily penetrate the skin when you determine that the squash is cooked.

The only part you want to eat are the strands. Be sure to remove the seeds and fiber before gently twisting the strands from the shell of the squash.

If zucchini and yellow squash are not cooked evenly, you may not have cut them uniformly in size and shape or stirred them properly during cooking. Every 2 minutes, bring the vegetables in the center of the dish to the outside edges and the vegetables along the edges to the center.

If you want to save even more calories, leave out the olive oil. (Vegetable oil will not add flavor, only calories.)

You will get uneven distribution of the garlic and basil flavor if you don't toss them with the squash before cooking to help the flavors blend.

ZUCCHINI

Have you run out of polite excuses for saying no to your neighbor's offers of prolific zucchini? If so, let's try some new and interesting ways to prepare them in the microwave.

If you just want to steam your zucchini, cut it into uniform slices and place in a 1-quart round casserole dish. Dot with a tablespoon of butter and cover with vented plastic wrap. Microwave on HIGH for 4 to 6 minutes or until crisp-tender.

If you are going to use whole squash, be sure to select ones that are uniform in size, so they will microwave more evenly. Small squash are best, as their skin and seeds are soft and moist.

If you want to use halves of the zucchini for stuffing, I suggest that you wash and cut lengthwise. Place squash skin-side down on 2 layers of paper towels on the floor of your microwave and cook on HIGH for 4 to 6 minutes.

Zucchini is a colorful vegetable that can be used for many different side dishes and main courses. If your family has a favorite stuffing, use it to personalize your zucchini boats.

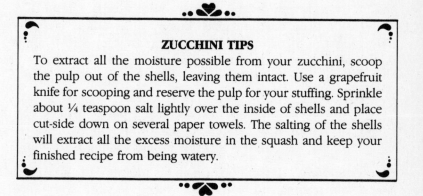

ZUCCHINI TIPS

To extract all the moisture possible from your zucchini, scoop the pulp out of the shells, leaving them intact. Use a grapefruit knife for scooping and reserve the pulp for your stuffing. Sprinkle about ¼ teaspoon salt lightly over the inside of shells and place cut-side down on several paper towels. The salting of the shells will extract all the excess moisture in the squash and keep your finished recipe from being watery.

Zucchini Crab Boats

Equipment: grapefruit knife, 6-cup glass measure, 8 × 12 or 9 × 13-inch casserole dish
Cooking time: 12 to 18 minutes
Standing time: none required
Serves: 3 to 4

 3 to 4 medium zucchini
¼ teaspoon salt
 2 tablespoons butter
 1 tablespoon white wine
 1 medium onion, minced
 1 clove garlic, minced
 1 celery stalk, minced
½ cup sliced fresh mushrooms
 1 6½-ounce can crabmeat, flaked and drained
 1 8-ounce can whole-kernel corn, drained
 1 medium tomato, diced
    pinch of pepper
½ cup seasoned breadcrumbs

Wash and cut zucchini in half lengthwise. Place on 2 layers of paper towels on the floor of your microwave and cook for 4 to 6 minutes on HIGH. Scoop out pulp and reserve. Sprinkle inside of shells with salt and invert on several layers of paper towels (see Box p. 145).

In the glass measure place butter, wine, onion, garlic, celery, mushrooms, and crabmeat. Microwave on HIGH for 5 to 7 minutes or until vegetables are soft, **stirring** every 3 minutes. Add reserved pulp, corn, tomato, pepper, and breadcrumbs to vegetable mixture, and mix well.

Stuff mixture into zucchini shells and place in casserole dish. **Cover** dish with wax paper and microwave on HIGH for 3 to 5 minutes or until zucchini is fork-tender and stuffing is steaming.

Troubleshooting: If you don't get all the moisture possible out of the shells, your stuffing will be too moist.

Suggestions: Try using canned or fresh shrimp, tuna, or lobster for a different taste.

Zucchini Lasagna

Ever since I discovered that lasagna could be made in the microwave without cooking the noodles first, I have been fascinated with trying different combinations of meat and vegetables along with the raw noodles and sauce. I was making lasagna at a food show one Saturday and forgot to bring the ground beef. Looking into space trying to decide what to do, I saw the Hillshire Farms booth.

I walked over, very quickly explained my problem, and asked if I could borrow a pound of smoked sausage. The result of that unplanned experiment was that everyone loved the smoked sausage taste in place of the ground beef and never knew it had been done totally by accident. My using zucchini was another unplanned experiment. One afternoon as I was making lasagna for dinner I kept staring at these two zucchini on the counter wondering what I was going to do with them. I sliced them thin and added them to my lasagna, and to my amazement zucchini lasagna was a real hit!

Equipment:	2-quart casserole dish, colander, 8 × 12 or 9 × 13-inch baking dish
Cooking time:	36 to 43 minutes
Standing time:	10 minutes
Serves:	6 to 8

- **2 cups thinly sliced zucchini**
- **1 pound hot or sweet sausage meat, crumbled**
- **4 cups spaghetti sauce**
- **8 uncooked lasagna noodles**
- **2 cups ricotta cheese**
- **1 egg, lightly beaten**
- **1 teaspoon parsley flakes**
- **¼ teaspoon garlic powder**
- **2 cups shredded mozzarella cheese**
- **½ cup Parmesan cheese**

Insert colander into casserole dish. Add crumbled sausage meat and microwave on HIGH for 4 to 6 minutes. Break up with a fork and place in a bowl with your spaghetti sauce.

Pour 1 cup of sauce and sausage into the bottom of the baking dish. Place 4 *uncooked* noodles evenly over the sauce, overlapping if necessary. Evenly distribute 1 cup of zucchini slices over noodles.

Combine ricotta, egg, parsley flakes, and garlic powder. Mix well. Spread half of this mixture over zucchini slices and sprinkle one cup mozzarella on top.

Cover this first layer with 1 cup sauce and repeat layering noodles, zucchini, ricotta, mozzarella, and sauce. **Cover** tightly with vented plastic wrap and microwave on HIGH for 15 minutes, **rotating** dish ½ turn every 5 minutes.

Reduce to 60 percent power or MEDIUM for 16 to 20 minutes until noodles are soft. Sprinkle top with Parmesan and microwave **uncovered** on HIGH power for 1 to 2 minutes until cheese melts.

Let **stand** 10 minutes before serving.

Troubleshooting: If your oven does not distribute its microwaves evenly, the sauce and noodles may overcook in spots, so be sure to rotate the dish frequently to avoid this problem.

Suggestions: If you have your own spaghetti sauce made with meatballs and/or sausage in it, just break them up with a fork and omit the sausage cooking step.

Veg-Kabobs

One day I was trying to think of interesting things to do with long wooden skewers. I opened the fridge, looked around, and decided to try an assortment of vegetables on my skewers. I started experimenting with a marinade and the results got such a rave I added veg-kabobs to my vegetable memory bank.

Equipment:	4 wooden skewers, meat rack or custard cups, 8 × 12 or 9 × 13-inch casserole dish
Cooking time:	4 to 7 minutes
Standing time:	5 minutes
Serves:	2 to 4

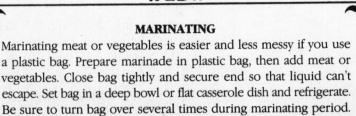

MARINATING

Marinating meat or vegetables is easier and less messy if you use a plastic bag. Prepare marinade in plastic bag, then add meat or vegetables. Close bag tightly and secure end so that liquid can't escape. Set bag in a deep bowl or flat casserole dish and refrigerate. Be sure to turn bag over several times during marinating period.

8 1-inch chunks green peppers (about 1 large pepper)
8 onion quarters
8 large fresh mushrooms
8 cherry tomatoes
8 1-inch chunks zucchini or yellow squash (about 1 medium
   squash)

MARINADE
½ cup wine vinegar
½ cup vegetable oil
1 teaspoon onion powder
1 clove fresh garlic, cut in half
¼ cup soy sauce
1 teaspoon oregano
½ cup water
   dash of pepper

On each skewer place 2 chunks of pepper, onion, mushroom, tomato, and squash.

In a plastic bag large enough to hold all ka-bobs, mix marinade ingredients together. Add kabobs, secure bag tightly so marinade will not leak out, and turn to coat each one with mixture. Once kabobs are coated, place bag in a dish large enough to hold it and refrigerate at least 2 to 3 hours or overnight, turning plastic bag over several times. (See Box p. 148.)

Discard marinade in its bag and place kabobs on meat rack or balance between inverted custard cups set in casserole dish. Microwave on HIGH for 4 to 7 minutes or until vegetables are crisp-tender to your taste. Halfway through cooking turn skewers over and re-arrange, bringing center ones to outside of dish.

Let **stand** for 5 minutes before serving.

Suggestions: Florets of broccoli or cauliflower add color and flavor. Try serving over rice, as an accompaniment to steak.

POTATOES

The one thing people always say they are able to do in their microwaves besides heat up leftovers is bake potatoes. But once I start asking a few questions, I find that very few people are achieving the perfect baked potato.

POTATO TIPS

Uniformly sized potatoes will cook in the same amount of time, far more evenly than potatoes of different sizes and shapes. Weighing them may help you if you question their size.

Any food that has a casing around it—such as potatoes, sausage, squash, egg yolks, tomatoes, peaches, and hot dogs—needs to be vented to allow the steam to escape. This can be done very easily with the tines of a fork. Pierce each end of the food deeply and you will avoid having your dinner decorating the inside of your oven.

For more even microwaving, place your potatoes on a meat rack to allow the microwaves to get under them as well as around the tops and sides. You can also use several chopsticks, evenly spaced and covered with 2 layers of paper towels, to elevate the potatoes off the floor of your microwave.

To achieve even cooking, always place the broadest end of the food to the outside of the oven and the smallest to the center. With potatoes, place them in the shape of wagon-wheel spokes, smallest end of the potato pointing toward the center of the oven.

During standing time, always have the shiny side of the foil toward the food you are trying to keep hot. The shiny foil reflects the heat back into the food, thereby keeping it hot longer.

Here are the best instructions I can give for the perfect microwaved potato.

Perfect Baked Potatoes

Equipment:	2 layers of paper towels, 4 squares of aluminum foil large enough to cover a potato
Cooking time:	approximately 4 minutes per potato
Standing time:	5 to 10 minutes
Serves:	1 person per potato

4 medium potatoes (see above)

Scrub potatoes well and pierce each with a fork twice to **vent** the steam.

Place potatoes in a wagon-wheel configuration (see Box p. 150) on 2 layers of paper towels over several chopsticks on the floor of your oven or on a paper-towel-covered meat rack. (see Box p. 150). Microwave on HIGH as follows:

1 potato	—	4 to 6 minutes
2 potatoes	—	7 to 8 minutes
3 potatoes	—	11 to 13 minutes
4 potatoes	—	14 to 16 minutes
6 potatoes	—	16 to 18 minutes

When finished, potatoes should be a bit firm in the center. Remove from oven and either wrap in aluminum foil, shiny side toward the potato, or place under an inverted casserole dish.

Let **stand** for 5 to 10 minutes before serving.

Troubleshooting: If your potatoes are shriveled up when microwaving time ends, it is because they are overcooked. Experiment with your oven and the size of potatoes you're using to find out just how long it takes to microwave a perfect potato. Always start with the shorter amount of cooking time, since it can always be increased.

If your potatoes are wet on the bottom it is because you failed to put them on 2 layers of paper towels. Moisture forms when food sits directly on the floor of the oven. This moisture must be absorbed with paper towels or it will go into your food.

If you forget to pierce your potatoes and they explode, see Keeping Your Oven Clean, p. 9.

If you place the potatoes in foil before microwaving, they will arch and ignite along with the paper towels. The foil goes on *after* the potatoes are cooked and removed from the microwave, shiny side toward the potato.

Once wrapped in foil or placed under an inverted casserole dish, the potatoes will finish cooking, remain hot, and not shrivel up for up to 30 minutes, giving you time to finish cooking the rest of your meal.

Suggestions: Try adding chili (see p. 74), Broccoli with Sour Cream and Mushrooms (see p. 165), cheese sauce (see p. 167), or a potato topping (see p. 102) to cover your perfect baked potatoes.

If given a choice, most people will choose the more attractively presented side dish; with a few extra ingredients you can turn your simple baked potatoes into the highlight of the meal.

If you are a real planner, you can bake, stuff, and freeze this side dish so that on a moment's notice you can defrost, heat, and serve. Be sure potatoes are completely cooled and wrapped well before freezing.

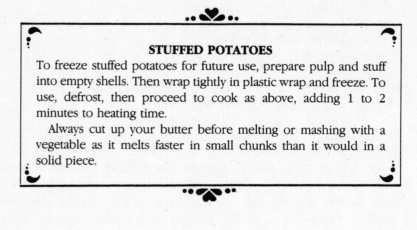

STUFFED POTATOES

To freeze stuffed potatoes for future use, prepare pulp and stuff into empty shells. Then wrap tightly in plastic wrap and freeze. To use, defrost, then proceed to cook as above, adding 1 to 2 minutes to heating time.

Always cut up your butter before melting or mashing with a vegetable as it melts faster in small chunks than it would in a solid piece.

Stuffed Baked Potatoes

Cooking time: baked potatoes—3 to 4 minutes; raw potatoes— 23 to 24 minutes
Standing time: none required
Serves: 1 per person

4 hot baked potatoes (see Perfect Baked Potatoes, p. 150)
5 tablespoons butter, cut up (see Box above)
¼ cup sour cream
 seasoned salt and pepper to taste
2 teaspoons onion powder
½ cup shredded sharp cheddar or cheese of your choice plus
 4 tablespoons for garnish
 dash of paprika

Remove a ¼-inch horizontal slice from the top of each hot baked potato. Using a teaspoon (a grapefruit spoon works well), remove potato pulp to a bowl, leaving skins intact. Mash pulp with butter and add sour cream, seasoned salt, pepper, onion powder, and shredded cheese, mixing together until smooth.

Divide mixture into empty shells and garnish with shredded cheese. Place on a paper plate covered with two layers of paper towel, in a wagon-wheel spoke configuration (see Box p. 150).

Cook on HIGH for 3 to 4 minutes until cheese melts and potatoes are hot. Sprinkle with paprika and serve.

Troubleshooting: If shells crack when you're scooping out pulp, don't worry. Just hold them together and fill with stuffing mixture; you will never notice the cracks or tears in the skins.

If the skins of the finished potatoes are moist, you forgot to place them on a paper-towel-lined plate before reheating.

If you're substituting mozzarella cheese for cheddar, put the garnish on only in the last 45 to 50 seconds; otherwise the mozzarella will toughen.

Paprika doesn't melt in the microwave as in a conventional oven, so add it last.

To help the centers of frozen potatoes heat evenly, **elevate** the dish on an inverted saucer or meat rack.

Suggestions: Try adding sautéed onions, mushrooms, and diced cooked bacon to the potato mixture for a change in flavor.

Scalloped Potatoes

Instead of baking your potatoes, how about scalloping them? If you have already tried my cheese sauce on p. 167 you already know how easy that is in the microwave, and now all you need to do is add a few veggies and some bacon and you're in business. Try serving this recipe with a side dish of smoked sausage for a quick and hearty dinner.

Equipment:	3-quart casserole dish
Cooking time:	25 to 30 minutes
Standing time:	5 minutes
Serves:	4 to 6

4 to 5 medium potatoes, peeled and thinly sliced
1 medium onion, peeled and thinly sliced
4 slices bacon, or 1 to 2 cups cubed ham
   salt and pepper
1 recipe of cheddar cheese sauce (see p. 167)

In the casserole dish, layer ¼ of the potatoes followed by ¼ of the onions. Cut one slice of bacon in quarters and arrange on top of onions, or cover onions with ham. Add salt and pepper and spoon ¼ of the cheese sauce over the top. Continue layering vegetables, meat, salt and pepper, and cheese sauce until all is used up, and **cover** with wax paper.

Elevate flat-bottomed dish on an inverted saucer and place on a turntable if available. Microwave on 50 percent power or MEDIUM for 25 to 30 minutes until potatoes are fork-tender. (If not using a turntable, be sure to **rotate** dish ¼ turn very 8 minutes.)

Let **stand, covered** for 5 minutes before serving.

Potato Pizza

Since you have to have some kind of browning dish in order to get halfway decent pizza dough out of your microwave, I started making potato pizza for my kids. They love mashed potatoes and this is one way to use up any leftovers and still put a hearty lunch or supper on the table.

The nice part is that you can add any toppings your family likes. I find the kids love preparing this version of pizza themselves and always seem to eat far more, while taking great pride in preparing the meal themselves.

Equipment:	2- or 4-cup glass measure, glass pie plate or round shallow dish
Cooking time:	9 to 10 minutes
Standing time:	2 minutes
Serves:	4

1½ **cups mashed potatoes**
¼ **cup fine regular or seasoned breadcrumbs**
1 **teaspoon parsley flakes**
1 **egg, slightly beaten**
 pinch of salt and pepper
4 **slices bacon, chopped**
1 **cup chopped onion**
½ **cup chopped green pepper**
1 **4-ounce can sliced mushrooms, drained**
1 **cup pizza sauce**
3 **tablespoons grated Parmesan cheese**
1 **cup shredded mozzarella cheese**

Mix together mashed potatoes, breadcrumbs, parsley flakes, and egg. Season with salt and pepper and lightly press in the base and slightly up the sides of a glass plate or round dish. Add bacon, onion, green pepper, and mushrooms to glass measure. Microwave on HIGH for 5 minutes. Drain off fat and arrange mixture over potatoes.

Top with pizza sauce and Parmesan. **Elevate** flat-bottomed dish on an inverted saucer and place on a turntable if available. (If not using a turntable, **rotate** dish ¼ turn every minute.) Microwave on HIGH for 3½ to 4 minutes until hot. Sprinkle mozzarella over the top and microwave on HIGH for 30 to 50 seconds, just until it begins to melt.

Let **stand** for 2 minutes before serving.

Suggestions: If you don't have any leftover mashed potatoes, just whip up some instant ones; no one will be the wiser.

SWEET POTATOES

Sweet potatoes and yams are sometimes confusing, so for those of you who aren't sure, light-colored skin and pale flesh are the characteristics of sweet potatoes, while those with a darker red-brown skin and bright orange flesh are traditionally referred to as yams.

When selecting your sweet potatoes be sure they are medium in size have no bruise spots—bruises guarantee a less tasty and less nutritious potato. Sweet potatoes do not store as long as white potatoes, so do not purchase them too far in advance.

Scrub sweet potatoes and pierce the skin several times with a fork to vent the steam. Place them on 2 layers of paper towel on the oven floor in a circle, pointing toward the center of the oven like the spokes of a wagon wheel. Place the largest end of the potato toward the outside of the oven, smallest end toward the middle of the oven. Microwave 1 sweet potato for 3 to 5 minutes, 2 for 6 to 8 minutes, 3 for 7 to 10 minutes, and 4 for 10 to 14 minutes.

Once finished microwaving, they should feel slightly firm in the center. Remove them from the oven and wrap in aluminum foil, shiny side toward the potato. Allow them to stand, covered, for 5 to 10 minutes before serving or using in the following recipe.

Sweet Potato Boats

Equipment: electric mixer
Cooking time: 12 to 18 minutes
Standing time: 5 to 10 minutes
Serves: 6

3 medium sweet potatoes
¼ cup orange juice
½ cup light brown sugar
¼ teaspoon salt
¼ teaspoon cinnamon
¼ teaspoon vanilla extract
6 tablespoons Cranberry-Orange Relish (see p. 192)
½ cup chopped pecans

Microwave pierced sweet potatoes in their jackets for 7 to 10 minutes on HIGH until tender. (See above for instructions.)

After **standing**, cut potatoes in half lengthwise and carefully scoop out pulp, leaving shells intact. Mash pulp and add orange juice,

¼ cup brown sugar, salt, cinnamon, and vanilla. Beat with an electric mixer until well blended.

Fill shells with mashed pulp and with the back of a spoon leave a well in the center of each potato. Fill each well with 1 tablespoon of the relish. Mix pecans with remaining brown sugar and sprinkle this mixture over potato halves.

Place potatoes on a paper plate lined with 2 layers of paper towels and microwave on HIGH for 3 to 5 minutes or until heated through.

Suggestions: Boats may be prepared ahead of time and refrigerated until ready to use. Add relish and pecan mixture just before microwaving.

PEPPERS

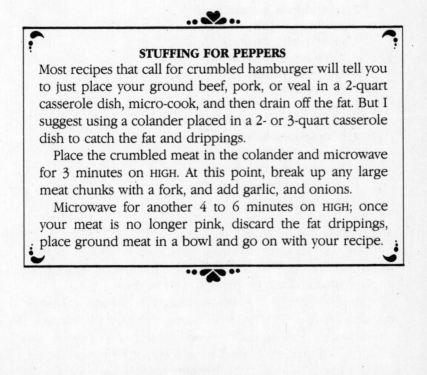

STUFFING FOR PEPPERS

Most recipes that call for crumbled hamburger will tell you to just place your ground beef, pork, or veal in a 2-quart casserole dish, micro-cook, and then drain off the fat. But I suggest using a colander placed in a 2- or 3-quart casserole dish to catch the fat and drippings.

Place the crumbled meat in the colander and microwave for 3 minutes on HIGH. At this point, break up any large meat chunks with a fork, and add garlic, and onions.

Microwave for another 4 to 6 minutes on HIGH; once your meat is no longer pink, discard the fat drippings, place ground meat in a bowl and go on with your recipe.

Red and Green Delight

Good old stuffed peppers seem to be the dish that inspires people to say, "Boy, I haven't had those in ages." The microwave version is prepared a bit differently from the conventional method, but the results are just as lip-smacking and very easy.

Equipment: colander, 2-quart casserole dish, 8 × 12 or 9 × 13-inch casserole dish
Cooking time: 19 to 23 minutes
Standing time: 5 minutes
Serves: 4

    4 large green peppers
  ¼ cup water
    1 pound lean ground beef
    1 medium onion, minced
    1 clove garlic, minced
    1 teaspoon seasoned salt
  ¼ teaspoon pepper
1¼ cups cooked rice
    1 egg
  ¼ cup seasoned breadcrumbs
    2 tablespoons ketchup
    1 16-ounce can whole tomatoes
    1 8-ounce can tomato sauce
    1 teaspoon chopped parsley
      pinch of thyme

Wash peppers and remove tops, seeds, and pith. Place pepper shells, open-side up, in 2-quart casserole dish. Pour water in bottom of dish and microwave on HIGH for 2 minutes. Remove peppers from dish and place upside down on paper towels to drain.

Crumble beef into colander placed in 2-quart casserole dish (see instructions p. 157) and microwave on HIGH for 3 minutes. Break up meat with a fork and add onion and garlic. Microwave again on HIGH for 4 to 6 minutes or until meat is no longer pink. Transfer meat to a bowl and mix in all the remaining ingredients except the whole tomatoes and tomato sauce and parsley and thyme.

Add ¼ cup of the tomato sauce to the meat mixture and mix

well. Divide mixture evenly into the peppers and mound the tops. Chop the whole tomatoes in the can and pour over the peppers. Pour the remaining tomato sauce over and around the peppers. Sprinkle with parsley and a pinch of thyme. **Cover** with vented plastic wrap, and **elevate** flat-bottomed dish on an inverted saucer. Place dish on a turntable if available. (**Rotate** dish ½ turn every 4 minutes if not using a turntable.)

Microwave on HIGH for 10 to 12 minutes until peppers are tender. Let **stand** 5 minutes before serving.

Suggestions: You may want to substitute ground pork or veal for the beef. Just add a salad and a nice wedge of Hint of Mint Cake (see p. 223) and dinner is complete.

TOMATOES

This tasty and attractive Greek side dish can accompany and accent virtually any meat or fish dish. Try it yourself and see how it brightens up any platter of food. Make it only when the good tomatoes are in season, though.

Yemistes Domates (Stuffed Tomatoes)

Equipment:	4-cup glass measure, two 2- or 3-quart casserole dishes
Cooking time:	27½ to 29½ minutes
Standing time:	5 minutes
Serves:	4

- 4 **large fresh tomatoes**
- 3 **tablespoons vegetable oil**
- 2 **medium onions, chopped**
- ½ **teaspoon dried dill**
- 1 **cup long-grain rice, uncooked**
- 2 **cups liquid (tomato pulp plus water)**
- ½ **cup currants**
- ⅓ **cup pignolias (pine nuts)**
- 2 **tablespoons breadcrumbs**
- ½ **cup tomato juice**

Starting with a tomato, stem-end up, cut a ¾- to 1-inch slice off the top. Scoop out and reserve the pulp and the tomato top. Repeat with remaining tomatoes.

In the glass measure, microwave oil and onions on HIGH for 3½ to 4 minutes or until soft.

Place onions in one of the casserole dishes and add dill, rice, and tomato pulp and water combined to make 2 cups. Add currants and pignolias and stir. Microwave, **covered** with a paper towel, on HIGH for 5 minutes; then reduce to 50 percent power or MEDIUM and microwave for 15 minutes. Let **stand** 5 minutes.

Stuff rice mixture into empty tomatoes, replace tops, and turn upside down in the other casserole dish. Sprinkle breadcrumbs lightly over tomatoes and add tomato juice.

Microwave **uncovered** on HIGH for 4 to 5½ minutes or until tomatoes are soft but solid.

To serve, make an X in the top of each tomato and open like a flower.

Hamburger Harry's Vegetable Melt

"While in New York to visit the Statue of Liberty, we had lunch at a restaurant called Hamburger Harry's on Chambers Street. Being vegetarians makes ordering lunch difficult at times, but Hamburger Harry's had a vegetable melt on the menu that we really enjoyed and feel it could be easily made in the microwave. Can you get the recipe and convert it to the microwave for me?" wrote a reader.

I called head chef Henry Walton at Hamburger Harry's and found him eager to help and very interested himself to learn the technique for microwaving his vegetable melt. He tells me he doesn't have microwave ovens in Hamburger Harry's. He uses a microwave at home, however, and admits he should take the time to do more experimenting.

Whether you're using this recipe as a main dish or taking the vegetables off the bread and using them for a side dish, you can microwave the vegetables ahead of time, reheat, and melt the cheese just before serving. Cutting the vegetables into uniform-sized pieces is especially important in this recipe to ensure that it cooks evenly. Be sure to note that Henry uses no spices, just allows all the natural flavors to blend. Never salt vegetables while cooking or you will find gray dehydration spots wherever the salt touches.

Equipment:	3-quart casserole dish, colander
Cooking time:	8 to 11½ minutes
Standing time:	none required
Makes:	4 open sandwiches

> **Florets only from 1 bunch broccoli**
> **Florets only from ½ head cauliflower**
> 1 **medium zucchini, halved lengthwise and sliced in thin half-moons**
> 1 **medium yellow squash, halved lengthwise and sliced in thin half-moons**
> ½ **small red pepper, cut in quarters and julienned**
> ½ **small green pepper, cut in quarters and julienned**
> 1 **medium carrot, halved lengthwise and sliced in thin half-moons**
> 2 **tablespoons water**
> 16 **slices of Monterey Jack cheese**
> 8 **slices whole wheat bread**

Place all prepared vegetables in the casserole dish, sprinkle water over the top, and **cover** with vented plastic wrap.

Microwave on HIGH for 7 to 10 minutes or until vegetables are crisp-tender, **stirring** twice. When done to your taste, drain vegetables.

For each serving, place 2 slices of whole wheat bread on a dinner plate and cover bread with ¼ of vegetable mixture. Top vegetables with 2 slices of Monterey Jack and microwave on HIGH for 45 to 75 seconds or just until cheese melts. If serving as a side dish, place vegetables in individual serving dishes and melt cheese over the top just before serving.

CANNED VEGETABLES

I have covered many fresh vegetables and even some frozen ones, but what do you do with canned vegetables? Obviously you must remember to remove them from their cans for heating since the metal cans reflect the microwaves. Living in a household of critics who don't like things prepared the same way too often, I have some interesting quickie things you can do to jazz up your canned veggies.

Mexican Corn

Equipment:	4-cup glass measure
Cooking time:	6 to 8 minutes
Standing time:	none required
Serves:	4

2 **tablespoons butter**
1 **medium onion, diced**
½ **medium green pepper, diced**
1 **16-ounce can whole-kernel corn, drained**

In the glass measure place butter, onion, and green pepper. Microwave on HIGH for 4 to 5 minutes, **stirring** once, then add drained canned corn. **Cover** and microwave on HIGH for 2 to 3 minutes more until vegetables are hot.

Mushroom-Decked Vegetables

Equipment:	4-cup measure
Cooking time:	6 to 8 minutes
Standing time:	none required
Serves:	4

2 **tablespoons butter**
1 **medium onion, diced**
4 **ounces fresh mushrooms, sliced**
¼ **teaspoon garlic powder**
1 **16-ounce can peas or French-cut string beans, drained**

In the glass measure place butter, onion, mushrooms, and garlic powder. Microwave on HIGH for 4 to 5 minutes, then add canned veggies. Microwave, **covered** with vented plastic wrap, on HIGH for 2 to 3 minutes more until vegetables are hot.

Hot Bean Salad

Equipment:	4- or 6-cup glass measure, 2- or 3-quart casserole dish
Cooking time:	12 to 16 minutes
Standing time:	none required
Serves:	6 to 8

1 16-ounce can each of cut green beans, red kidney beans, yellow wax beans, and lima beans
4 slices bacon, diced
1 medium onion, chopped
½ green pepper, chopped
½ cup sugar
1 tablespoon cornstarch
  dash of pepper
¾ cup cider vinegar

Open all or any combination of the canned vegetables, drain, empty into the casserole dish, and set aside.

In the measuring cup microwave bacon on HIGH for 3 to 4 minutes until crisp. Drain on paper towels. Discard all but 2 tablespoons of the bacon fat.

To bacon drippings add onion and green pepper. Microwave on HIGH for 4 to 5 minutes until crisp-tender. Add sugar, cornstarch, pepper, and vinegar. Microwave on HIGH for 4 minutes until mixture thickens, **stirring** twice.

Add bacon to beans and pour in hot liquid. **Cover** with vented plastic wrap and microwave on HIGH for 6 to 8 minutes until vegetables are hot; stir after 4 minutes.

Beets with Bacon

Equipment:	8- or 10-inch browning dish
Cooking time:	5 to 7 minutes
Standing time:	none required
Serves:	4 to 6

6 slices bacon, diced
2 16-ounce cans shoestring-cut beets
1 to 2 teaspoons fresh lemon juice (see Box p. 227)
⅛ teaspoon salt
¼ teaspoon pepper

Preheat browning dish for 5 to 7 minutes or according to manufacturer's directions.

Once hot, add bacon to dish. Microwave on HIGH for 3 to 4 minutes or until bacon bits are crisp.

Drain all but 2 tablespoons of bacon fat and add shoestring-cut beets (or beets you have diagonally sliced into thin sticks). Add lemon juice, salt, and pepper, stirring well.

Microwave on HIGH for 2 to 3 minutes, until beets are hot, stirring and adjusting spices.

Sauces

Sour Cream Sauce to Top Any Vegetable

Equipment: 4- or 6-cup glass measure
Cooking time: 6 to 8 minutes
Standing time: none required
Makes: 3/4 cup

  2 tablespoons butter
  8 ounces fresh mushrooms, sliced, or 1 8-ounce can sliced mushrooms, drained
½ teaspoon onion powder
  dash of pepper
  1 tablespoon white wine
½ cup sour cream
  1 teaspoon chopped chives

In the glass measure, combine butter and mushrooms. Microwave on HIGH for 3 to 4 minutes until tender. Whisk in onion powder, pepper, wine, sour cream, and chives. Microwave on 60 percent power or MEDIUM for 3 to 4 minutes until heated through, **whisking** twice.

WHISKING SAUCES

The use of a whisk for stirring sauces in the microwave is a must. When you make a sauce over the range you stand and constantly stir it to eliminate lumps, but in the microwave you stir only occasionally, and if you don't do a good job your sauce will not be smooth. I suggest buying a small whisk just for sauces, to guarantee a smooth lump-free sauce every time. Because the whisk is made of metal, be sure not to leave it in the microwave when cooking.

White Sauce

Maybe it's just me, but every time I make a white sauce on my stove top I wind up decorating the stove, the counter, and usually a few drips on the floor. Sound familiar? Probably not, if you're a neat cook, which I'm not.

When I discovered that I made no mess (you read right) making a white sauce in the microwave, I was elated. Believe me, try it in the microwave once and you will never make white sauce on your stove top again.

A white sauce in the microwave does demand constant attention since you must whisk it every minute for about 5 minutes—but it saves so much fuss you won't mind. I take a plain veggie and spruce it up with a dab of cheese sauce and my family is delighted. I sometimes just put plain cheese sauce over baked potatoes and add bacon bits. Anything that changes the humdrum into something special makes all the difference in the attitudes of your eaters.

Equipment:	4-cup glass measure
Cooking time:	5 to 7 minutes
Standing time:	none required
Makes:	1 cup

2 tablespoons butter
2 tablespoons all-purpose flour
¼ teaspoon salt

     pinch of pepper
1 **cup milk less 2 tablespoons**
2 **tablespoons white wine**

Place butter in glass measure and microwave **uncovered** on HIGH for 30 to 45 seconds or until melted. Whisk flour, salt, and pepper into melted butter.

Whisk until smooth, then gradually add milk and wine, continually **whisking** to keep mixture smooth.

Microwave mixture uncovered on HIGH for 4 to 6 minutes, **stirring** every minute, until sauce thickens and coats a spoon.

Troubleshooting: Sauce will get rubbery if you don't continually stir to keep it smooth.

If cheese does not completely melt after whisking for 1 minute, microwave the sauce on HIGH for 1 minute and whisk again.

CHEESE SAUCE VARIATION
Use ½ cup shredded American, Swiss, cheddar, or your favorite cheese.

Prepare white sauce as above and stir shredded cheese into hot white sauce, whisking until cheese melts and sauce is smooth.

PASTA SAUCES

I have always said that my boys could eat some form of tomatoes every night, and, keeping that in mind, it's no wonder that spaghetti and meatballs is their all-time favorite. I advocate using the microwave to save time, energy, heat in the kitchen, and dishes. However, some things just need to be cooked on a conventional stove and spaghetti and macaroni are good examples.

You need such a large container to properly microwave pasta that it doesn't save you time or energy. But spaghetti sauce is another story; it microwaves beautifully. I cook my meatballs and sausage separately and add to my sauce—or you can just use your colander for crumbled hamburger and sausage. (See Box p. 61.)

I have several versions, using meat, clams, mussels, shrimp, and scallops. If you have a favorite recipe, use my techniques and times and do some experimenting with your ingredients.

Meatballs and Sausage in Spaghetti Sauce

Equipment:	9-inch glass pie plate, deep 3-quart casserole dish with cover if available
Cooking time:	56 to 70 minutes
Standing time:	none required
Serves:	4 to 6

MEATBALLS
- **1 pound ground beef**
- **½ cup flavored breadcrumbs**
- **¼ cup milk**
- **1 tablespoon A-1 Sauce**
- **1 egg**
- **1 medium onion, minced**
- **¼ teaspoon garlic powder**
- **1 pound sweet sausages with fennel, or your favorite Italian brand**

SAUCE
- **2 28-ounce cans Italian crushed tomatoes**
- **1 8-ounce can tomato sauce**
- **2 to 3 cloves garlic, minced**
- **8 ounces fresh mushrooms, sliced**
- **1 tablespoon crushed dried basil**
- **2 teaspoons crushed dried oregano**
- **¼ teaspoon fennel seeds**

Combine all meatball ingredients except sausages together, mixing well. Shape meat mixture into 14 to 18 *uniformly sized* and shaped meatballs and arrange in a circle in pie plate.

Microwave **uncovered** on HIGH for 4½ minutes. Turn meatballs over and rearrange in dish. If you have a turntable, I suggest using it.

Once rearranged, continue microwaving on HIGH for 3½ to 5½ minutes until brown and no longer pink, drain, and set aside.

Place sausages in a round or square dish large enough to hold it, pierce the casings well, and **cover** the dish with vented plastic wrap. Microwave on HIGH for 4 minutes, turn sausages over, rearrange in dish, and microwave for 4 to 6 minutes more on HIGH until sausages are no longer pink.

In the casserole dish, combine all the sauce ingredients and microwave **covered** (if using plastic wrap, vent back one corner) on HIGH for 5 minutes. Add meatballs and sausages. Reduce to 50 percent power or MEDIUM and cook **uncovered** for 35 to 45 minutes, **stirring** several times. (If you only have HIGH on your oven, see Box p. 170.) Dish should not be covered so sauce will thicken; however, if it is spattering your oven, cover the top with a paper towel. Place on turntable if available. (If not using turntable **rotate** dish ¼ turn every 10 minutes.)

Serve over hot cooked macaroni.

Troubleshooting: If you have a hot spot in your oven and do not use a turntable, you may find the sauce overcooking in that area. To avoid this, turn dish more frequently.

If your macaroni turns cold during serving, cover it with vented plastic wrap and microwave on HIGH for 90-second intervals until hot. Be sure to stir well to distribute the heat.

Red Clam Sauce

Equipment:	deep 3- or 4-quart casserole dish
Cooking time:	20 to 23 minutes
Standing time:	none required
Serves:	4

- **4 dozen fresh small clams in their shells**
- **4 tablespoons olive oil**
- **3 to 4 cloves garlic, minced**
- **¼ cup bottled clam juice**
- **¼ cup white wine**
- **1 28-ounce can Italian crushed tomatoes**
- **1 to 2 tablespoons chopped fresh basil or 1½ tablespoons dried crushed basil**
- **hot cooked linguine (about 1 pound)**

Scrub clams very well, drain, and set aside. In casserole dish, combine olive oil and garlic. Place on turntable if available. (If not using turntable, **rotate** dish ¼ turn every time you stir.) Microwave on HIGH for 2 minutes, stir, and add clam juice, wine, tomatoes, and basil.

Microwave on HIGH for 8 to 9 minutes or until boiling. Add clams, **cover** (if using plastic wrap, vent back one corner), and reduce to 80 percent power or MEDIUM-HIGH and microwave for 10 to 12 minutes until all clams are open. Stir every 2 to 3 minutes. Serve over hot linguine.

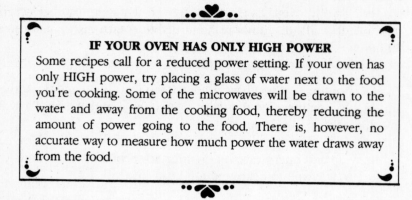

IF YOUR OVEN HAS ONLY HIGH POWER

Some recipes call for a reduced power setting. If your oven has only HIGH power, try placing a glass of water next to the food you're cooking. Some of the microwaves will be drawn to the water and away from the cooking food, thereby reducing the amount of power going to the food. There is, however, no accurate way to measure how much power the water draws away from the food.

Seafood Sauce

Equipment: 3- or 4-quart deep casserole dish with cover if available
Cooking time: 21 to 29 minutes
Standing time: 3 minutes
Serves: 4 to 6

2 **dozen small clams or mussels**
¼ **pound peeled and deveined shrimp**
½ **pound fish fillets (flounder or sole or your favorite) cut into 1-inch chunks**
¼ **pound fresh or frozen scallops**
8 **ounces fresh mushrooms, sliced**
1 **large onion, minced**
4 **tablespoons olive oil**
3 **to 4 cloves garlic, minced**
½ **cup bottled clam juice**
1 **28-ounce can crushed Italian tomatoes**
1 **bay leaf**

  1 **teaspoon crushed dried thyme**
  1 **tablespoon fresh or dried chopped basil**
     pinch of saffron
     salt and pepper to taste

Defrost any frozen fish and scrub clams, then set aside.

In casserole dish put the olive oil, garlic, mushrooms, and onions. Microwave **uncovered** on HIGH for 4 to 5 minutes until onions are soft.

To onion mixture add clam juice, tomatoes, bay leaf, thyme, basil, saffron, and salt and pepper and place on a turntable if available. (If not using turntable **rotate** dish ¼ turn every time you stir.) Microwave **covered** (if using plastic wrap, vent back one corner) on 80 percent power or MEDIUM-HIGH for 10 to 12 minutes, stirring every 3 to 4 minutes.

Remove the bay leaf and add the clams, fish, scallops, and shrimp. Microwave on HIGH for 8 to 12 minutes until all the clams are open and the fish is flaky. Let dish **stand** 3 minutes before serving.

Troubleshooting: If the fish is overcooked when served it is because you microwaved it perfectly and it overcooked while standing. Be sure to slightly undercook and allow it to finish during standing time.

(Discard any clams that are not open instead of continuing to microwave and overcooking all the fish.)

Suggestions: Instead of serving over spaghetti or linguine, try serving in soup bowls and dipping French bread in the sauce.

Fruit

APPLES

I found an interesting letter in my mail and thought I would share it with you. It said, "I love to make apple crisp in my regular oven but don't know how to convert it to the microwave. Also, can you tell me which varieties of apples are better to use for cooking?"

Rather than take an uneducated guess about cooking apples, I went straight to the expert, Albert Bishop of Bishop's Orchards in Guilford, Connecticut. Albert knows his apples and now so will you.

McIntosh apples are great for eating, but they split if you use them for baked apples. These delicious eating apples don't stand up well in long-cooking recipes, but the microwave cooks so quickly that I feel they do better in a microwaved pie than they would in a conventional one. For applesauce, a mix of McIntosh and almost any other apple except Red Delicious produces a nice taste.

Cortland apples, I have found, seem to be the best all-around baking and cooking apple. The flesh of Cortlands stays white longer than other apples when you are slicing them for a fresh fruit or Waldorf salad. They hold their shape very well for baked apples and in slices for pie.

Macoun (sometimes spelled Magowan) and Red Delicious apples are excellent eating apples, while Red Delicious are also good cut up in salads. Neither of these two varieties is recommended for pies, while Golden Delicious are good pie and eating apples.

Stayman apples are good all-around firm cooking apples that hold their shape when cut into slices for cakes. Rome apples are also good to cook with and hold their shape in cakes, while Greenings are too tart for eating apples and are best in pies.

That's a little background on apples, but your taste buds are the best judge of your preference. Take your family apple picking at one of your local orchards this year and try baking them, putting them in pies, cakes, and applesauce (you can freeze or can the applesauce and use it all year).

Tempting Baked Apples

Equipment: custard cups or 1-quart casserole dish
Cooking time: 2 minutes for 1 apple, and add 1 minute for each additional apple
Standing time: none required
Serves: 1 apple per person

For each apple:
2 teaspoons butter
1 tablespoon brown sugar
1 tablespoon raisins
1 teaspoon chopped pecans or walnuts
1 tablespoon apple juice
dash of cinnamon and nutmeg

Carefully peel rim of apple skin from the top of each apple to allow the steam to escape. Core the apples, being sure not to cut through the bottoms. Cream butter and sugar together. Fill cavity with raisins and nuts, then mound butter and sugar mixture on top.

Place 1 or 2 apples in custard cups, and 3 or more in casserole dish. Drizzle apple juice over tops and sprinkle with cinnamon and/or nutmeg.

Microwave, **covered** with vented plastic wrap, on HIGH for 2 minutes for 1 apple, and 1 minute more for each additional apple. Baste with pan juices halfway through cooking and use a turntable if available. (If not using a turntable, **rotate** dish ½ turn after minute.)

Suggestions: Serve hot baked apples with a scoop of ice cream or flavor your whipped topping with a touch of cinnamon.

Apples and Stuff

Equipment: pastry blender and 9-inch round baking dish
Cooking time: 14 to 16 minutes
Standing time: 5 minutes
Serves: 6

   4 to 5 apples, peeled, cored, and thinly sliced
   ½ to ¾ cup sugar
   2 tablespoons all-purpose flour
   1 teaspoon cinnamon
   dash of salt
   ¼ cup sliced and drained maraschino cherries
   ¼ cup raisins
   ¼ cup chopped almonds

TOPPING
   ½ stick butter
   1 cup flour
   ½ cup sugar
   ½ teaspoon baking powder
   pinch of salt
   1 egg
   1 tablespoon butter
   1 teaspoon cinnamon

Combine sugar, flour, cinnamon, and salt. Toss apple slices in sugar mixture and add cherries, raisins, and nuts. Allow apple mixture to stand while preparing topping.

Cut butter into flour, sugar, baking powder, and salt, using a pastry blender or 2 table knives until mixture is crumbly. Add egg and mix well with a fork.

Evenly spread apple filling in bottom of a buttered 9-inch round baking dish. (See Box p. 202.) Sprinkle crumb topping over filling, dot with butter, and sprinkle with cinnamon.

Microwave on HIGH for 14 to 16 minutes or until apples are tender. **Elevate** flat-bottomed baking dish on an inverted saucer and use a turntable if available. (If not using a turntable, **rotate** dish ½ turn after 7 minutes.)

Let **stand** on a hard, heat-proof surface for 5 minutes. Serve warm with ice cream or whipped topping.

Suggestions: A neat way to cut and core an apple at the same time, while still getting even slices, goes like this: peel and place apple on cutting board and cut four large pieces, leaving the square core standing. Turn each of the four pieces cut-side down and slice.

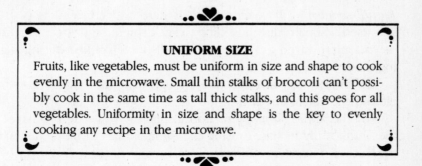

UNIFORM SIZE

Fruits, like vegetables, must be uniform in size and shape to cook evenly in the microwave. Small thin stalks of broccoli can't possibly cook in the same time as tall thick stalks, and this goes for all vegetables. Uniformity in size and shape is the key to evenly cooking any recipe in the microwave.

Apple Crisp

Equipment:	9-inch round baking dish
Cooking time:	8 to 11 minutes
Standing time:	5 minutes
Serves:	6

5 cups peeled, cored, and thinly sliced apples
¼ cup apple juice

TOPPING
¼ cup butter
¼ cup dark brown sugar
½ cup flour
¼ cup chopped walnuts
½ teaspoon cinnamon

In a medium bowl melt butter on HIGH for 45 to 55 seconds. Mix in sugar, flour, nuts, and cinnamon until you have a crumbly mixture.

Place apples in buttered 9-inch round (see Box p. 202) baking dish and sprinkle with apple juice. Crumble topping over apples.

Elevate flat-bottomed container on an inverted saucer and place on turntable if available. (If not using a turntable **rotate** dish ½ turn halfway through cooking.) Microwave on HIGH for 8 to 11 minutes until apples are tender.

Let **stand** for 5 minutes and serve warm with whipped topping.

Troubleshooting: If your topping is hard and crusty, it is because you used a square dish and didn't check shielding tips on page 202; or you microwaved too long and the dish overcooked during standing time.

If the center wasn't cooked enough, you may have forgotten to elevate and rotate the dish.

If the apple slices were not all tender, you may not have cut them uniformly in size, causing the thinner ones to be tender while the thicker ones were still raw.

Suggestions: When you want something special to serve in footed glasses, substitute cream sherry for the apple juice. A really rich treat.

Applesauce

For years I stood over a large hot pot adding apples and stirring constantly, trying to keep those sneaky few from sticking to the bottom, when I made applesauce. The day of scrubbing off stuck-on apples is over, but the recipe I have is just for plain old-fashioned applesauce.

So, let's get creative and add some strawberries, blueberries, or even raspberries that you may have in the freezer or can buy frozen. Don't get me wrong; applesauce in its plain state is wonderful and freezes well for use all winter—but a little added color and flavor can only enhance a good basic product.

Equipment: deep 2- or 3-quart casserole dish
Cooking time: 10 to 12 minutes
Standing time: none required
Makes: 8 to 10 cups

8 **apples, a variety of your choice—peeled, cored, and
   quartered**
½ **cup apple cider or juice**
½ **cup sugar (to taste)**
⅛ **teaspoon salt**
½ **teaspoon cinnamon**
⅛ **teaspoon nutmeg**

Place apples and cider or apple juice in casserole dish. **Cover** with
vented plastic wrap and microwave on HIGH for 10 to 12 minutes or
until apples are tender, **stirring** well every 3 minutes.

Mash with a potato masher (or use a food processor) then add
sugar and spices to taste. Cool and serve with pork dishes or as a
dessert.

Suggestions: Once applesauce is sweetened to taste, add berries of
your choice, mixing carefully so that their color doesn't run. For a
darker sauce, substitute brown sugar for white when sweetening.

Package in little lunchbox containers and freeze. Pop frozen into
lunchboxes in the morning and they will defrost and be chilled for
lunch.

APPLE PIE FILLINGS

Do you have 6 or 8 good baking apples on hand that you just want to
do something with? Does good old everyday apple pie with a little
twist of something different sound challenging?

Is sugar a problem in your household or are you just trying to
cut down for health or dieting reasons? If so, how about trying a
filling that doesn't add any sugar but uses naturally sweet cider or
apple juice? No, it won't be soup, as the juice will be thickened before
you add the apples. However, if you don't mind adding sugar but still
want something different, how about adding some cheddar cheese to
America's Favorite?

Apple Cheese Filling

Equipment:	8- or 9-inch microwaved pie crust, dough cut-outs
	or lattice top (see p. 207)
Cooking time:	10 to 12 minutes
Standing time:	10 minutes
Serves:	6

**6 to 8 apples, a variety of your choice—peeled, cored, and
sliced thin**
¾ to 1 cup sugar
2 tablespoons flour
1 teaspoon cinnamon
dash of nutmeg
dash of salt
¼ cup shredded sharp cheddar cheese
2 tablespoons butter

Combine sugar, flour, spices, salt, and cheese in a medium bowl. Add apples, tossing to coat. Let sit for 5 minutes.

Fill baked pie crust (see p. 207) with apple mixture and dot with butter. Place a sheet of wax paper on microwave floor. On the wax paper place an inverted saucer and carefully set the pie plate on top. Microwave on HIGH for 10 to 12 minutes, or until apples are tender, **rotating** dish ¼ turn every 3 minutes. (If a turntable is available, place wax paper, inverted saucer, and then pie on top.)

Let **stand** for 10 minutes, then place lattice top or cutouts over the apples.

Troubleshooting: If the center of your pie does not completely cook it is because you forgot to elevate it so that the microwaves could cook from underneath as well as from the top and sides.

If your crust is soft and mushy, you probably did not completely precook it. Follow the directions in the pie crust recipe (see p. 207) and make sure you completely cook the crust before adding your filling.

A two-crust pie will not allow the filling to cook, so don't even try it.

If you find the lattice top too difficult to make, just cut the dough with the open end of a glass or use cookie cutters.

Suggestions: Try using cookie cutters appropriate for the nearest holiday for the cut-outs to go on top of the filling to replace the top crust.

Sprinkle cinnamon and sugar over fluted edges of pie crust and cut-outs.

Naturally Sweet Apple Pie Filling

Equipment:	6-cup glass measure or high-sided 2-quart bowl, microwaved 8- or 9-inch pie crust
Cooking time:	13 to 16 minutes
Standing time:	10 minutes
Serves:	6

- **6 to 8 apples, a variety of your choice—peeled, cored, and sliced thin**
- **¾ cup cider or frozen apple juice concentrate**
- **3 tablespoons cornstarch**
- **⅛ teaspoon salt**
- **1 teaspoon cinnamon**
- **dash of nutmeg, preferably freshly grated**
- **2 tablespoons butter**

In glass measure or bowl, combine cider and cornstarch. Microwave on HIGH for 3 to 4 minutes until thickened, **whisking** every minute. (See Box p. 166.) Cool. Add all remaining ingredients except butter. Place in cooled baked pie shell and dot with butter.

Place a sheet of wax paper on the floor of your microwave. Place pie plate on an inverted saucer in center of the oven and microwave on HIGH for 10 to 12 minutes until apples are tender, **rotating** dish ¼ turn every 3 minutes. (If a turntable is available, place wax paper, inverted saucer, and pie plate on top.)

Let **stand** for 10 minutes, then add lattice or cut-out top, or just leave fruit top uncovered and add whipped topping before serving.

Suggestions: Instead of putting lattice or cut-outs on top of baked fruit, try taking 6 slices of American cheese and rolling them to resemble cornucopias, adding a maraschino cherry in the middle of each, and evenly space them over the filling of the finished pie.

PEACHES

You see those lovely fuzzy peaches sitting at all the roadside stands in cute little baskets. The price is right, you can't resist the lovely aroma, you buy some, and now they sit on your kitchen counter. Now what?

Rather than letting the peaches get brown spots and go bad, which they do in the blink of an eye, I suggest you preserve a hefty amount for use during the year. Make a batch into jelly, leave a few to be eaten fresh, and bake with the rest.

I like to prepare a medium sugar syrup and add sliced peaches and freeze. One year I just peeled, halved, and pitted my peaches, and placed them in the syrup. Once they cooled, I put maraschino cherries in the center of each one before freezing. This syrup can be used for any fruit you want to preserve—pears, pineapple, and plums work very well.

I stopped at Bishop's Orchards in Guilford, Connecticut, and asked them what they recommend using to keep peaches from browning when freezing them. They don't feel lemon juice does a good job, and it leaves a lemon flavor. They recommend a product called Fruit Fresh, which not only stops browning but also protects the flavor of any fruit you use it with.

I have frozen peaches without using this ascorbic acid product and sometimes I've been lucky and had no browning, but other times I had terribly discolored fruit. The only way to guarantee perfectly colored fruit after preserving is to use some brand of this product.

No matter what you choose to do with this luscious fruit, you must start by removing the skins. To do this best, I suggest filling a 2- or 3-quart casserole dish with enough water to cover several peaches. Microwave on HIGH for 4 to 5 minutes or until the water is boiling. Using a paring knife, make a small X in the bottoms of 3 or 4 peaches and drop them into the boiling water.

Let them stand in the water for about 1 minute, then plunge them into a bowl of cold water. Once cooled down enough to hold, the skin should peel off in strips. Place peeled fruit in a brine of 3 teaspoons of salt mixed into 2 quarts of water. This brine will keep the fruit from turning brown before you are ready to use it.

If you are going to freeze some of the fruit for later use, you will have to begin by making a sugar syrup. There are three categories for this syrup—thin, medium, and heavy. The one you use is a matter of your personal taste.

FREEZING IN SUGAR SYRUP

Type of Syrup	Sugar	Water or Fruit Juice
Thin	1 cup	3 cups
Medium	1 cup	2 cups
Heavy	1 cup	1 cup

To prepare syrup, combine sugar and liquid in a container large enough to hold them. Microwave on HIGH for 2 to 3 minutes until sugar is dissolved. Then bring to boil on HIGH for 3 to 4 minutes more.

Once syrup is boiling, add sliced or halved peaches and microwave on 50 percent power or MEDIUM for 2 minutes and cool. Once cool, package in air-tight containers, label the contents, and date. If you're using an ascorbic acid product, add according to manufacturer's directions. Fruit packaged properly for freezing will keep for at least 6 months.

PEACH CAKES

When using peaches in baking, I have found that they turn brown if left untreated with ascorbic acid. I either treat them before using, or I use the ones I have put in sugar syrup (see directions p. 181), being sure to drain them very well before baking so that I don't add any extra liquid to my recipe.

For all of you who want an easy, quick method for using up your fruit, try this upside-down peach spice cake. I brought this to a church bake sale and no one believed it came out of a microwave.

Peach and Spice Supreme

Equipment: 12-cup bundt pan
Cooking time: 16½ to 17½ minutes
Standing time: 10 minutes
Serves: 8 to 10

1 **package instant vanilla pudding, prepared**
2 **peaches, skinned, pitted, and sliced**
1 **boxed spice cake with pudding in the mix, prepared according to box directions, beating 4 minutes (I prefer Pillsbury)**

Grease and dust bundt pan with brown or granulated sugar. Pour prepared vanilla pudding into bottom of pan and attractively arrange peach slices over pudding. Pour prepared cake batter over peaches and pudding and let sit for 5 minutes.

If available, place bundt pan on a turntable and microwave on 30 percent power or LOW for 11 minutes. (If not using turntable, **rotate** dish ¼ turn every 3 minutes.)

Change power setting to HIGH and microwave 5½ to 6½ minutes or until cake comes away from sides of pan. (If you have only HIGH power on your oven, bake 12 minutes on HIGH.)

Let **stand** for 10 minutes on a hard, heat-proof surface before inverting onto a serving platter.

Troubleshooting: You may find that some of the pudding remains in the pan when inverted if you allow it to cool too long. Invert after no more than 15 minutes of standing time, and if some of the pudding has remained in the pan, scoop out and carefully place on top of the cake.

Suggestions: Try using pears or your own canned apple slices in place of the peaches.

Banana Peach Dream

This cake takes a bit more time and trouble to assemble all the necessary ingredients, but it's well worth every second you spend on it.

Equipment:	12-cup bundt pan
Cooking time:	16½ to 17½ minutes
Standing time:	10 minutes
Serves:	8 to 10

1 **boxed yellow cake mix with pudding (I prefer Pillsbury)**
½ **cup mashed bananas**
½ **cup crème de banana liqueur**
4 **eggs**
¼ **cup vegetable oil**
½ **cup water**
1 **cup whipping cream**
½ **cup vanilla ice cream**
2 **cups sliced fresh peaches**

Grease and dust bundt pan with sugar and put aside. In large mixing bowl combine cake mix, bananas, crème de banana liqueur, eggs, oil, and ½ cup water. Blend well and beat at medium speed on an electric mixer for 4 minutes.

Pour into prepared bundt pan and let sit for 5 minutes. Place on turntable if available and microwave on 30 percent or LOW for 11 minutes. (If not using turntable, **rotate** dish ¼ turn every 3 minutes.)

Increase power to HIGH and microwave for 5½ to 6½ minutes more until cake comes away from sides of pan. (If you have only HIGH power on your microwave, bake for 12 minutes.)

Let **stand** for 10 minutes on a hard, heat-proof surface, then invert onto serving platter and cool before serving.

Beat cream till thick but not stiff. Add ice cream by spoonfuls, beating just till smooth. Frost cake with cream mixture and decorate with peach slices. Serve right away or put in freezer before serving.

Troubleshooting: If you cool cake in the microwave you may find the moisture build-up makes the cake stick to the pan; remove cake from oven as soon as it is finished baking.

BLUEBERRIES

Have you ever tried picking your own blueberries at one of the farms in your area? If you haven't tried it you should. Take your largest pot—you will crush the blueberries if you use any type of bag—and find one of the area farms that have opened their bushes for picking and try your hand.

Whether picking them yourself or buying them, be sure you select large, dark blueberries that are plump, firm, dry, and without stems. If buying them already picked, avoid stained containers, which indicate wet or leaky berries.

Blueberries are extremely perishable and should be used or frozen within 2 to 3 days of picking. To ensure their freshness, package them without washing, in 1- or 2-cup portions, and freeze. When you are ready to use them, take out the quantity you need and then wash. *Never* wash blueberries until you are ready to use them.

Here is an easy-to-make pudding recipe that is a bit different but must be refrigerated for 24 hours. If you're in a hurry, make instant vanilla pudding and add fresh blueberries.

Old-Fashioned Blueberry Pudding

Equipment:	deep 2- or 3-quart bowl or casserole dish, 1-quart round mold or lettuce crisper, small plate or saucer that fits across top of mold, 2- or 3-pound weight, rubber knife or spatula
Cooking time:	5 to 8 minutes
Standing time:	none required
Refrigeration time:	24 hours
Serves:	6

  3 cups (1½ pints) blueberries, washed and stemmed
1½ tablespoons sherry
  ½ cup honey
    dash of nutmeg
  8 thin slices white bread, crust removed
    strawberries and whipped cream for garnish

In the casserole dish, combine blueberries, sherry, honey, and nutmeg, and **cover** with wax paper. Microwave on HIGH for 4 to 6 minutes or until boiling. Continue cooking on HIGH for 1 to 2 minutes until the berries split and the juices are released. Remove from the microwave and set aside to cool.

Line the round mold or lettuce crisper with the bread by laying a slice on the bottom and surrounding it with diagonally cut slices placed around the sides. There should be no spaces showing. Pour the cooled blueberry mixture into the mold and cover the top of it with bread slices. Do not overlap any of the bread. Trim off any excess.

Place the small plate on the pudding so that it rests right on the top, covering it completely. On top of the plate place the 2- or 3-pound weight to hold it down firmly. Chill weighted dish for 24 hours.

When ready to serve, remove plate and weights, and loosen edges with rubber knife or spatula. Invert mold onto serving plate and garnish with strawberries and whipped cream. Serve at room temperature, cut into wedges.

Blueberry Streusel Coffee Cake

I am using a packaged cake mix for the base of my blueberry coffee cake because this version is quick and easy to put together. Whether you are breakfast eaters or late-night snackers, this treat is sure to please everyone.

When I ran this recipe in my newspaper column I was inundated with letters asking me to convert this recipe for use in conventional ovens. I said, "Sorry, I only convert to the microwave, not to the conventional oven!" Everyone had a good laugh, but I really have done this recipe only in the microwave, and it is super.

Equipment: 12-cup bundt pan
Cooking time: 16½ to 17½ minutes
Standing time: 10 minutes
Serves: 8 to 10

brown or granulated sugar for dusting pan
1 **boxed yellow cake mix with pudding (I prefer Pillsbury), prepared according to box directions, beating 4 minutes**
2 **cups blueberries, washed**

STREUSEL
¾ **cup packed light brown sugar**
⅓ **cup butter, softened**
¼ **cup all-purpose flour**
½ **teaspoon ground cinnamon**
½ **cup chopped pecans**

ICING
1 **cup confectioner's sugar**
1½ **ounces cream cheese, softened**
1 **tablespoon milk**
1 **teaspoon vanilla extract**

Grease and dust bundt pan with brown or granulated sugar. Fold blueberries into cake batter and pour half the batter into bundt pan.

Using a fork, blend all streusel ingredients together and sprinkle half over batter. Place the remaining batter in pan and sprinkle with remaining streusel topping. Place bundt pan on turntable, if available.

Microwave on 30 percent power or DEFROST for 11 minutes, then change to HIGH for 5½ to 6½ minutes or until cake comes away from sides of pan. (If your oven has only HIGH power, microwave 12 to 13 minutes. If you have no turntable, **rotate** pan ¼ turn every 3 minutes.)

Let **stand** on a hard, heat-proof surface for 10 minutes then invert onto serving plate. Blend icing ingredients together until smooth and drizzle over cool cake.

Troubleshooting: I have found that if the cake is difficult to release from the pan you may have let it stand too long. Do not allow cakes to stand for more than 10 to 15 minutes before inverting onto your serving platter.

BANANAS

Has your counter ever held green-tipped yellow bananas crying out to be desserts of some kind? Other than banana bread, I had never experimented much with cooking bananas, but I worked on it and found the kids especially loved the results.

Before cooking with bananas survey their degree of ripeness. Green-tipped ones are best used for cooking, while completely yellow ones are best eaten raw; very ripe brown-speckled bananas should be mashed for milkshakes or cake and bread recipes.

When selecting your bananas always look for those that are not bruised and do not have splits in the skin. Always leave your bananas at room temperature, uncovered, until they are ripe. Once ripe, refrigerate and use them up within one or two days. If they're very ripe and you can't use them right away, peel and wrap them in plastic wrap, then freeze. They go straight from the freezer into blender drinks and they're great.

For my first experiment, I peeled four green-tipped bananas and halved them lengthwise. On the cut end I inserted a wooden stick, placed them on a plate, and froze them for about 2½ hours and turned them into:

Chocolate Peanut Boats

Equipment:	Popsicle sticks or skewers
Cooking time:	2 to 4 minutes
Standing time:	none required
Serves:	8

    4 bananas, peeled and halved lengthwise
  ½ cup peanut butter chips
  ½ cup chocolate chips
    3 tablespoons solid shortening (I prefer Crisco)
      toasted chopped nuts or colored sprinkles

Insert Popsicle sticks halfway into banana halves, place on a lightly greased platter, and freeze for 2 to 2½ hours. When bananas are frozen, place peanut butter chips, chocolate chips, and shortening in a small bowl. Microwave on 50 percent power or MEDIUM for 2 to 4 minutes, **stirring** each minute, until the chips are soft and shiny.

Once chips are soft, mix until completely melted. Either dip frozen bananas in the melted liquid or spoon it over the bananas. Be careful to catch excess drippings. Before the glaze sets, roll or spoon nuts or sprinkles over coated bananas.

Suggestions: You may substitute 1 cup of either chocolate chips or peanut butter chips—or try using butterscotch chips for a real treat. If you have a favorite chocolate fondue recipe, it will work well, but forget marshmallow—it's just too messy.

The kids went wild over these little banana boats, so I know they are good, but the counter still held more bananas. So Strawberry-Banana Cheese Pie was next. This about did it for my supply of bananas and my waistline.

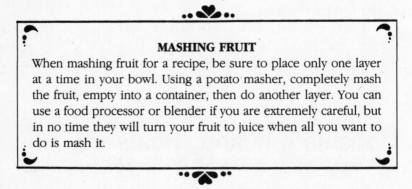

MASHING FRUIT

When mashing fruit for a recipe, be sure to place only one layer at a time in your bowl. Using a potato masher, completely mash the fruit, empty into a container, then do another layer. You can use a food processor or blender if you are extremely careful, but in no time they will turn your fruit to juice when all you want to do is mash it.

Strawberry-Banana Cheese Pie

Equipment:	1-quart bowl, potato masher
Refrigeration time:	2 to 3 hours
Cooking time:	8 to 10 minutes
Standing time:	none required
Serves:	6

1   prebaked 9-inch pie crust or 1 prepared 9-inch crumb
    crust
1   quart strawberries, cleaned and hulled

¾ **cup water**
1 **cup sugar**
3 **tablespoons cornstarch**
1 **tablespoon Grand Marnier liqueur (optional)**
1 **tablespoon strawberry or strawberry-banana Jell-O powder (for color)**
1 **8-ounce package cream cheese**
2 **bananas, sliced**
 whipped cream for garnish

Reserve 1 cup whole strawberries and place remaining berries in bowl and mash (see Box p. 188). Add water and sugar to mashed berries, mixing well. Microwave on HIGH 5 to 6 minutes until mixture is boiling.

Soften cornstarch with a little water and add to mixture, **stirring** well. Microwave on HIGH for 2 to 3 minutes or until mixture thickens, stirring once. Stir in Grand Marnier and powdered Jell-O. Cool to lukewarm.

Brush sides and bottom of pie crust with 2 tablespoons lukewarm strawberry glaze. Place cream cheese in a small bowl and soften on 50 percent power or MEDIUM for 50 to 65 seconds. Spread softened cream cheese in bottom of pie shell. Slice bananas and place over cream cheese. Gently toss reserved whole strawberries with remaining glaze and pour over banana and cream cheese. Refrigerate for 2 to 3 hours and garnish with whipped cream.

When ready to slice, see Box p. 211.

Strawberry-Banana Daiquiris

When you've run out of ideas for bananas, freeze the leftover ones for this treat. I know this is a no-cook recipe, but I just couldn't talk about bananas without giving you my favorite summer drink recipe. Don't tell anyone you found this in a microwave cookbook; let them think you've been making this wonderful concoction forever.

Equipment: blender
Blender time: 1 minute
Serves: 2 to 3

1 6-ounce can frozen lime juice
1 frozen banana
½ to ¾ cup frozen strawberries
½ cup rum
2 cups ice cubes

Place frozen lime juice in glass blender container and blend on HIGH for 1 minute. Add bananas, strawberries, and rum. Blend for another minute until fruit is pulverized. Add ice cubes and continue blending until thick.

Pour into footed glasses and garnish with a large strawberry.

Suggestions: Try using your two favorite fruits blended together for a delicious summer cooler.

CRANBERRIES

How many times have you walked past those neatly stacked bags of fresh cranberries in the food store and thought about all the super cooks who make their own cranberry sauce? Well, super cooks, move over, because the microwave makes cranberry sauce so easy that anyone can make it from scratch.

When you boil cranberries on your conventional range you have to be sure to keep stirring to avoid sticking, but this won't happen in your microwave. The key is to be sure you use a deep, large container and use wax paper to help keep the spatters in the pot.

In my house, they prefer the cranberry sauce jellied, but I know many of you like to leave the berries whole so I will give you instructions for both methods. For those of you who like cranberry-orange relish I have also included my recipe for you to try.

Whole-Berry Cranberry Sauce

Equipment:	deep 3- or 4-quart casserole dish or bowl
Cooking time:	17 to 24 minutes
Standing time:	none required
Serves:	8 to 10

1 pound fresh cranberries
1½ cups water
2 cups sugar

Place water and sugar in bowl or casserole dish (if flat-bottomed, **elevate** on an inverted saucer) and microwave on HIGH for 3 to 4 minutes. Meanwhile, wash and pick over cranberries to be sure all are red and firm. Stir sugar syrup well and add cranberries, then **cover** with wax paper.

Microwave on HIGH for another 4 to 6 minutes or until the cranberry skins split open, stirring well. Reduce to 50 percent power or MEDIUM and microwave until the sauce thickens, about 10 to 14 minutes, stirring twice. Pour into a mold or attractive serving dish and cool. Once cool, refrigerate.

Jellied Cranberry Sauce

Equipment:	deep 3- or 4-quart casserole dish or bowl, food mill or mesh strainer, potato masher
Cooking time:	14 to 22 minutes
Standing time:	none required
Serves:	8 to 10

1 pound fresh cranberries
2 cups sugar or to taste
1½ cups water

Sort and wash cranberries, then place them in casserole dish or bowl. Add water and **cover** with wax paper. (If you're using a flat-bottomed container, **elevate** on an inverted saucer.)

Microwave on HIGH for 6 to 10 minutes until all berries have split. Carefully, put berries and water through a food mill. If one isn't available, mash with a potato masher and strain to eliminate skins.

Add sugar to taste, cover with wax paper, and microwave on 50 percent power or MEDIUM for 8 to 12 minutes until sauce thickens, **stirring** every 2 minutes.

Pour into an attractive serving dish or mold and cool. Once cool, refrigerate.

Cranberry-Orange Relish

Equipment: deep 3- or 4-quart casserole dish or bowl
Cooking time: 12 to 18 minutes
Standing time: none required
Serves: 10 to 12

1 pound fresh cranberries
2 cups sugar
½ cup orange juice
½ cup orange liqueur (I prefer Triple Sec) or water
1 tablespoon grated orange zest

Combine all ingredients in casserole dish or bowl, **cover** with wax paper, and microwave on HIGH for 12 to 18 minutes or until cranberries burst open and are soft, **stirring** every 4 minutes. (If dish is flat-bottomed, **elevate** on an inverted saucer.)

Skim the foam from the surface and place in a decorative serving dish, cool, and refrigerate.

Baking

MUFFINS

Muffins always taste so good in the morning or for that late-night, what-do-you-have-to-eat? snack. My mail tells me that many of you are having problems with your muffins getting hard several hours after baking. The general rule for baking anything in muffin pans or custard cups: You must use *two* muffin papers, one to hold the cake and one to absorb the moisture formed between the cake and the pan.

This is the same problem faced when putting bread or potatoes flat on the floor of the microwave. Moisture forms between the food and the floor of the oven. If you do not have *two* paper towels or muffin papers to absorb the moisture, it remains in the food, causing it to become hard later.

Then we have the problem of appearance of the muffins. Our eyes are used to seeing golden-brown tops on our muffins and of course we can't get this effect in the microwave. However, you can use a variety of toppings to fool the eye into believing there is a browned muffin underneath. Try covering your favorite recipe with crumbled cookies, leftover cake, muffins, sweet rolls, or coffee cakes that are dried and crumbled, graham cracker crumbs mixed with cinnamon and sugar, or the following streusel topping.

Streusel Topping

Makes enough to swirl inside a bundt cake or top 1 recipe of muffins

    1 cup all-purpose flour
    ½ cup sugar
    ½ cup packed dark brown sugar
    2 teaspoons ground cinnamon
    6 tablespoons butter
    1 egg yolk
    ¼ cup chopped nuts, pecans, peanuts, or walnuts

In a medium bowl, mix flour, both sugars, and cinnamon. With 2 table knives or pastry cutter, cut in butter and egg yolk until crumbly. Add nuts and use as a topping for muffins or coffee cakes.

Cover and refrigerate leftover topping.

Suggestions: This topping can be placed over any canned pie filling for an easy cobbler.

Surprise Muffins

Here is a recipe for muffins to accompany your lunch or dinner. They are tasty and make a nice substitute for bread.

   Equipment: muffin pan or custard cups, muffin or cupcake papers
Cooking time: 20 to 40 seconds per muffin
Standing time: none required
     Makes: 10 to 12 muffins

    1 cup all-purpose flour
    1 tablespoon sugar
  1½ teaspoons baking powder
    ½ teaspoon paprika
    ¼ teaspoon salt
    ½ cup shredded cheddar cheese

2 slices bacon, cooked and crumbled
2 tablespoons chopped green pepper
2 tablespoons chopped onion
½ cup milk
¼ cup cooking oil or melted butter
1 egg

Place all ingredients in a bowl and mix quickly and lightly only until particles are moistened.

Using 2 muffin papers for each muffin, fill cups half-full.

For 1 muffin, microwave	20 to 40 seconds
2 muffins	30 to 90 seconds
4 muffins	1 minute to 2½ minutes
6 muffins	2½ to 4½ minutes

When muffins have finished microwaving, remove to a wire rack to cool. Eat warm with butter or cold.

Troubleshooting: If your muffins got hard shortly after baking, you did not use two muffin papers. This step is essential, since there is no other way to absorb the moisture short of having it go into the dough and make it hard.

Suggestions: Minced leftover meats may be substituted for the bacon, and scallions may be used instead of onions for more color.

Lemon Squares

Before I squeeze my lemons, or any citrus fruit for that matter, I microwave each piece for 15 to 20 seconds on HIGH, let it stand for 2 minutes on the counter, then roll it between the palms of my hands. Look out; the flavor and juice it releases will surprise you each and every time you do it.

I received a note from a lovely woman who said, "I walked into the kitchen this morning to find my husband strategically placing our morning grapefruit in the microwave. 'What are you doing?' I asked. 'The Microwhiz lady says to place them in a circle, but I only have 2 pieces,' he replied. Well, after placing them he set the oven for 40 seconds, because they were so big he thought they would need the longer time. I never said a word, but I thought you were both crazy. After the oven shut off, and they finished standing, he rolled them in his hands and cut them open with a grin on his face I haven't seen in 20 years. I just had to write and thank you for not only the juiciest fruit we have ever had, but making my 72-year-old husband real proud of his new microwaving skills."

Every time I squeeze a lemon I can't help but think of that charming couple.

Equipment:	pastry blender, 8-inch round or square baking dish, electric mixer
Cooking time:	7½ minutes
Standing time:	none required
Makes:	16 squares

1 cup sifted flour
½ cup sugar
½ cup butter
¼ cup sifted confectioner's sugar

FILLING
2 eggs
¾ cup sugar
3 tablespoons fresh lemon juice
1 teaspoon grated lemon zest
¼ teaspoon baking powder
2 tablespoons sifted flour

Combine 1 cup sifted flour and ½ cup sugar in a medium bowl. Cut in butter using pastry blender or 2 table knives until mixture is crumbly. Press mixture into the bottom and halfway up the sides of baking dish. If using a flat-bottomed dish, **elevate** on an inverted saucer and place on a turntable if available.

Microwave on HIGH for 4 minutes. (If not using a turntable, **rotate** dish ½ turn every 2 minutes.)

Place eggs, sugar, lemon juice, lemon zest, baking powder, and 1 tablespoon flour in medium bowl. Beat until blended, using an electric mixer at MEDIUM speed. Pour over crust.

Elevate dish on an inverted saucer, place on a turntable if

available, and microwave on HIGH for 3½ minutes or until top is bubbly. (If not using turntable, **rotate** dish ¼ turn after each minute.)

Cool in dish on hard, heat-proof surface and when cool sprinkle with confectioner's sugar and cut into 2-inch squares.

Troubleshooting: If you had burnt edges on your squares, you either overbaked them, forgot to rotate the dish, or used a square baking dish without shielding.

If the lemon filling was rubbery, you overcooked it.

If the center of the dish wasn't cooked, you used a flat-bottom dish and forgot to elevate it.

Suggestions: Dough can be a base for lemon meringue square by adding prepared lemon pudding and topping with meringue (see p. 209). Don't throw those lemon rinds away until you place them in a 4-cup glass measure, add 2 cups water, then microwave for 10 minutes on HIGH. It will not only help remove any crusted-on spots in your oven but deodorize it too.

Cone Cakes

When my children were young I always found that sending cupcakes to school made a huge mess for the teacher. To alleviate the paper-and-crumb mess, I started putting my batter into flat-bottomed ice cream cones in my regular oven. One day I was in a hurry and tried them in the microwave—they baked almost instantly.

Once they are cool I frost the tops, add sprinkles, nuts, or chocolate chips, and the kids get to eat cake and holder all-in-one with much less mess and crumbs. Be sure to place the cones on 2 layers of paper towels to absorb the moisture, and set them on a rack to cool once baked, and you are in business.

Equipment:	rack for cooling
Cooking time:	1½ to 3 minutes for every 6 cones
Standing time:	none required
Makes:	24 to 30 cones

   1 **boxed cake mix, any flavor, prepared according to package directions**
  24 **to 30 flat-bottomed ice cream cones**
     frosting (homemade or canned) or whipped topping
     sprinkles, nuts, and/or decorations

Place about 2 heaping tablespoons of cake batter into each cone.

Place 2 layers of paper towels on the floor of your microwave and place up to 6 cones at a time in a circle.

Microwave on HIGH for 1½ to 3 minutes or until cake springs back when touched lightly. Cool on a wire rack for 5 to 10 minutes, then frost and decorate.

Suggestions: Sometimes I drop chocolate chips into the batter before baking for a surprise in the middle.

CUPCAKES

What about cupcakes for the adults? Cupcakes can be made in micro-safe muffin pans, which turn out small cupcakes, or in custard cups, which produce larger cakes. In either utensil you will need 2 cupcake papers, 1 to hold the cake and the other to help absorb the excess moisture that forms.

Since microwaved cupcakes rise higher than conventionally baked ones, fill each paper only ⅓ full. Be sure to cut through the batter with a knife tip or a toothpick to eliminate air spaces.

Arrange the custard cups in a circle on the floor of your microwave and rotate after half the baking time. Cook until almost dry on top, but don't worry if small moist spots appear, as they will dry as the cake cools. If you overbake them, they will be hard and dry.

As soon as they have finished baking, remove them from their containers and set on a wire rack to cool. Once cool, decorate with your favorite icing and add chocolate shots, nuts, cherry halves, various colored sprinkles, or whatever you may fancy for more eye appeal.

Homemade batter using baking soda can stay up to a week in your refrigerator; batter using baking powder will last for 3 to 4 days in case you don't want to bake them all at once. When baking packaged cake mixes, fill your pans only half-full and use the leftover batter for cupcakes.

As a general rule of thumb, bake cupcakes on HIGH as follows: 1 cupcake for 25 to 35 seconds; 2 for 40 to 80 seconds; 4 for 80 to 100 seconds; 6 for 1½ to 2½ minutes.

Gram's Butterfly Cupcakes

For Christmas one year, the children gave their teachers muffin pans filled with their Gram's Butterfly Cupcakes—and were they a hit; try them yourself.

> *Equipment:* no special equipment required
> *Cooking time:* 10 to 12 minutes (from baking through decorating)
> *Standing time:* none required
> *Makes:* 25 to 30 cupcakes

25 to 30 baked yellow cupcakes in their papers
1 batch lemon or vanilla pudding, prepared
strawberry jam

For each cupcake, cut a 1½-inch circle out of the top and set aside. Fill the hole with pudding.

Cut the circle in half and stand the two halves in the pudding, cut-side down with the outer crust edges facing each other to form wings.

Put a dab of jelly between the wings to form a butterfly.

Suggestions: My mom always uses lemon pudding, but you could use chocolate or butterscotch and put a strip of whipped cream or melted chocolate between the wings.

Fruit Squares

All I can tell you about this recipe is that I found it in a newspaper article years ago and my family looks forward to it every fall, when I always have an abundance of apples. The original recipe was an apple square that you baked in a conventional oven for 55 minutes.

One night I needed a dessert for my husband's lunch the next day, but I didn't have an apple in the house. I did have a can of cherry pie filling, however, and so what the heck, I gave it a try. I don't have to tell you that cherry squares became our anytime-of-year treat, and it microwaves in about one-quarter the conventional cooking time.

I use this recipe often when I demonstrate microwave cooking, and I can't remember how many times I've put this recipe together while talking (which I do a great deal of) about some other aspect of microwaving and forgot to put the egg into the crust. It is a bit more like a fruit cobbler without the egg, but it works well, and if no one knows it is supposed to be a fruit square recipe that isn't crumbly, they love it.

Any fruit pie filling or your own homemade version will make a fine center for this recipe. Remember, don't panic if you forget the egg; just rename it a fruit cobbler.

> *Equipment:* pastry blender, 9-inch round or square baking dish
> *Cooking time:* 16 minutes
> *Standing time:* 5 minutes
> *Yields:* 16 small or 12 large squares

- **1 stick butter**
- **2 cups flour**
- **1 cup sugar**
- **1 teaspoon baking powder**
  pinch of salt
- **1 egg**
- **1 21-ounce can cherry or any other flavor pie filling**
- **2 tablespoons butter**
- **1 teaspoon cinnamon**
  confectioner's sugar for decoration

In a medium bowl, cut butter into flour, sugar, baking powder, and salt until mixture is crumbly (as in making a pie crust), using a pastry blender or table knife. Add egg and mix well with a fork. Spread a little more than half of the mixture into ungreased baking dish. (See Box p. 202.) Spread fruit filling over crumb mixture. Sprinkle remaining crumb mixture over fruit filling. Dot with butter and sprinkle with cinnamon.

If dish is flat-bottomed, **elevate** on an inverted saucer and place on a turntable if available. (If turntable is not available, **rotate** dish ¼ turn every 4 minutes.)

Microwave on HIGH for 16 minutes.

Let **stand** on a hard, heat-proof surface for 5 minutes. When completely cool, sprinkle confectioner's sugar on top and cut into squares.

Apple-Cherry-Nut-Filling

Substitute this filling for canned pie filling and follow microwaving instructions for fruit squares.

Makes enough filling for a 9-inch round or square baking dish.

2 **pounds apples (6 to 8)**
¾ **to 1 cup sugar, to taste**
2 **tablespoons all-purpose flour**
1 **teaspoon ground cinnamon**
   dash of salt
½ **cup sliced maraschino cherries, drained**
½ **cup raisins**
¼ **cup chopped walnuts**

Peel, core, and thinly slice apples. Combine sugar, flour, cinnamon, and dash of salt.

Toss apples with sugar mixture and add cherries, raisins, and nuts. Let stand while preparing crust for fruit squares.

Suggestions: This also makes an interesting pie filling to use with the pie crust recipe on p. 207.

Brownies

Can you feel your taste buds come to attention when you just picture a soft, chewy, bumpy-textured, rich, chocolaty, spattered-with-nuts brownie? It's not the same reaction you get from sharp cheese, but it's the next best thing.

Your microwave can produce brownies just as I have described, or it can produce the most tasty, mouth-watering, gourmet dog bones your pooch has ever had the pleasure of devouring. Whether your brownies are from a packaged mix or Grandma's recipe box, they still need to be microwaved properly. The Fido treat is made when you bake in square pans or fail to shield a square pan (see Box p. 202). Overbaking in the microwave will also accomplish a bricklike result, so be careful.

Use round dishes to bake brownies in (see Box below.) To avoid uneven baking, elevate your flat-bottomed dishes on an inverted saucer, don't overbake, and your brownies are a sure winner. But what about preparing them for lunchboxes?

How about baking them in cupcake papers, using a muffin pan or custard cups to support them while baking? This not only works very well, but it's so much easier for the kids to handle in school. When baking cupcakes, muffins, or brownies, be sure you use 2 papers for every cake. One paper holds the cake and the other collects the moisture that forms. As soon as baking is finished, remove the cake to a rack for cooling and discard the wet outside paper.

Chocolate brownies *look* more natural than blond brownies, but they microwave equally as well. Why not be a bit creative and add peanut butter chips, coconut, chopped maraschino cherries, miniature marshmallows, or raisins to your next batch?

Once the brownies are cool, top with your favorite frosting or glaze and package them for lunch boxes or mid-morning snacks at work or school. Take an extra minute to enclose a little note with each package telling the recipient you hope this luscious chocolate treat brightens up their day.

SHIELDING SQUARE DISHES

Round containers in the microwave tend to eliminate overcooked corners and edges. Microwaves overcook whatever sits in square corners, making it necessary to shield them from overcooking. The use of a round dish eliminates any overcooked spots.

Shielding is necessary if you are using square containers to bake in, and this is possible only if your oven allows the use of aluminum foil. There are two ways to shield.

Method 1 has you cut triangles of aluminum foil just big enough to cover each corner. Lay them on top of the container but do not overlap, crimp, or allow the foil to touch itself.

Method 2 uses a piece of foil the exact size of the top of your square container. Cut the center out of the piece of foil, leaving a 2-inch border all around the outside edges, like a picture frame. Do not mold the foil to the dish. Lay this flat sheet of foil over the dish, but, again, do not crimp, fold, overlap, or allow the metal to touch itself, as it will arch and probably start a fire and ruin your oven.

Equipment: 8- or 9-inch round baking dish, or muffin pan or custard cups (see p. 202)
Cooking time: 6 to 10 minutes (2 to 4 minutes in cupcake papers; see p. 198)
Standing time: 5 minutes
Makes: 16 squares (or 12 to 16 cupcakes)

⅔ **cup butter**
1 **cup dark brown sugar**
2 **ounces unsweetened chocolate, melted**
1 **cup all-purpose flour, sifted**
¼ **cup sweetened cocoa mix**
¼ **teaspoon salt**
½ **teaspoon baking powder**
2 **eggs, slightly beaten**
1 **teaspoon vanilla extract**
½ **cup chopped walnuts or pecans**

Lightly grease the baking dish and set aside. In a medium bowl, combine butter, brown sugar, and melted chocolate. Microwave on 50 percent power or MEDIUM for 2 to 3 minutes or until melted. Set aside.

Sift together flour, cocoa, salt, and baking powder and add to butter mixture. Stir in eggs, vanilla, and then nuts until blended.

Pour into prepared dish, **cover** with wax paper, and **elevate** flat-bottomed dish on inverted saucer, on a turntable if available, in center of microwave. (If not using a turntable, **rotate** dish ½ turn every 2 minutes.)

Microwave on HIGH for 4 to 7 minutes. Microwave just until no moist spots appear, but do not overbake.

Let **stand** on hard, heat-proof surface for 5 minutes before cutting.

Troubleshooting: If you are using a boxed mix rather than a scratch recipe, follow box directions for microwaving times but substitute a round pan. Should the boxed mix not have microwaving instructions, call or write the brownie company and I am sure they will send them to you (see p. 214).

BROWNIE CUPCAKES
These are great for lunchbox treats. Use the preceding brownie recipe.

Line muffin pan or 4 custard cups with 2 cupcake papers in each space. Fill papers no more than half full, and if using custard cups place in a circle on the floor of your microwave.

Microwave on HIGH for 2 to 4 minutes, **rotating** dish or cups ½ turn after 2 minutes.

Once done, and no moist spots appear, remove outer wet paper and place brownie cupcakes on a wire rack to cool.

Troubleshooting: Failing to use 2 cupcake papers will result in tough hard brownies, since the moisture that should be absorbed by the second paper will go instead into the brownie, where it hardens after baking.

Be sure to bake just until there is no wet batter on the top of the cake. Mark the recipe with the time and dish you used so there won't be so much guesswork the next time you use the recipe.

MELTING CHOCOLATE

If you usually mold chocolate by melting it in little jars set into a pan of water on your stove top, are you in for a surprise. To melt in the microwave, place ½ to 1 pound of chocolate caps (special chocolate for molding) or squares in a bowl and microwave on 50 percent power or MEDIUM for 3 to 4 minutes, stirring every 2 minutes. The chocolate will appear solid—then suddenly you will have smooth, hot, melted chocolate. Should your chocolate be old or too thick, add very small amounts—less than ⅛ tea-spoon at a time—of solid shortening such as Crisco, not butter. This will help smooth out the chocolate. If you microwave the chocolate on HIGH power, it will burn.

Chocolate Pudding Cake

Equipment:	deep 8-inch round or square baking dish, 4-cup glass measure
Cooking time:	9 to 11 minutes
Standing time:	10 minutes
Serves:	6

CAKE
 2 **tablespoons butter**
 1 **cup all-purpose flour**
 ¾ **cup sugar**
 2 **tablespoons cocoa**
 2 **teaspoons baking powder**
 ½ **teaspoon salt**
 ½ **cup milk**
 1 **teaspoon vanilla extract**
 ½ **cup chopped pecans or walnuts**

PUDDING
 ¾ **cup light brown sugar**
 ¼ **cup cocoa**
 1¼ **cups water**
    whipped cream for topping

Slice butter, place in a custard cup, and microwave on HIGH for 35 to 45 seconds or until melted. Sift flour, sugar, cocoa, baking powder, and salt into a medium mixing bowl. Stir in milk, melted butter, vanilla, and nuts. Pour into baking dish.

In the glass measure, mix brown sugar, cocoa, and water together well. Pour over batter but do not stir. **Shield** if using a square dish, and **elevate** flat-bottomed dish on an inverted saucer. (See Box p. 202.)

Place on turntable if available and **cover** with a paper towel, then microwave on HIGH for 9 to 11 minutes. (If not using turntable, **rotate** ½ turn after 5 minutes.)

Let **stand**, covered, on a hard, heat-proof surface for 10 minutes.

Serve in individual dessert bowls, cake down with pudding on top. Garnish with whipped cream and serve warm or cold.

Troubleshooting: If the cake is very heavy, you forgot to sift the dry ingredients, which is a *must*.

Pudding is thin when hot but thickens up as cake cools.

If pudding boils over the sides of the dish, your baking dish is too shallow.

If the cake leaves marks on the paper towel, it is only because cakes rise so high so quickly that they usually touch the towel, then go back down to their normal height. Not to worry.

Donnkenny Chocolates

My friends at the Donnkenny Company in Manhattan—I always wear their clothes and stop in to see what's new several times a year—were slightly reluctant microwavers. Everyone in the office had microwaves at home but used them only for leftovers. We got them a microwave for the office and I started teaching everyone how easy microwaving is. The gang at Donnkenny loves desserts, especially chocolate ones, and I came up with one that is easy yet looks impossible to do at the office. It's perfect for impromptu office parties and great at home, too.

Equipment:	6-cup glass measure, 16 to 18 7-ounce paper drinking cups, serving plate large enough to hold all the little mounds of cake
Cooking time:	6½ to 10½ minutes
Standing time:	2–3 minutes
Makes:	16 to 18 individual cakes

1 boxed chocolate cake mix, 2-layer size, prepared according to box directions (but substitute crème de cacao for ½ of the liquid called for)

SAUCE
- **¼ cup butter**
- **¼ cup sugar**
- **1 heaping teaspoon cornstarch**
- **¼ cup Hershey's chocolate syrup**
- **½ cup water**
- **1 tablespoon plus 1 teaspoon crème de cacao**
- **1 small container whipped topping or whipped cream chocolate curls or sprinkles**

Prepare cake mix according to box directions but substitute ½ of the liquid called for with crème de cacao. Beat batter for 4 minutes. (Batter may be prepared at home and brought into the office.) Fill 7-ounce *paper* drinking cups half full of batter and cut through the batter with a knife to eliminate any air holes. Arrange 6 to 8 cups at a time, in a circle, on the floor of the microwave.

Microwave on HIGH for 2½ to 4½ minutes or until almost dry on top, **rotating** cups once during baking.

Let cups **stand** for 2 to 3 minutes, then shake cups or use a thin knife to loosen the edges of the cake around the cup and remove mounds of cake. Place cakes upside down on a large flat dish. Whisk all sauce ingredients together in glass measure and microwave on HIGH for 4 to 6 minutes or until sauce comes to a full boil, **whisking** after 3 minutes. (Prepare sauce at home and heat at the office before pouring over mounds.)

Pour hot sauce over cake mounds and let stand for ½ hour. Top mounds with whipped cream and chocolate curls or sprinkles before serving.

Troubleshooting: If you try to remove the cake from the cups while too hot, they just won't come out. I usually just shake the cups over the serving plate several times and the cakes drop out.

Try to get the sauce over the top of each mound, as they are best when the sauce soaks into the cake.

If you want to do this at the office, bring the cake mix and sauce mix all prepared and just microwave at work.

Suggestions: You can use any flavor cake mix that you feel the chocolate sauce will complement.

Basic Pie Crust

In case you haven't tried it yet, pie crust won't brown in the microwave. You can, however, substitute orange juice for water or add several drops of yellow food coloring to the dough, which will give color to the crust once baked.

Remember, work as fast as you can with pie dough and handle it as little as possible. Always micro-cook your pie crust before adding any filling to ensure it is cooked properly.

Equipment:	pastry blender or electric mixer or food processor, rolling pin
Cooking time:	pie crust, 7 to 9 minutes; cut-outs, 2 to 3 minutes
Standing time:	none required
Makes:	1 bottom crust and lattice or cut-out tops

    1½ **cups all-purpose flour**
    ¾ **teaspoon salt**
    1 **tablespoon butter, room temperature**
    ½ **cup shortening**
    4 **to 5 tablespoons cold water or cold orange juice**
    5 **to 6 drops yellow food coloring (optional)**

Mix flour and salt together, then cut in butter and shortening using pastry blender, 2 table knives, electric mixer, or food processor. Cut together until mixture resembles coarse crumbs. Do not mix together by hand, as this tends to make a sticky dough.

Mix food coloring with cold water or cold orange juice and sprinkle, 1 tablespoon at a time, over flour mixture while stirring with a fork. Add just enough water to form a smooth ball of dough. (You don't want cracked or sticky dough.)

Clear a section of your counter, and, using your hands, flour it well. Form dough into 1 large and 1 small ball. Flatten large ball and roll out with a rolling pin to ⅛-inch-thick circle.

Gently place pastry in pie plate, being careful not to stretch. Trim and flute the edges as you would for a conventional pie, pricking dough under fluted edges, along sides, and bottom. Let crust sit 10 minutes before baking.

Microwave on 60 percent power or MEDIUM for 7 to 9 minutes, **rotating** dish ¼ turn every 2 minutes, or place on a turntable. As soon as brown spots begin to appear, crust is done. If crust bubbles up, gently push bubbles down.

Since a two-crust pie won't work, use the remaining dough to make a lattice top, or use cookie cutters to cut shapes that can be placed over fruit filling to substitute for the top crust.

Suggestions: The use of amber-colored pie plates may also help add the appearance of color to the crust.

Take whichever crust cut-outs you wish, or lattice strips, and sprinkle a mixture of 1 tablespoon sugar and ¼ teaspoon cinnamon over cut-outs. Place on wax paper and microwave on HIGH for 2 to 3 minutes until dry and puffy. Do not overcook. Loosen from wax paper while warm and place on baked fruit pie.

Meringue for Pie

No matter what you do to a meringue topping in the microwave, it won't brown. The microwave will do the cooking, but if you feel the peaks still need to have brown tips, pop it under your regular broiler for 2 to 3 minutes.

This is the basic meringue recipe my mother taught me. Sometimes I just sprinkle tossed coconut or graham cracker crumbs over it for color, while other times I use my regular broiler to give it a touch of color—the choice is yours.

Equipment:	electric mixer
Cooking time:	3 to 5 minutes
Standing time:	none required
Makes:	enough to cover a 9-inch pie

> **3 egg whites**
> **¼ teaspoon cream of tartar**
> **½ teaspoon cornstarch**
> **6 tablespoons sugar**
> **1 baked 9-inch pie, lemon or lime**

Place egg whites, cream of tartar, and cornstarch in a small deep bowl and beat with electric mixer until foamy white clouds begin to form. Add sugar 1 tablespoon at a time. Continually beat until stiff straight peaks form when you lift the beater out of the bowl. Spread onto pie, being sure to touch it to the edges of the crust. Place on turntable if available, and microwave on 50 percent power or MEDIUM for 3 to 5 minutes until set. (If not using turntable, **rotate** dish ½ turn after 2 minutes.)

For brown-tipped meringue, place under preheated broiler for 2 to 3 minutes, watching carefully.

Suggestions: Try lightly sprinkling the uncooked meringue with toasted chopped nuts, toasted coconut, cornflake crumbs, or graham cracker crumbs for color.

Holiday (or Any Day) Cheesecake

Cheesecake in the microwave? Fact or fiction? Not only is it a fact, it's quick, easy, and delicious. But before we talk filling, let's cover the crust.

A two-crust pie in the microwave just doesn't work; however, a single crust works quite well and is very flaky and puffy, but doesn't brown. To compensate for the lack of browning, you can add 3 to 4 drops of yellow food coloring, substitute orange juice for part of your liquid, brush your crust with egg yolk before microwaving, or flour a pastry cloth with whole wheat flour instead of all-purpose flour. The use of amber glass pie plates also can help put a little darker cast to the appearance of the pie crust.

Instead of a regular pastry crust, try something different with your next pie. Try graham crackers, ginger snaps, chocolate or vanilla wafers, or a crust made with 2 tablespoons of butter softened and mixed with 1½ cups of coconut.

To prepare crumbs for your pie crust, crush your cookies, wafers, or crackers in a plastic bag, then roll gently with a rolling pin. If you have a food processor fitted with a steel blade, you can make this job a real quick one. Mix about 1¼ cups of crumbs with 5 to 6 tablespoons of melted butter and 3 tablespoons of sugar, until evenly moistened. Then press your crumb mixture firmly over the bottom and sides of a 9-inch glass pie plate. Microwave on HIGH for 1½ to 2 minutes and then quickly press the crumbs against the pie plate again.

This holiday cheesecake can be served with your favorite pie filling either spread on top or served alongside, and the pumpkin cheesecake filling is really unique. Don't turn up your nose, it's delicious and so different for the fall when you can use either fresh, frozen, or canned pumpkin—but fresh is by far the tastiest.

MELTING BUTTER

To get butter to melt faster with less spatter and spitting in your microwave, slice it before melting and cover the top of the custard cup or bowl with a paper towel or paper napkin.

```
            ..❤️..
┌─────────────────────────────────────┐
│                                       │
│            CRUMB CRUST TIP            │
│  To prevent part of the crumb crust  │
│  from sticking to the dish           │
│  when serving, place a hot, moist terrycloth towel all around the │
│  outside of the pie plate and allow it to stand for 3 to 4 minutes │
│  before slicing and serving. The heat from the towel will help │
│  loosen the crust from the dish, and when you slice and remove, │
│  you won't leave half of the crust behind. │
│                                       │
└─────────────────────────────────────┘
            ••❤️••
```

CRUMB CRUST TIP

To prevent part of the crumb crust from sticking to the dish when serving, place a hot, moist terrycloth towel all around the outside of the pie plate and allow it to stand for 3 to 4 minutes before slicing and serving. The heat from the towel will help loosen the crust from the dish, and when you slice and remove, you won't leave half of the crust behind.

Equipment:	9-inch glass pie plate or round baking dish, electric mixer
Cooking time:	14 to 21 minutes
Standing time:	none required
Serves:	8

CRUST (or see p. 210 for other crusts)
- **5 tablespoons butter**
- **1¼ cups graham cracker crumbs**
- **3 tablespoons sugar, white or brown**

Microwave butter in pie plate **uncovered** on HIGH for 30 to 45 seconds until melted. (See Box p. 210.) Add crumbs and sugar, stirring with fork until evenly moistened. Spread crumb mixture evenly over bottom and sides of dish, and if dish is flat-bottomed, **elevate** on inverted saucer and place on turntable if available. (If not using turntable, **rotate** dish ½ turn once.)

Microwave uncovered on HIGH for 1½ minutes. When finished, quickly press crumbs against sides of dish.

FILLING
- **2 8-ounce packages cream cheese**
- **¾ cup sugar**
- **⅓ cup sour cream**
- **¼ teaspoon salt**
- **4 eggs**
- **2½ teaspoons fresh lemon juice (see Box p. 227)**
- **¼ teaspoon vanilla extract**

Microwave cream cheese in a large bowl **uncovered** on 50 percent power or MEDIUM until soft, about 60 seconds. Using an electric mixer, beat until smooth. Beat in sugar, sour cream, and salt. Add eggs one at a time, beating well between additions. **Stir** in lemon juice and vanilla.

Elevate flat-bottomed bowl on inverted saucer and place on turntable if available. Microwave filling uncovered on HIGH for 4 to 6 minutes until very hot, stirring every 2 minutes. (If not using turntable, **rotate** ¼ turn every 2 minutes.) Pour hot cheese filling over crumb crust and spread evenly. Elevate on inverted saucer and place on turntable if available. (If not using turntable, rotate dish ½ turn every 4 minutes.)

Microwave uncovered on 50 percent power or MEDIUM for 7 to 12 minutes or until filling is almost set. The center of the filling should be a bit wobbly when the dish is jiggled.

Filling will become firm as it cools. Cool completely and refrigerate, **covered**, for 6 to 8 hours before serving. (See Box p. 211.)

Troubleshooting: If your cheese filling comes over the sides of the pie plate while baking, it is because you forgot to put the microwave power down to 50 percent or MEDIUM and are cooking your cheesecake on HIGH. The microwave cooks so quickly that on HIGH the cheese boils right over.

If you find the center of the cheesecake not quite set enough, you could have forgotten to elevate your flat-bottomed pie plate.

Suggestions: Try frosting the top of a chilled cheesecake with 1 cup sour cream or top with two cups fresh strawberries, raspberries, blueberries, or sliced peaches.

Pumpkin Cheesecake

I am not a lover of pumpkin pie but I do make them for Thanksgiving. I was giving a class one Thanksgiving and I had a small bowl of leftover pumpkin. I brought it to class and the girls had a ball tasting this new recipe until we got all the ingredients just right.

Equipment:	electric mixer, 9-inch glass pie plate
Cooking time:	14 to 21 minutes
Standing time:	none required
Serves:	8 to 10

CRUST
5 tablespoons butter
1¼ cups graham cracker or ginger snap crumbs
3 tablespoons sugar

Microwave butter in pie plate, **uncovered**, on HIGH for 45 to 55 seconds. (See Box p. 210.) Add crumbs and sugar, stirring with a fork until evenly moistened.

Spread crumb mixture evenly over bottom and sides of dish. **Elevate** flat-bottomed dish on inverted saucer and place on turntable if available. (If not using turntable, **rotate** dish ½ turn after 60 seconds.) Microwave uncovered on HIGH for 90 seconds. As soon as oven turns off, press crumbs against the dish.

FILLING
2 8-ounce packages cream cheese
½ cup sugar
¼ cup sour cream
1 cup canned, frozen, or fresh pumpkin
⅛ cup light molasses (optional)
3 eggs
1 teaspoon vanilla extract
¼ teaspoon ground ginger
2 teaspoons cinnamon
¼ teaspoon nutmeg
¼ teaspoon ground cloves

Remove cream cheese from metal wrapper, place in bowl, and microwave on 50 percent power or MEDIUM for 1 minute or until soft. Beat with electric mixer until smooth. Beat in sugar, sour cream, pumpkin, and molasses. Add eggs one at a time, beating very well between additions. Stir in vanilla and spices.

Elevate bowl on inverted saucer and microwave **uncovered** on HIGH for 4 to 6 minutes or until very hot, stirring every 2 minutes. Pour hot filling over crumb crust and spread evenly.

Elevate flat-bottomed dish on inverted saucer and place on

turntable if available. (If not using a turntable, **rotate** dish ½ turn every 3 minutes.) Microwave uncovered on 50 percent power or MEDIUM for 7 to 12 minutes or until filling is almost set. The center should still be a bit wobbly, as it will firm up as cake cools. Cool completely and refrigerate, **covered**, for 6 to 8 hours before serving. (See Crumb Crust Tip Box p. 211.)

Troubleshooting: If your pumpkin filling rises over your pan and comes out all over the oven, it is because you forgot to reduce the power to 50 percent or MEDIUM.

If the center of your pie is not set enough, it may be because you forgot to elevate your flat-bottomed dish.

CAKE MIXES

If you've been wishing you could contact the individual cake mix companies, wish no more. Each major company has a toll-free telephone number you can call, or on each box you will find an address you can write to and request any microwaving information they have on their products.

The booklet you receive when you call Betty Crocker, at 1-800-328-6787, is loaded with all kinds of recipes using Bisquick, Gold Medal flour, and their various boxed cake mixes.

You can reach Pillsbury at 1-800-328-4466; in my experience, their mixes produce the best results in the microwave. I have never received any additional mailings from Betty Crocker, but Pillsbury has sent updated recipe pamphlets. I never have enough new recipes to try, and I am sure you will enjoy your copies.

For those of you who regularly use Duncan Hines cake mixes, you can reach them at 1-800-543-7276; in Ohio call 1-800-582-3945. Be sure to ask them to put you on their mailing list so you will receive updates on their products.

Pineapple Upside-Down Cake

I thought you might be interested in my very first experiment in microwave cake baking. Since pineapple upside-down cake was liked by all, I tried a one-layer version using an 8 × 8-inch square pan. It was fun and came out pretty well, but I figured that there had to be a reason why the edges of the square cake were sort of dry and hard—of course at this point I didn't know about shielding.

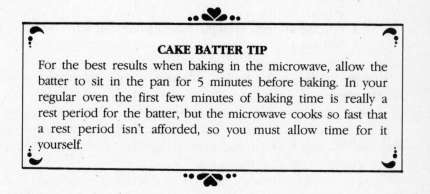

CAKE BATTER TIP

For the best results when baking in the microwave, allow the batter to sit in the pan for 5 minutes before baking. In your regular oven the first few minutes of baking time is really a rest period for the batter, but the microwave cooks so fast that a rest period isn't afforded, so you must allow time for it yourself.

I went to my file of family recipes and found my mother-in-law's recipe for pineapple upside-down cake. Her recipe also called for using a single-layer 9 × 13-inch pan. I did as much reading as I could and found out that the microwaves overcook anything in square corners, making round pans a much better choice. If round works well, I thought, how about a bundt shape?

Sure enough, the bundt shape microwaves beautifully. The brown sugar glaze that cascades down the sides of the cake adds color to an otherwise very bright yellow cake. Once it's inverted onto a serving plate, people don't really believe you baked this cake in a microwave.

I always keep an extra jar of cherries in the fridge, a yellow-cake mix on the shelf, and a can of pineapple slices beside it, as my "emergency company is coming" dessert, so I am never caught unable to say, "Dessert, hot out of the microwave, in twenty minutes."

Equipment: 12-cup bundt pan, electric mixer
Cooking time: 17 to 19 minutes
Standing time: 5 minutes
Serves: 8 to 10

⅓ **cup butter**
⅔ **cup firmly packed light brown sugar**
1 **8½-ounce can sliced pineapple, drained and juice reserved**
8 **maraschino cherries**
1 **boxed yellow-cake mix with pudding, 2-layer size**
3 **eggs**
⅓ **cup oil**
1 **cup liquid (reserved pineapple juice and water to make a full cup)**

Grease and lightly sugar bundt pan, using either granulated or light brown sugar.

In a small bowl, microwave butter for 35 to 50 seconds and mix in brown sugar. Press brown sugar mixture into bottom of greased and sugared bundt pan. Attractively arrange fruit and press pineapple slices and cherries into brown sugar.

Prepare cake mix with eggs, oil, and pineapple juice and water, beating at medium speed with electric mixer for 4 to 5 minutes. Pour over pineapple slices and let sit for 5 minutes.

Microwave on 30 percent power or LOW for 11 minutes, on a turntable if available, then change power to HIGH and microwave for 6 to 8 minutes or until cake comes away from sides of pan and no raw batter spots appear. (If not using turntable, **rotate** cake ¼ turn every 5 minutes.)

(If you have only HIGH on your oven, microwave for 12 to 14 minutes on HIGH or until the cake comes away from the sides of the pan and no moist spots appear.)

Let **stand** on a hard heat-proof surface for 5 minutes, then invert onto serving plate. Serve warm or cold with a mound of whipped cream if you choose.

Troubleshooting: Butter may appear to glaze tops of pineapple slices when cake is inverted, as some of the brown sugar is still in the pan. Scoop out any brown sugar and drizzle it over the top of the cake.

If you are baking with only HIGH power, be sure your bundt pan is 12 cups, and don't fill over half-full or the cake will rise over the top of the pan and onto the floor of your microwave.

Single-Layer Pineapple Upside-Down Cake

Equipment:	8 × 8-inch square or 8- or 9-inch round baking dish, electric mixer
Cooking time:	9½ to 11½ minutes
Standing time:	5 minutes
Serves:	6

- ¼ **cup butter**
- ½ **cup firmly packed light brown sugar**
- 1 **8½-ounce can sliced pineapple, drained and juice reserved**
- 8 **maraschino cherries**
- 1 **9-ounce single-layer yellow-cake mix**
- 2 **eggs**
  reserved pineapple juice plus water to make liquid called for on box directions

Combine butter and brown sugar in baking dish. (See Box p. 202 for square dishes.) Microwave on HIGH for 60 to 90 seconds or until butter and sugar melt. Stir together well.

Arrange pineapple rings in brown sugar mixture, placing maraschino cherries in center of rings and where they meet. Set dish aside. Blend cake mix, eggs, and pineapple juice and water in medium mixing bowl with electric mixer for 4 minutes. Pour batter evenly over fruit.

If using a flat-bottomed dish, **elevate** on inverted saucer and place on turntable if available. (If not using turntable, **rotate** dish ½ turn after 5 minutes.)

Microwave for 8½ to 10 minutes on HIGH until a wooden toothpick inserted into the center of the cake comes out clean.

Let **stand** on a hard, heat-proof surface for 5 minutes, then immediately invert onto serving platter and remove dish. Serve warm or cool and add whipped topping if desired.

Troubleshooting: Do not overbake cake or it will toughen.

Brown sugar may remain in pan once inverted, so spoon over hot cake and let it drizzle down the sides.

FILLED CAKES

My son Bill once asked me, "Why is it, Mom, when we buy an ice cream cake at the ice cream store it never has any cake with it?" That was a really good question that I couldn't answer, so I set to work with my microwave to see what I could do about getting a cake and ice cream into one shape.

I remembered my mother making a filled cake using this method, so I tried it one Halloween as a surprise for the kids' afterschool treat. I used a chocolate cake, pumpkin-flavored ice cream, and covered the outside in chocolate whipped cream. Rich it was, and the kids loved it.

Try your hand, using any flavor cake and ice cream your family prefers. If the idea sounds interesting but you're not into ice cream, I have a few other ideas that may spark your interest.

Most cake-mix manufacturers suggest you begin the baking process on 30 percent power or LOW, then change to HIGH. If your oven has only HIGH, you must be sure the pan is not more than ½ full and bake it for 10 to 13 minutes—the time varies according to the flavor. To be sure of the exact directions, call or write the cake-mix company whose brand you prefer (see p. 214).

TESTING CAKES FOR DONENESS

To test the doneness of your cake, first make sure it is coming away from the sides of the pan. Next, check that there are no wet batter spots on the top of the cake. You can then test with a toothpick. If all three things test out, remove the cake from the microwave.

STANDING TIME IN BAKING

Standing time in cake baking is very important. The last part of the cake to cook is the bottom, and most of this is done in standing time. Once the baking process is finished, remove the cake to a hard, heat-proof surface—not a wire rack—because you want to trap as much heat as possible in the cake. Let the cake stand for 10 minutes so that the bottom will cook completely. If after the 10-minute standing period you invert the cake onto a serving plate and there is still raw batter on the bottom, put the cake back in the pan and microwave on HIGH for another 2 minutes and allow to stand again.

SOFTENING ICE CREAM

To soften hard frozen ice cream, place the container on the floor of your oven and microwave on HIGH for 30 seconds, then let stand for 2 minutes. Repeat this process once or twice until the ice cream reaches the proper consistency. Please be careful and don't melt it.

Chocolate Ice Cream Cake

Equipment:	electric mixer, bundt pan (preferably 12-cup)
Cooking time:	17 to 19 minutes
Standing time:	none required
Serves:	8 to 10

1 **box chocolate cake mix, prepared according to box directions**
2 **pints ice cream, any flavor**
2 **tablespoons cocoa**
1 **8-ounce container whipped topping or fresh whipped cream**

Prepare cake mix according to box directions, beating for 4 minutes. Prepare bundt pan by greasing and sugaring (see Box p. 217). Place cake batter in pan and allow to sit for 5 minutes.

Place filled pan on turntable if available, and microwave on 30 percent power or LOW for 11 minutes. Then, change power to HIGH for

6 to 8 minutes or until cake comes away from the sides of the pan and no wet spots appear. (Microwave for 12 minutes if your oven has only HIGH power. If not using turntable, **rotate** pan ½ turn every 4 minutes.)

Let **stand** on a hard, heat-proof surface for 10 minutes, then invert pan onto serving plate and cool.

When cake is completely cool, slice off a 2-inch top and put it aside. Leaving the sides and bottom of the cake intact, scoop out all the remaining cake and freeze the shell.

Soften ice cream in microwave (see Box p. 219) and stuff into frozen cake shell. Replace cake top and freeze.

Combine cocoa with whipped topping and frost frozen cake. Decorate with sprinkles, chocolate shots, or chocolate shavings. If you prefer, melt chocolate blocks and drizzle different colors on the frozen cake instead of whipped topping (see Box p. 204).

Suggestions: Any flavor cake mix and ice cream will do—your choice.

Island Dream

Equipment: electric mixer, bundt pan (preferably 12-cup)
Cooking time: 16½ to 18 minutes
Standing time: 10 minutes
Serves: 8 to 10

1 **box yellow, lemon, cherry, or pineapple cake mix, prepared according to box directions**
2 **pints cherry vanilla ice cream or rainbow sherbet**
1 **12-ounce container whipped topping or 1 pint whipping cream, whipped**
1 **8-ounce bag shredded coconut**
11 **slices pineapple**
11 **maraschino cherries**
1 **fresh pineapple top**

Prepare cake mix according to box directions but beat for 4 minutes. Grease and sugar bundt pan, place batter in pan, and allow to sit for 5 minutes.

Place on turntable if available and microwave on 30 percent power or LOW for 11 minutes. Change power to HIGH and microwave for 5½ to 7 minutes or until cake comes away from the sides of the pan and no wet spots appear. (If your oven has only HIGH, bake for 12 minutes. If not using turntable, **rotate** pan ½ turn every 4 minutes.)

Let **stand** on a hard, heat-proof surface for 10 minutes, then invert onto serving platter and cool.

Once cake is cooled, slice off a 2-inch top slice and set aside. Leaving the bottom and sides intact, scoop out the inside of the cake, making a hollow shell, and freeze.

Soften the ice cream (see Box p. 219) and scoop it into the frozen shell, replace cake top, and frost with whipped topping. Sprinkle coconut over topping and cut pineapple slices in half. Stick the cut ends of half the pineapple slices into the cake, making little handles all along the bottom of the cake. Repeat this process along top edge of cake. Press cherries along bottom edges between pineapple slices. Freeze until ready to serve.

When ready to serve, remove some of the leaves at the bottom of the pineapple top and place it into the center opening in the bundt cake.

Strawberry Heaven

Equipment:	electric mixer, bundt pan (preferably 12-cup)
Cooking time:	16½ to 18 minutes
Standing time:	10 minutes
Serves:	8 to 10

1 **boxed yellow or strawberry-flavored cake mix, prepared according to box directions**
1 **pint whipping cream, whipped, or one 16-ounce container whipped topping**
1 **pint frozen strawberries, drained**
1 **pint fresh strawberries, washed and hulled**

Prepare cake mix according to box directions and beat for 4 minutes. Grease and sugar bundt pan, pour in batter, and let sit for 5 minutes.

Place on turntable if available. (If not using turntable, **rotate** pan ½ turn every 4 minutes.)

Microwave on 30 percent power or LOW for 11 minutes, then change power to HIGH and microwave for 5½ to 7 minutes or until cake pulls away from the sides of the pan and no wet spots appear. (If your oven has only HIGH, microwave for 12 minutes.)

Let **stand** for 10 minutes on a hard, heat-proof surface, then invert onto serving platter and cool.

When cake is cool, remove a 2-inch slice off the top and set aside. Leaving the sides and bottom intact, scoop out all the remaining cake.

Mix drained strawberries into half the whipped topping and place in cake shell. Replace top and frost with remaining whipped topping and decorate with whole fresh strawberries all over the top and sides.

Suggestions: Substitute any other fruit for the strawberries, being careful to drain off any juice.

Choco-Mocha Surprise

Equipment:	electric mixer, bundt pan (preferably 12-cup)
Cooking time:	16½ to 17½ minutes
Standing time:	10 minutes
Serves:	10

CAKE
- 1 box chocolate cake mix with pudding
- ½ cup crème de cacao
- ¾ cup water
- ½ cup vegetable oil
- 3 eggs

FILLING
- 1 pint heavy cream or 1 16-ounce container whipped topping
- 1 heaping teaspoon confectioner's sugar
- 2 teaspoons instant powdered chocolate-coffee beverage
- 1 tablespoon crème de cacao
- 1 banana, sliced thin
- chocolate shots or shavings for decoration

Grease bundt pan and dust with sugar or cocoa.

In a large mixing bowl put cake mix, crème de cacao, water, oil, and eggs. Beat on MEDIUM for 4 minutes, then pour into prepared pan and let sit for 5 minutes.

Place pan on turntable if available and microwave for 11 minutes on 30 percent power or LOW. Change power to HIGH and bake for 5½ to 6½ minutes or until cake comes away from the pan and no wet spots appear. (If not using turntable, **rotate** pan ¼ turn every 3 minutes; if using only HIGH power, bake for 12 minutes.)

Let **stand** for 10 minutes on a hard, heat-proof surface, then invert onto serving platter and cool.

Once cool, cut a 2-inch slice off the top off the cake and set aside. Leaving bottom and sides intact, scoop out the insides of the cake.

If using whipping cream, add cream, sugar, and instant chocolate-coffee beverage to a medium bowl. Beat until peaks are stiff. Fold in crème de cacao. If using whipped topping, just fold in instant coffee and crème de cacao.

In cake shell, spread a layer of mocha cream, then top with bananas. Finish filling shell with mocha cream and replace top. Frost cake with mocha cream and decorate with chocolate shots or shavings.

Marbled Hint of Mint

This is a fun cake that has (you guessed it) a hint of mint to the flavor—it can be served frosted or just dusted with confectioner's sugar.

Equipment: electric mixer, bundt pan (preferably 12-cup)
Cooking time: 16½ to 17½ minutes
Standing time: 10 minutes
Serves: 8 to 10

  1 **boxed yellow-cake mix, 2-layer size**
  1 **box instant pistachio pudding, 4-serving size**
  4 **eggs**
  ½ **cup water**
  ½ **cup crème de menthe**
  ½ **cup vegetable oil**
  ½ **teaspoon almond extract**
  ⅓ **cup chocolate syrup**

Grease and sugar bundt pan and set aside. (If using a tube pan or small bundt, never fill more than ½ full; reserve leftover batter for cupcakes.)

Combine cake mix, pudding, eggs, water, crème de menthe, oil, and extract in a mixing bowl. Blend ingredients on LOW speed, then change to MEDIUM for 4 minutes. Pour all but 1 cup batter into prepared pan.

Combine reserved batter and chocolate syrup, blending well. Marble chocolate batter through pistachio batter with a table knife.

Place on turntable if available and microwave on 30 percent power or LOW for 11 minutes. Increase power to HIGH and continue microwaving for 5½ to 6½ minutes or until there is no raw batter on top of the cake and it begins to come away from the sides of the pan. (If not using turntable, **rotate** ½ turn halfway through baking time; if your oven has only HIGH, bake for 12 to 14 minutes.)

Let **stand** for 10 minutes on a hard, heat-proof surface, then invert onto a serving platter. When cool, dust with confectioner's sugar or spread with your favorite frosting.

Easy Holiday Fruitcake

Thanks to all my wonderful readers in Connecticut for sending me their traditional fruitcake recipes, I have come up with the alternative to the usual tired, heavy, rum-soaked fruitcake that takes hours to bake in a conventional oven. Mine is lighter and can hold whatever varieties of fruit and nuts the baker enjoys.

I prefer baking in a round container with an open center as opposed to the conventional loaf shape. The loaf shape in the micro-wave has a tendency to overcook in the square corners and along the edges. If you don't have a bundt or tube pan for the microwave, you can improvise by using a deep round micro-safe baking pan or glass bowl, with a glass of water in the center.

You must leave the glass, which should be filled at least halfway, in the dish until the cake has finished baking and gone through standing time. Be sure to grease and sugar the outside of the glass just as if it were part of the pan; failing to do so will cause the cake to stick.

Several of the recipes I've received called for using a packaged nut, date, or banana bread mix. My thought was to use a gingerbread mix for color and flavor. If you want to try this method, begin with the bread mix of your choice, and to it add 1 egg, 1 cup water, 1 cup raisins, chopped nuts, and a 16-ounce container of fruit mix for fruitcakes. Line a glass loaf pan with wax paper and pour in the batter. You must shield the edges of your loaf pan or use an 8-inch round pan. (See Box p. 202.)

Elevate the pan and microwave on 50 percent power or MEDIUM for 9 minutes, rotating the dish ½ turn every 3 minutes. Then increase the power to HIGH and microwave for 4 to 7 minutes or until the center tests done with a toothpick. Let stand on a hard, heat-proof surface for 5 to 10 minutes before removing from pan to cool.

I put together many of the ideas I received and came up with the following version. I am trying to make it as simple and easy as possible to encourage more of you to try your new skills. I have mentioned many different kinds of fruits and nuts; feel free to substitute any and all of your favorites in my recipe. I am using orange liqueur but you may substitute orange juice or just water for all the liquid. Once you have a basic recipe, just make changes to suit your individual palate.

Equipment: electric mixer, bundt pan (preferably 12-cup)
Cooking time: 17 to 20 minutes
Standing time: 10 minutes
Serves: 8 to 10

- 1 **boxed spice or applesauce spice cake mix**
- 1 **cup seedless raisins**
- 1 **cup chopped pecans and/or walnuts**
- 1 **16-ounce container candied fruit**
- 3 **eggs**
- ½ **cup orange liqueur (balance of liquid required on cake mix directions should be either water or orange juice)**
- ¼ **teaspoon cinnamon**
- ¼ **teaspoon ground cloves**
- ⅛ **teaspoon nutmeg**
- 2 **tablespoons apple jelly**
- 6 **maraschino cherries**
- 24 **whole white almonds**

Prepare bundt pan by greasing and dusting with brown or granulated sugar. Place raisins, nuts, and candied fruit in a bowl and add 3 tablespoons of the dry cake mix, tossing together until mixed and coated. Set aside.

In a large mixing bowl, place balance of cake mix, eggs, liquid, cinnamon, cloves, and nutmeg. Beat with electric mixer for 4 minutes on MEDIUM.

Blend fruit into batter, mixing until well blended. Pour batter into prepared pan and let sit for 5 minutes. If using smaller than a 12-cup bundt pan, be sure to fill pans only ½ full. Place on turntable if available. (If not using turntable, **rotate** dish ¼ turn every 3 minutes.)

Microwave on 30 percent power or LOW for 11 minutes. Increase power to HIGH and bake for 6 to 9 minutes until the cake pulls away from the sides of the pan and there are no moist spots visible.

Let **stand** on a hard, heat-proof surface for 10 minutes, then invert onto a serving platter and glaze with apple jelly. Place whole maraschino cherries and white almonds along the top to form flowers.

Troubleshooting: If you do not mix the nuts and fruit with the dry cake mix, they will stick together and clump up in the bottom of the cake.

Let stand for no longer than 15 minutes before inverting onto your serving platter to avoid cake sticking to the pan.

ITALIAN EASTER PIES

A traditional part of most Italian Easter tables are the Ricotta Cheese and Italian Ham Pies. I had made them the regular way but never attempted them in the microwave until Easter 1985, when I felt confident that I knew enough people who had eaten and baked these pies for so many years that they would be able to help me get them to taste perfect.

What a job I had converting them to the microwave! The filling for the Ricotta Cheese Pie is supposed to be very heavy—almost the consistency of soft ice cream—when you put it into the crust. Because it is a milk product, the actual cooking of the pie is done on a reduced power setting. I used 50 percent power or MEDIUM to do the actual cooking of the filling in the crust and found it worked very well.

In one experiment, I beat the filling and put it right into the shell without heating it first. This produced filling cascading over the pie pan and onto the oven floor. To solve this problem, I heated the filling on HIGH for 4 to 5 minutes, stirring every minute until it was hot. Then I placed it over the graham cracker crust and microwaved at 50 percent power or MEDIUM. It bakes only until the cheese is set, as it completely firms up while cooling.

The crust on the Italian Ham Pie was a problem. It had a bread dough crust that came out paler than the pie and not looking as nice as I would have liked. So I baked just the filling in a pan alone. The results were wonderful and very tasty.

I used several different types of meat in my pie, but if your family likes only ham or salami, using just those varieties of meat will achieve the same great flavor and appearance.

I received many letters from people who had baked the Italian Ham Pie with a crust for more years than they cared to remember and all said the crustless version done in the microwave was superb. You be the judge.

CITRUS JUICE TIP

To get the most juice from your citrus fruit, microwave lemons, limes, oranges, and grapefruit for 15 to 20 seconds per piece of fruit on the floor of your microwave. If doing several at one time, place in a circle. Allow fruit to stand for 1 to 2 minutes, then roll between the palms of your hands. The fruit will give a surprising amount of juice along with added flavor to both the juice and the zest (the colored part of the skin).

Ricotta Cheese Pie

Equipment:	9-inch glass pie plate or round baking dish, electric mixer
Cooking time:	20 to 35 minutes
Standing time:	none required
Serves:	10

CRUST
   3 **tablespoons butter**
   ¾ **cup graham cracker crumbs**
   2 **tablespoons confectioner's sugar**

Microwave butter in pie plate or baking dish **uncovered** on HIGH 30 to 45 seconds or until melted. Add crumbs and sugar, stirring with a fork until evenly moistened.

Spread crumb mixture evenly over bottom of dish, **elevate** flat-bottomed dish on inverted saucer, and microwave uncovered on HIGH for 1½ minutes. Place dish on turntable if available, or **rotate** dish ½ turn after 1 minute.

FILLING
   3 **pounds whole-milk ricotta cheese**
   3 **large eggs**
   ¾ **cup confectioner's sugar**
   ½ **cup milk**
   2 **tablespoons flour**
   1 **teaspoon lemon extract**
   1 **teaspoon vanilla extract**
      grated zest of 1 lemon (see Box p. 227)

Beat ricotta cheese and eggs until smooth in large bowl. Add sugar, milk, flour, flavorings, and lemon zest. Beat together until well blended. Place bowl on turntable if available and microwave on HIGH for 4 to 6 minutes until cheese mixture is hot. (If not using turntable, **rotate** dish ½ turn after 3 minutes.) **Stir** well every minute. Mixture will be thick and creamy.

Place hot mixture into prebaked crumb crust and **elevate** on inverted saucer. Microwave on 50 percent power or MEDIUM for 15 to 18 minutes or until cheese is set and center does not look soft. Let cool completely and refrigerate.

Troubleshooting: If cheese mixture boils over sides of pan, you either did not get it hot enough before placing the mixture in the crust, or you microwaved on HIGH instead of 50 percent or MEDIUM.

If the top of the pie is unevenly cooked, you need a turntable in your microwave.

If the center of the pie is not as firm as the outside edges when served, you may have forgotten to elevate it.

Crustless Italian Ham Pie

Equipment:	2 8-inch glass pie plates or 2 10-inch round casserole dishes
Cooking time:	18 to 21 minutes
Standing time:	5 minutes
Serves:	10

1 pound ham, salami, pepperoni, or any other ham of your choice, cubed very small
5 eggs
1 basket cheese,* cut in small cubes
⅛ pound grated Romano cheese
pepper to taste (about 1 teaspoon)

Place eggs in large bowl and beat. To beaten eggs add all other ingredients, folding together well by hand, being careful not to break the cheese.

Place mixture in pie plate or round casserole dish and **elevate** on inverted saucer. (If using crust, place filling in prebaked crust.) Bake for the first 3 minutes on HIGH, and then reduce to 50 percent power or MEDIUM and continue baking for 15 to 19 minutes until eggs are set and not runny.

Let **stand** on a hard, heat-proof surface for 5 minutes and serve warm or cold. Be sure to refrigerate any leftovers.

Suggestions: Mixture may be made the day before, tightly wrapped, refrigerated, and baked just prior to serving.

Basic Butter Cookie Batter

I never know just when, but it seems whenever the kitchen is completely cleaned up, someone wants a 10:00 P.M. snack. On those occasions I open the refrigerator, pull out my hidden bowl of cookie

---

*Basket cheese is a fresh, creamy cheese packed in a basket, sold around Easter in Italian markets and specialty stores.

batter, and 2 to 3 minutes later a glass of milk awaits a plate of cooling cookies. How did you do that, Mom? I'll never tell!

Cookie batter stays fresh in the fridge for 2 to 3 weeks. I always roll the entire batch into balls before storing; then I need only a sheet of wax paper on the floor of my microwave to produce my late-night snack.

The most important thing I can tell you when microwaving is always to start with the shortest amount of baking time the recipe gives. You can always put food back into the microwave and cook it longer, but once your cookies are burned, it's all over, whether your sweet tooth has been satisfied or not.

COOKIE TIPS

For light, fluffy cookies, beat batter well with an electric mixer.

For evenly baked cookies, uniformly sized and shaped things cook more evenly in the microwave. Preroll the entire batch into 27 equal-size balls. Place 9 cookies (3 rows of 3 cookies each) evenly spaced on either a sheet of wax paper or a micro-safe cookie sheet.

To prevent burning, start with the shorter amount of baking time, and if uncooked spots remain on the tops of the cookies, continue baking at 20-second intervals until tops of cookies are baked.

To eliminate burned cookies, microwave each batch for only 2 minutes on HIGH and check for wet spots, then continue baking at 20-second intervals until dry. Remember, cookies continue cooking for about 30 to 60 seconds after being removed from the oven, and with their high sugar content they will burn if overcooked. Cook just until there are no raw dough spots on top of the cookies. Be sure to note how long a batch of 9 takes in your oven so you will be prepared for other batches.

Cooking time: 2 to 3 minutes per batch of 9 cookies
Standing time: none required
Makes: 27 cookies

½ cup butter
½ cup sugar
 1 egg
1½ cups all-purpose flour
½ teaspoon cream of tartar
¼ teaspoon baking soda
¼ teaspoon salt
½ teaspoon almond extract
½ teaspoon vanilla extract

Soften butter and cream together with sugar and egg until well blended. Add flour, cream of tartar, baking soda, salt, vanilla, and almond extract to butter mixture. Beat until well blended and chill until firm.

Using 1 tablespoon of dough per cookie, roll dough into 27 balls. (See Box p. 230.) Place 9 balls (3 rows of 3 cookies each) on wax paper cut to fit the floor of your microwave.

Bake on HIGH for 2 to 3 minutes until just set and no raw dough spots appear. (See Box p. 230.)

VARIATIONS

THUMB-PRINT COOKIES. Roll balls of dough in finely chopped nuts (I prefer peanuts, but use your favorite) and bake. As soon as the cookies are baked, make a depression in the top of the cookie with your thumb and fill with jelly.

CHOCOLATE CHIP. Substitute ½ cup packed dark brown sugar for granulated or use granulated plus 2 teaspoons cocoa. Substitute ½ teaspoon vanilla extract for almond and add 1 cup chocolate chips.

PEANUT BUTTER CHIP. Substitute ½ cup packed dark brown sugar for granulated, and ½ teaspoon vanilla for almond flavoring, then add 1 cup peanut butter chips.

CHOCOLATE PEANUT-BUTTER CHIP. Substitute ½ cup brown sugar for granulated and ½ teaspoon vanilla extract for almond. Add ½ cup chocolate chips, ½ cup peanut butter chips, and ¼ cup chopped nuts.

CHOCOLATE. Substitute ½ teaspoon vanilla extract for almond and add 2 teaspoons cocoa.

LEMON. Substitute 2 teaspoons fresh lemon juice for almond extract and add 1 teaspoon grated lemon zest.

COCONUT. Stir in 1 cup plain, toasted, or colored flaked coconut.

ORANGE-RAISIN. Substitute 1 teaspoon orange extract for almond and add ½ cup raisins and 1 teaspoon grated orange zest.

SPICE. Substitute ½ teaspoon vanilla extract for almond, add 2 tablespoons molasses, 1 teaspoon cinnamon, and ¼ teaspoon each of nutmeg, ginger, and cloves.

Having had my share of cookie crumblers always wanting something different, I started making my own "dress-up" cookies.

I always keep a package of both chocolate and vanilla wafers, a bag of marshmallows, a can of ready-to-spread frosting, a jar of Marshmallow Fluff, and various-flavored chocolate bars on hand.

At a moment's notice I can slice a marshmallow in half, place it on top of a wafer cookie, and microwave on 50 percent power or MEDIUM for 15 to 30 seconds or until it melts. Place an opposite-flavor wafer on top and you have an instant cookie treat. When doing this, I always arrange my cookies on a paper plate in a circle. The paper plate catches the moisture, and by placing them in a circle I get more even melting.

You can leave the top cookie off and place a piece of chocolate bar over the marshmallow, which melts, quickly adding a frosting. A crunch bar or chocolate peanut bar also adds a different flavor to the marshmallow. Spread quickly with a knife and watch the eyes light up.

Now get creative and spread the wafers with Marshmallow Fluff or ready-to-spread frosting. Add M & M's, nuts, chocolate pieces, or sprinkles for a different look and flavor.

Another idea is to microwave the frosting or fluff for 15 to 30 seconds on 50 percent power or MEDIUM, and once it starts to melt add a second cookie to make a sandwich. You can make a game out of having the kids design their own combinations.

One final thought is to mix colored sprinkles into the frosting before adding it to the cookies. A combination of many different colors is so pretty and your little ones will love the "dressed up" effect.

Jams and Jellies

If you would love to make jelly and jam but don't have the time, couldn't possibly use the whole batch, don't have canning jars, and aren't interested in standing over that hot steamy pot of boiling fruit, have I got a solution for you.

Micro-jam is just for you small-batch, out-of-time, no-fuss cooks. It is also for those of you wanting homemade jams or quick gifts. A pretty footed glass or coffee mug makes a great little "hello" gift. I will give you both refrigerator and freezer instructions, but just be sure the container you use is freezer-safe.

Micro-jam is so easy that you can prepare it fresh before breakfast. I buy my fruit at the peak of ripeness: less-ripe fruit will not have the same sweetness when used in jam. Instead of making all the batches immediately, I prepare my fruit by cleaning, peeling, hulling, chopping, or mashing, and freeze the prepared fruit in measured packages.

My freezer then has measured and labeled packages of fruit ready for me to add sugar, pectin, and lemon juice, making jam preparation a snap. Let me point out how important it is that your fruit is uniform in size. If you're chopping it, the pieces must be even and uniform; if it's mashed (a potato masher works beautifully), be sure all fruit is completely pulverized.

If you decide to store the jam for any length of time, you must sterilize your jars. Jar sterilization has to be done on top of your stove, as the microwave cannot provide the constant high temperatures needed and cannot melt the paraffin that is used to seal certain types of canning jars.

Before starting your jam, be sure you are using a large enough container to prepare it. Once boiling, the jam will go over the sides if the container is not large enough, so be sure never to use anything smaller than 2 quarts—and the larger the better.

Tiny Batch
Strawberry Fridge Jam

Equipment:	2- or 3-quart deep casserole dish or bowl, potato masher
Cooking time:	8 to 9 minutes
Standing time:	none required
Makes:	1½ cups

2 cups or 1 pint ripe strawberries, cleaned and hulled
1½ cups sugar
1½ teaspoons powdered fruit pectin

Using potato masher, completely mash cleaned, hulled berries. Place in casserole dish or bowl and stir in sugar until completely absorbed. Add pectin and stir very well.

Cover with wax paper and microwave on HIGH 3 to 4 minutes or until mixture comes to a full boil. Stir and reduce to 60 percent power or MEDIUM and continue microwaving, **uncovered**, for 5 minutes until mixture is slightly thickened. It will completely thicken as it cools.

Skim off any foam with metal spoon and pour into glasses. Once cool, cover with plastic wrap and refrigerate. If using canning jars, be sure to sterilize and seal jars properly.

Suggestions: You may substitute 1 10-to-12-ounce package of frozen strawberries.

Medium Batch
Strawberry Freezer Jam

Equipment:	deep 3-quart casserole dish or bowl, freezer-safe jars, potato masher
Cooking time:	9 to 17 minutes
Standing time:	none required
Makes:	3½ cups

1 **quart fresh strawberries, cleaned and hulled, to make 2½ cups mashed berries**
½ **box powdered fruit pectin (1¾-ounce size)**
3 **cups sugar**

In casserole dish or bowl, mash strawberries. Add pectin and stir thoroughly. **Cover** with wax paper and microwave on HIGH for 5 to 9 minutes or until mixture comes to a full boil all around the edges and center of dish. Stir twice during cooking time.

Completely mix in sugar and microwave **uncovered** on HIGH for 4 to 7 minutes until mixture comes to a full rolling boil, stirring every minute to prevent mixture from boiling over. After mixture comes to full boil, boil for 1 minute.

Skim off foam with a metal spoon and let jam cool slightly. Pour into freezer containers and freeze. Some canning jars can be used in the freezer, but be sure to check that they are freezer-safe before using.

Suggestions: Be sure to measure pectin carefully and label left-over for next batch. You may substitute 20 ounces of frozen strawberries for fresh.

Full Batch Strawberry Jam

Equipment:	4-quart (or larger) deep casserole dish or bowl, potato masher
Cooking time:	21 to 25 minutes
Standing time:	none required
Makes:	8 cups

    2 **quarts washed and hulled strawberries (5 cups mashed strawberries)**
    1 **1¾-ounce box powdered fruit pectin**
6½ **cups sugar**

Place berries in casserole dish or bowl and mash with potato masher completely. Completely stir in pectin and **cover** with wax paper.

Microwave on HIGH for 10 to 12 minutes or until mixture comes to a full boil, **stirring** twice during cooking.

Stir in sugar thoroughly and microwave **uncovered** on HIGH for 10 to 12 minutes until mixture comes to a full boil. Boil for 1 full minute.

Skim off foam with metal spoon and pour into hot sterilized jars or freezer containers. (If using freezer containers, cool jam first so as not to melt plastic.)

Blueberry Jam

   Equipment: 3- or 4-quart deep casserole dish or bowl, potato masher
Cooking time: 15 to 19 minutes
Standing time: none required
      Makes: 3 pints

1½ **pints fresh blueberries, washed and stemmed**
   1 **tablespoon fresh lemon juice**
  ½ **box powdered fruit pectin (1¾-ounce size)**
2¼ **cups sugar**

Place berries in casserole dish or bowl and mash completely. Stir in lemon juice and pectin.

Cover with wax paper and microwave on HIGH for 9 to 11 minutes or until mixture comes to a full rolling boil all around the dish and in the center. Stir 3 times during this period. Stir in sugar and microwave on HIGH for another 5 to 7 minutes or until mixture comes to another full boil, stirring twice during this period. Boil for 1 full minute.

Skim off any foam and place in sterilized canning jars or decorative glasses. (If using plastic, be sure to cool first so as not to melt the container.)

Suggestions: If using frozen blueberries, be sure you start with 2 cups mashed berries.

Peach Jam

Equipment:	3- or 4-quart deep casserole dish or bowl, potato masher
Cooking time:	11 to 17 minutes
Standing time:	none required
Makes:	3½ cups

1 pound peaches, skinned, pitted, and mashed (2 cups prepared fruit)
1 tablespoon fresh lemon juice
½ box powdered fruit pectin (1¾-ounce size)
2¾ cups sugar

Place mashed fruit in casserole dish or bowl and mix in lemon juice. Next, completely stir in powdered pectin and **cover** with wax paper.

Microwave on HIGH for 7 to 10 minutes until mixture comes to a full rolling boil all around the sides of the container and in the center, **stirring** once. Immediately add sugar and stir.

Microwave on HIGH for 3 to 6 minutes or until mixture comes to a full rolling boil again. Stir after 3 minutes and then every minute to avoid the jam boiling over. Once mixture is completely boiling, boil for 1 minute more on HIGH.

Skim off any foam and place in sterilized canning jars, decorative glasses, or completely cool and place in plastic freezer containers.

Grape Jelly or Any Fruit Jelly Made from Frozen Juice Concentrate

Equipment: 3- or 4-quart deep casserole dish or bowl
Cooking time: 13 to 19 minutes
Standing time: none required
Makes: 4 cups

1 6-ounce can grape juice or any fruit juice concentrate
2 cups water
1 box powdered fruit pectin (1¾-ounce size)
3¾ cups sugar

Place juice concentrate and water in casserole dish or bowl. Completely mix in powdered fruit pectin and **cover** with wax paper. Microwave on HIGH for 5 to 8 minutes or until mixture comes to a full boil, **stirring** every 2 to 3 minutes. Immediately add the sugar and stir until dissolved.

Microwave again on HIGH for 7 to 10 minutes or until mixture comes to a full rolling boil, stirring twice. Once boiling, allow jelly to boil hard for 1 minute.

Skim off any foam and pour into sterilized glass jars, or completely cool and place in plastic freezer containers.

Candy and Popcorn

CANDY

If you pour and mold your own candy at home, the microwave is the place to melt your chocolate caps (see Box p. 204).* Place caps in a bowl and microwave for 90 seconds on HIGH, stirring every 30 seconds. The caps will appear hard, but keep stirring, as lack of stirring will cause the chocolate to burn.

For those of you who would rather have the chocolate melting while you answer the phone, set the microwave at 50 percent power or MEDIUM and microwave the caps for 3 to 4 minutes. Stir well after 3 minutes, and if not soft enough microwave at 30-second intervals until it is.

It is so simple to make your own filled candy. All you need to purchase is a mold for shaping the chocolates. These molds are readily available at most confectionery stores or through mail-order catalogs. You paint the melted chocolate into the mold, being sure there are no air holes or spaces that aren't completely covered with chocolate, place in the fridge, and let harden.

Using my filling recipe, prepare various flavors and fill your chocolate shells. Once the filling is packed in the shell, cover the top with more melted chocolate, being sure to seal the edges. Return to the fridge until the bottom has set, then pop out of

*Chocolate caps, or molding chocolate, can be bought in specialty gourmet stores or through mail order.

the mold your completed filled candy. Be careful not to touch the cold pieces, as your fingers will leave prints on the shiny cold surface.

Soft-Center Fillings

½ **pound butter**
1 **teaspoon vanilla extract**
1 **teaspoon salt**
1 **cup minus 2 tablespoons sweetened condensed milk**
6 **cups *sifted* confectioner's sugar**

Cream butter, vanilla, and salt in a large bowl. Blend in milk until smooth. Add sugar gradually, blending with a wooden spoon until smooth and stiff—there will be a little leftover sugar.

Turn onto a clean wooden board and knead in remaining sugar carefully. Mixture should be smooth, not sticky.

FLAVORS

CHOCOLATE WALNUT. Use 1 ounce premelted unsweetened chocolate plus walnut chunks or chopped walnuts.

COCONUT. Place ¼ cup coconut in your blender for 30 seconds to chop fine and add to basic filling.

LEMON. Use 1 to 2 teaspoons lemon extract and grated lemon zest to taste. You may want to add yellow food coloring. When using extract, you may want to add a bit more sugar.

ORANGE. Use 1 to 2 teaspoons orange extract and grated orange zest to taste. You may want to add red and yellow food coloring and a bit more sugar.

CHERRY. Mince maraschino cherries and 1 teaspoon juice from the jar.

English Toffee

My house doesn't hold major sweet tooths, but when they like something, look out. I tried this recipe at the suggestion of a friend who loved the results but thought the constant stirring over her regular stove was a bit tiring.

I took my first test batch to a food and nutrition show and walked around giving samples and asking for comments and suggestions about the recipe. All I heard was, "May I try another piece?" or, "I don't know if the recipe is right, but it tastes delicious." Not one person cared how I had made it—only that it was very tasty.

I heartily suggest this recipe to all of you trying to find that magic potion that will add a few ounces to your tiny figure. Or you could always give it away.

Equipment:	3-quart deep bowl or casserole dish, cookie sheet, small glass bowl
Cooking time:	21 to 28 minutes
Standing time:	none required
Makes:	2 pounds

2 **cups butter**
2 **cups sugar**
5 **tablespoons water**
  pinch of cinnamon
1 **teaspoon vanilla extract**
1 **pound chocolate squares, for melting**
¼ **pound almonds, chopped and toasted (see Box p. 241)**

Slice butter and place in bowl or casserole dish along with sugar. Microwave on HIGH for 3 minutes. Whisk in water. Continue whisking and add cinnamon and vanilla. **Elevate** flat-bottomed container on inverted saucer and place on a turntable if available. (If not using turntable, **rotate** bowl ¼ turn each time you whisk.)

Microwave·**uncovered** on HIGH for 18 to 25 minutes, **whisking** well every 5 minutes. While toffee is cooking, cover a regular cookie sheet with aluminum foil; then butter the foil well.

When toffee has reached the hard-crack stage (see Box p. 241), pour it over the buttered foil. Let cool.

USING A CANDY THERMOMETER

If using a candy thermometer, the temperature must reach 300 degrees to be considered at hard-crack stage. Be sure not to leave thermometer in microwave unless it is microwave-safe. If not using a thermometer, you must test the candy by dropping a ½ teaspoon into a bowl of cold water. When hard brittle threads form, the candy is done.

TOASTING NUTS

To toast chopped nuts in the microwave, lay them flat in a glass pie plate and add 1½ teaspoons vegetable oil. Microwave on HIGH for 2½ to 3 minutes until light brown. Stir nuts every 30 to 45 seconds.

In a small glass bowl, melt ½ pound chocolate squares on HIGH for 90 seconds, **stirring** every 15 seconds until melted. Pour over cooled toffee and sprinkle with toasted almonds (see Box p. 241) and let cool. Once cool, turn toffee over and repeat chocolate and nut procedure. When completely cool, crack it with a hammer into bite-size pieces.

Note: I used sweet butter in one experiment and found the taste very rich, but the toffee wasn't quite as hard.

POPCORN

Popcorn seems to be a favorite treat made by almost everyone. If you do not have at least a 600-watt microwave, I do not suggest trying to make popcorn in yours, as you may find it does a terrible job. The main reason popcorn doesn't perform well is because it has such a low moisture content, and once the kernels begin popping there is very little moisture left in the remaining unpopped ones to attract the microwaves.

DANGER   There are some basic rules for making popcorn that you must adhere to for safety reasons. Never try popping popcorn in a plain brown paper bag, as it may catch on fire. Also, do not try to micro-pop corn by putting oil and kernels in a casserole dish. Both these methods are dangerous and can cause a fire in your oven. However, if you want to use your microwave, purchase a popper made for the microwave or buy the specially designed bags filled with kernels.

If you use the microwaveable bags of kernels, try elevating them on an inverted saucer. By allowing the microwaves to get under as well as around the bag you will get more of the kernels to pop. Pop only one bag at a time and allow the microwave to cool down for 10 to 15 minutes between batches. The oven fills up with a great deal of steam from the hot kernels.

Do not reuse the microwaveable bags, and be very careful when opening them. There is a great deal of trapped steam that escapes as the bag is opened and it may burn you. The most important tip I can give you is not to leave your oven unattended when popping corn. If anything should go wrong, be right there to shut off your oven.

You can revitalize stale or grocery-store popcorn in the microwave on HIGH for 45 to 90 seconds. Test to see if kernels are warm after 30 seconds and toss them around in their bag. Try adding grated cheese, garlic or onion powder, seasoned salt, or melt 2 to 3 tablespoons of butter in a custard cup for 50 seconds and add 1 tablespoon of chili powder to it. Sprinkle over your popcorn for an interesting zing to your next batch.

Microwave Dinners

Are you thinking, "How can I get this quick-cooking wizard to put a meal from start to finish on the table *hot?*" I *know* that's what you're thinking because it's a common request. I have put together a few examples of taking a meal-in-a-dish recipe, combining it sometimes with an added vegetable, and always with a dessert to show you how to do it.

It takes a bit of planning, but it can be done. Don't forget that properly covered food will stand, finish cooking, and stay hot for at least 15 to 20 minutes, giving you time to cook another dish. Organization is the key; if you can get everything organized, you'll find it works quite well.

I suggest mapping out your week's menu and making a shopping list in advance. Label your meats and freeze in the portions you need for each dish. This will eliminate guesswork later. Defrost according to your menu and line up all your necessary ingredients on the counter before you begin cooking. This saves time and makes preparation go much smoother.

Choose desserts that are best served hot and microwave them while you're eating, or prepare the dessert early in the day or just before you begin dinner preparation. All in all—it can be done—but it takes a bit of planning on your part. Remember, you make the wizard perform, so get your act together.

I hate to tell you to do something that I don't do myself, and I do not cook rice, egg noodles, or any macaroni products in my microwave as I feel no time or energy is saved.

What I suggest is this: cook a double batch on your conventional stove and freeze enough for another meal. Defrost and reheat in the microwave while the main dish is standing. This will save you time and energy, which is our goal when microwaving.

ONE-DISH MEALS

I have selected four stick-to-your-ribs main dishes (Beef Bourguignonne, Swiss Steak, Chicken Cacciatore and Chicken Parmesan) that can be served either with rice or precooked noodles reheated in microwave— or you can add a green salad and some hot rolls you have baked in your conventional stove and reheated in the microwave.

These main dishes are followed by two complete microwave menus for the fearless among you.

Beef Bourguignonne

Equipment: 3-quart casserole dish with cover if available
Cooking time: 49 to 59 minutes
Standing time: 10 minutes
Serves: 6

1 box frozen sliced carrots
5 slices bacon, quartered
2 pounds tender beef, sirloin or top round steak, sliced into ¼-inch-wide strips
⅓ cup flour
¼ teaspoon garlic powder
¼ teaspoon paprika
1 cup Burgundy wine
½ cup water
1 tablespoon A-1 Sauce
2 teaspoons instant beef bouillon
1 large onion, thinly sliced
18 fresh mushroom caps, or 1 8-ounce can mushroom caps, drained
2 cloves garlic, minced
½ teaspoon thyme
1 bay leaf
salt and pepper to taste

Place box of frozen carrots on 2 layers of paper towels on floor of microwave and cook on HIGH for 4 minutes. Be sure box is not covered in a foil wrapper (if it is, remove it). Set aside.

Place bacon in casserole dish and microwave on HIGH for 4 minutes. Reserve drippings.

Coat beef strips with flour, garlic powder, and paprika. Add coated strips to bacon drippings and toss to coat. Whisk together wine, water, A-1, and bouillon, and add to beef. Add onion, mushrooms, carrots, garlic cloves, thyme, bay leaf, and salt and pepper.

Cover with casserole cover or vented plastic wrap and place on turntable if available. Microwave on HIGH for 5 minutes, then reduce to 50 percent power or MEDIUM and microwave for 40 to 50 minutes, **stirring** (and **rotating** dish ¼ turn if not using turntable) every 15 minutes, until beef is fork-tender.

Let **stand**, covered, for 10 minutes before serving.

Troubleshooting: Forgetting to use a tender cut of meat and not tenderizing with a meat mallet or carefully with the edge of an unbreakable saucer, may make fork-tender texture difficult.

Using a spoon will not give you as smooth a gravy as using a whisk will.

Out of Burgundy? White wine will do but won't give you as much color.

Try to keep the meat under the liquid to keep it from drying out.

Suggestions: Serve over noodles or rice.

Swiss Steak

Equipment:	Meat mallet, 10-inch browning dish with cover (if using a smaller browning dish without cover, you will also need a 3-quart casserole dish with cover)
Cooking time:	48 to 58 minutes
Standing time:	10 minutes
Serves:	6

1 **box frozen broccoli spears or chopped broccoli**
2 **pounds round steak, ½-inch-thick or 2 pounds Swiss steaks**
3 **to 4 tablespoons flour**
   garlic salt
2 **tablespoons olive oil**
1 **onion, sliced thin**
1 **cup sliced fresh mushrooms, or 1 4-ounce can, drained**
1 **16-ounce can crushed tomatoes**
1 **8-ounce can tomato sauce**
¼ **cup Burgundy wine**
½ **teaspoon dried basil**
½ **teaspoon dried oregano**
½ **cup sliced pitted black olives (optional)**

Place frozen box of broccoli on 2 layers of paper towels and microwave on HIGH for 4 minutes. If box is covered in a foil wrapper, remove it before microwaving.

Preheat browning dish according to manufacturer's instructions. Sprinkle one side of meat with flour and garlic salt and pound in with meat mallet. Repeat on other side and cut into serving-size pieces.

Once browner is preheated, add olive oil and move around to coat dish. Add enough pieces of meat to cover dish and microwave **uncovered** on HIGH for 1 minute, then turn over and cook for 2 more minutes. Preheat browner for 2 to 3 minutes and repeat process with remaining meat. If browner is too small to hold the entire recipe, transfer to larger casserole dish. Cover meat with sliced onion and mushrooms. Place broccoli over onions and add tomatoes, tomato sauce, wine, basil, oregano, and olives if using.

Cover with casserole top or vented plastic wrap, place on turntable if available, and microwave on HIGH for 5 minutes.

Reduce to 50 percent power or MEDIUM for 45 to 55 minutes, **stirring** every 15 minutes (and **rotating** dish ¼ turn if not using turntable) until meat is fork-tender. Let **stand**, covered, for 10 minutes before serving to tenderize.

Troubleshooting: Forgetting to use a tender cut of beef and not tenderizing with a meat mallet or carefully with the edge of an unbreakable saucer will not produce fork-tender meat.

Be sure to slice vegetables in uniform size so that they all will cook to the same degree of doneness.

If you don't have your manufacturer's instructions for your browning dish, heat 5 to 7 minutes on HIGH.

Try to keep meat under sauce to keep it moist.

Suggestions: Serve over noodles or with mashed potatoes.

Chicken Cacciatore

This is my friend Ann Parry's recipe for Chicken Cacciatore. Ann used to make this in her electric frying pan, letting it simmer away and use up lots of electricity.

I find it a quick and easy dinner to put together when I am late getting in. I always have a package of cooked spaghetti in my freezer, and I use a little extra sauce in the preparation so there is plenty for the spaghetti.

Equipment:	6-cup glass measure, 12 × 8 or 13 × 9-inch casserole dish
Cooking time:	31 to 36 minutes
Standing time:	5 minutes
Serves:	4

> 2 tablespoons olive oil
> 2 cloves garlic, minced
> 1 medium onion, thinly sliced
> 1 medium green pepper, diced
> ½ cup thinly sliced celery
> 1 cup sliced fresh mushrooms
> ¼ cup white wine
> 1 32-ounce jar spaghetti sauce with mushrooms
> 2- to 3-pound frying chicken, cut up

In the glass measure place oil, garlic, onion, green pepper, celery, and mushrooms. Microwave on HIGH for 4 to 5 minutes until crisp-tender. Add wine and spaghetti sauce and mix well.

Cut chicken breasts in half and break thigh bones at joints of chicken legs. Arrange chicken pieces in casserole dish with meatiest parts of the chicken to the outside of the dish. Pour vegetables and sauce over chicken pieces and **cover** with vented plastic wrap.

Microwave on HIGH for 15 minutes. Rearrange chicken pieces and microwave another 12 to 16 minutes on HIGH until chicken is no longer pink.

Let **stand**, covered, for 5 minutes before serving.

Troubleshooting: Chicken takes the longest to cook at the joints, therefore breaking the leg and thigh joints will enable more even cooking; failing to do so may add time to cooking.

Olive oil adds flavor; if you're dieting or it's not available, just skip it.

Be sure vegetables are cut in uniform size and shape so they will cook evenly.

Suggestions: Serve over spaghetti or rice. A large can of crushed tomatoes along with ¼ teaspoon of oregano and ¼ teaspoon basil may be substituted for the spaghetti sauce.

Chicken Parmesan

Equipment: meat mallet, meat rack
Cooking time: 8 to 10 minutes
Standing time: 5 minutes
Serves: 2 to 4

2 **whole boneless chicken breasts, skinned and cut in half**
¼ **cup butter**
½ **cup cornflake crumbs**
1 **teaspoon garlic powder**
1 **cup spaghetti sauce**
1 **cup shredded mozzarella cheese**

Pound chicken breasts with meat mallet or edge of an unbreakable saucer until flat.

In a small bowl melt butter on HIGH for 45 to 55 seconds. Mix cornflake crumbs and garlic powder together on paper plate. Dredge chicken cutlets in butter, then in cornflake crumbs. Place cutlets on meat rack and **cover** with wax paper.

Microwave on HIGH for 7 to 9 minutes until meat is no longer pink.

Let **stand**, covered, for 5 minutes.

Add 1 to 2 tablespoons of sauce to top of each cutlet and cover with mozzarella. Microwave on HIGH power for 40 to 50 seconds, just until cheese begins to melt.

Troubleshooting: If you fail to cover chicken with wax paper, it will decorate the inside of your oven with cornflake crumbs.

If you want to use a meat mallet, be sure to use the flat side and not the tenderizing part, or it will cut the cutlets.

Suggestions: Breadcrumbs or Shake-and-Bake can be used, but you will not get the fried effect and color you get with cornflake crumbs.

COMPLETE MICROWAVE DINNERS

> **MENU**
>
> Scalloped Potatoes and Polish Sausage
> Green-Bean Bake
> Choco-Nut Meringue Squares

(Prepare squares either just before dinner or earlier in the day.)

Equipment:	electric mixer, 8- or 9-inch round baking dish, 4-cup glass measure, 1- and 3-quart round casserole dishes
Cooking time:	49 to 65 minutes (for entire meal)
Standing time:	none required
Serves:	4 to 6

Choco-Nut Meringue Squares

Makes 16 squares

CRUST
1⅓ **cups flour**
¼ **cup sugar**
¼ **cup finely chopped walnuts**
½ **cup butter**

COMPLETE MICROWAVE DINNERS

FILLING
1 (3- to 4-ounce) package chocolate pudding, cooking variety
2 cups milk

MERINGUE
3 egg whites
¼ teaspoon cornstarch
¼ teaspoon cream of tartar
6 tablespoons sugar

Combine flour, sugar, and nuts in medium bowl and cut in butter until mixture is crumbly. Press mixture into bottom of baking dish.

Microwave on HIGH for 2 minutes, **rotate** dish ¼ turn, and microwave 2 minutes more until set. If dish is flat-bottomed, **elevate** on inverted saucer and use turntable if available.

Combine pudding and milk in measuring cup and whisk until well blended. Microwave on HIGH for 5 to 7 minutes, **whisking** every 2 minutes until thick. Set aside to cool.

Place egg whites, cornstarch, and cream of tartar in a deep bowl. Beat with electric mixer until foamy white clouds are formed. Add sugar, 1 tablespoon at a time, while you continue beating until firm stiff peaks are formed when you lift the beater.

Pour pudding over crust and frost meringue over pudding, being sure to seal the meringue onto edges of the crust so it won't shrink.

Microwave at 50 percent power or MEDIUM for 3 to 5 minutes until the meringue is set, rotating dish ¼ turn every 2 minutes.

Green-Bean Bake

1 box frozen green beans, cooked
4 slices bacon
¼ cup flavored breadcrumbs
½ can onion rings
½ 10¾-ounce can cream of mushroom soup, undiluted

Microwave paper-covered box of green beans on 2 layers of paper towels for 6 to 8 minutes on HIGH.

Place bacon slices in 1-quart round casserole dish and microwave on HIGH for 2 to 3 minutes. Remove bacon, crumble, and set aside. Reserve drippings.

Add breadcrumbs to bacon drippings and stir. Microwave on HIGH for 2 minutes, stirring once. Drain any excess fat and set aside.

Combine cooked beans, bacon, onion rings, and soup in 1-quart casserole dish. Mix together well and top with breadcrumbs. Set aside, then heat on HIGH for 4 to 5 minutes while main dish is standing.

Scalloped Potatoes and Polish Sausage

> **4 to 5 medium potatoes, peeled and thinly sliced**
> **1 medium onion, peeled and thinly sliced**
>   **salt and pepper to taste**
> **1 pound Polish sausage or Kielbase**
>
> **CHEESE SAUCE**
> **2 tablespoons butter**
> **2 tablespoons flour**
> **1 cup milk**
> **2 tablespoons white wine**
> **1 cup shredded sharp cheddar cheese**
>   **dash of salt and pepper**

In measuring cup melt butter on HIGH for 45 to 50 seconds. Whisk in flour until smooth. Whisk in milk and wine, whisking until well blended.

Microwave on HIGH for 4 to 6 minutes, whisking every 2 minutes until thick. Once sauce is thick enough to coat a spoon, blend in cheese, salt, and pepper, and microwave on HIGH for 1 to 2 minutes until cheese melts. Set aside.

In the 3-quart casserole dish, layer ¼ of the potatoes and onion slices, then sprinkle on salt and pepper, and pour ¼ of cheese sauce on top. Continue layering until all ingredients are used, ending with cheese sauce.

Elevate flat-bottomed dish on inverted saucer and place on turntable if available. (If not using turntable, **rotate** dish ¼ turn every 5 minutes.) Microwave on HIGH for 5 minutes. Reduce to 50 percent power or MEDIUM and microwave for 15 to 20 minutes until potatoes are almost fork-tender.

Cut sausages into chunks or, if they are in links, be sure to pierce to keep from exploding, and arrange on top of potatoes. Microwave on HIGH for 4 to 7 minutes until sausages are done, rotating dish ½ turn every 3 minutes.

Let **stand, covered** with wax paper, for 5 minutes before serving.

MENU

Stuffed Chicken Legs
Sweet Potato Boats (page 156)
Corn Bread

Equipment: electric mixer, 4-cup glass measure, meat rack, 8- or 9-inch clear glass round baking dish
Cooking time: 45 to 58 minutes (for entire meal)
Standing time: none required
Serves: 4 to 6

(Stuff chicken legs and set aside to cook while stuffing sweet potatoes. Microwave corn bread first and cover lightly to keep warm.)

Corn Bread

¾ **cup all-purpose flour**
¾ **cup yellow cornmeal**
1 **tablespoon sugar**
1 **tablespoon baking powder**
½ **teaspoon salt**
¼ **teaspoon chili powder**
2 **eggs, beaten**
½ **cup milk**
⅓ **cup oil**

Combine all ingredients and stir just until smooth. Pour batter into baking dish and **elevate** on an inverted saucer in the center of your microwave. Microwave on 50 percent power or MEDIUM for 6 minutes, **rotating** dish ¼ turn after 3 minutes.

Increase power to HIGH and microwave 2 to 6 minutes more, rotating dish every 2 minutes. Check for doneness by looking through bottom of clear glass dish; there should be no unbaked batter appearing in the center.

Let **stand** for 10 minutes before removing from dish. Serve warm.

Prepare sweet potatoes for baking (see p. 156); they can be heated while the chicken legs stand.

Stuffed Chicken Legs

       2 tablespoons butter
       2 cloves garlic, finely minced
       ½ cup chopped celery
       ¼ cup chopped mushrooms
       ¼ cup chopped onions
       1½ cups breadcrumbs (flavored
           do very well)
       ½ teaspoon salt
       ⅛ teaspoon pepper
       ¼ teaspoon poultry seasoning
       1 egg, slightly beaten
       6 chicken legs, with thigh joints
           cracked

   GLAZE
       2 tablespoons honey
       2 tablespoons soy sauce

Place butter, garlic, celery, mushrooms, and onions in glass measure. Microwave on HIGH for 3 minutes. **Stir**, microwave on HIGH for 3 minutes more. Stir in breadcrumbs, salt, pepper, poultry seasoning, and egg. Mix lightly but well.

Lift up skin on top of chicken leg and place 1 heaping tablespoon of stuffing between the skin and the meat. Wrap skin around stuffing and meat and secure skin under the leg with a wooden toothpick. If you do not toothpick the skin over the stuffing, it may shrink during cooking and leave stuffing exposed.

Place stuffed legs on meat rack in wagon-wheel-spoke design, with the meaty end of the leg to the outside of the dish. Combine glaze ingredients and brush on chicken. Microwave on HIGH for 18 to 25 minutes or until juices run clear, rearranging legs and **rotating** dish every 5 to 7 minutes.

Let **stand, covered** with plastic wrap, for 5 to 10 minutes before serving.

Remove plastic wrap from sweet potatoes and microwave on HIGH for 4 to 5 minutes. Serve with warm corn bread.

A Couple of
Neat Tricks

Drying Herbs

I have heard many complaints that herbs lose their flavor when you dry them in the microwave. Years ago, I had a very bad (and buggy) experience when I didn't properly wash my herbs first before drying, so I urge you either to wash or to check them very carefully before even thinking about preserving them.

I wash mine first, shake out as much excess water as possible, discard any part that is flowering, and lay them in a single layer between 2 paper towels. Don't crowd them; instead, do several batches. I then heat on HIGH for 2 minutes (using a 600-watt oven; if your wattage is less, increase time by 30 seconds for each 50 watts below 600 watts), leaving me with a partially dried herb.

Once the herbs are partially dried, I gather the stalks together, tie with string, and hang them from a cup hook in my kitchen. I find they retain their flavor and add a nice aroma to my kitchen. Try drying a batch completely and see if you are satisfied with it. Remember, if you wash your herbs first, they may need an extra minute on HIGH because of the extra moisture.

If you dry them completely in the microwave, allow them to stand for 5 to 10 minutes before snipping off the stems. To help in getting your herbs to flake, just run a knife or the sharp edge of a spoon over them or place them in a plastic bag and rumple it—the dried herbs will flake off the stems.

I usually save a tablespoon of each herb I dry and place them together with a cup of water in a micro-safe bowl and boil them for 3 or 4 minutes in my microwave. I sometimes add a pinch of cinnamon or apple pie spice to the herbs for a real country-kitchen smell. The mixed herbs add a lovely aroma to my kitchen as well as to the inside of my microwave.

Inedible Cookie Ornaments

Several years ago, I started making inedible cookie ornaments to entertain my preschoolers. Before baking, I punched a hole right into the top of the cookie so that when the children finished decorating with markers or paint I could string them with yarn, ribbon, or heavy twine. The result was a lovely necklace created by each little artist.

I found my inedible-cookie recipe adapted very well to the microwave because the bottoms don't brown as they do when baked in a conventional oven, where they bake for 30 minutes. In the microwave it takes only 2 to 3 minutes on HIGH.

From the preschool stage we went to entering school and birthday parties. I found these ornaments made great placecards or favors that the birthday child could decorate prior to the party—or serve as a prize for the guest with the most creative piece. It is very easy to find cookie cutters in almost any shape to match your party theme.

During the early years of school, I sent enough ornaments for the entire class every holiday. The children loved having a special decoration to wear for each holiday.

One Christmas my children and I needed something special to add to the candy and cookie tins that we worked so hard preparing for our family and friends. Back to our flour, salt, and water recipe. Together we painted and varnished the prettiest snowmen, with the year written across their chests. We made little holes in the tops for the ornament holders and had the perfect little "From Our House To Yours" gift to tie on the outside of our tins.

Try your hand and see what talented artists your house holds. It is not only easy but fun, and that's what family projects using the microwave should be.

Here are some tips for goof-proof ornaments:

Smooth ornaments: kneading is very important; don't skimp on the amount of time you spend.

For holes: place holes before baking or ornaments will crack if you try to do it after they become hard.

Do not roll dough too thin or it will burn. Try to keep the thickness uniform for even cooking of all ornaments.

Hard dry ornaments: moisture forms between the ornament and the wax paper. By removing the ornament as soon as it is cool enough to touch, and turning it over, the moisture should dry out. Do not store in covered containers as the ornaments will get soft and mold.

Breakage: accidents do happen, and some may crack, so make extras.

Equipment:	cookie sheet (optional), wire rack for cooling
Cooking time:	3 minutes (but start the day before)
Standing time:	none required
Makes:	15 to 20 ornaments, depending on size

> **1 cup flour**
> **½ cup salt**
> **½ cup water**

Combine flour and salt in medium bowl. Mix with a wooden spoon. Add water a little at a time to form a smooth ball.

Knead the dough for 5 to 7 minutes, until smooth and firm. (This is very important for nice, smooth ornaments; see above.) Place dough in a plastic bag to prevent drying, and take out small pieces as you need them. Roll out a piece of dough on a floured surface as you would cookie dough and cut out or use cookie cutters to make shapes and designs of your choice.

Put cut-out ornaments on a sheet of wax paper, about 5 to 6 per baking batch, and place in a circle. The wax paper can be placed on a cookie sheet, but it is not necessary. Let sit overnight before baking.

Place a sheet of wax paper with ornaments on the floor of your microwave and bake on HIGH for 3 minutes. Remove from microwave, and as soon as they are cool enough to touch, remove from wax paper and turn them over to cool and dry out on wire rack.

Once the cookies are hard and dry, decorate with paints, markers, crayons, and varnish if you like, to seal.

Troubleshooting: If you have burned edges, the dough was rolled too thin.

If you have curled edges, the dough was too thick in the middle and too thin on the edges. Check your cookie cutters; some tend to flatten the edges.

If you have moist bottoms, you left them on the wax paper too long and moisture penetrated into the dough.

If you have browned bottoms, the dough was overcooked for its thickness.

Index